FROMENTAL HALEVY

For my husband Nissim

FROMENTAL HALEVY

HIS LIFE & MUSIC
1799-1862

BY RUTH JORDAN

KAHN & AVERILL
LONDON

First published in 1994 by
Kahn & Averill
9 Harrington Road, London SW7 3ES

Copyright © 1994 by Ruth Jordan

British Library Cataloguing-in-Publication Data

A catalogue record for this book
is available from the British Library

ISBN 1–871082–51–X

Typeset in Baskerville by York House Typographic
Printed by Redwood Books, Trowbridge, Wilts

CONTENTS

LIST OF ILLUSTRATIONS

ACKNOWLEDGMENTS

My first word of thanks goes to Georges Lubin, editor of the unequalled George Sand *Correspondance* who, as early as 1981, when I first mentioned my interest in Halévy, generously responded with information about relevant printed and Ms collections at the Bibliothèque nationale. My second goes to Philippe Guillemin, Counsellor for Cultural Affairs at the French Embassy in London, whose name opened many doors in Paris.

For the interest taken and help offered I am grateful to the staff of the various departments of the Bibliothèque national and Bibliothèque de l'Opéra, Eve Harbon and staff of the Bibliothèque Alliance israëlite universelle, the Director and Catherine Rochon of the Conservatoire national supérieur de musique et de danse, Bruno Chenique of Les Appels d'Orphée, Antoinette Romain, Conservateur en chef of the Musée d'Orsay, Aline Dardel of the Bibliothèque-Museé de l'Opéra, Mme B. Favre, Gérard Ganvert, Karl and Marthe Leich-Galland.

Many thanks to Margot Cohn of the Department of MS & Archives at the Jewish National and University Library in Jerusalem; the staff of the British Library in Bloomsbury; the National Sound Archives in South Kensington; Jews' College Library; Francesca Franchi of the Covent Garden Archives; Nick Collins, Nancy Cowan, Richard Hobbs, Elbie Lebrecht, Norman Lebrecht, Patrick Mills, Sister Margaret McDonald of the Sisters of Sion, my students at the Spiro Institute who studied *La Juive* through excerpts before the complete opera conducted by Antonio de Almeida on CD/cassette became available; and finally friends and acquaintances whose keen interest in the project was a source of encouragement and joy.

FOREWORD

*M*OST PEOPLE WHOM I ASKED whether they had heard of Fromental Halévy thought they had. Wasn't he that fellow who wrote librettos for Offenbach? He was not; the librettist was his nephew Ludovic. Some facetiously suggested that Fromental was a kind of Swiss cheese. Only one person, a man in his seventies, immediately plunged into a rendition of Cardinal Brogni's aria *Si la rigueur* from the first act of *La Juive*. He remembered it from a 78 rpm record he heard in his youth. He had never seen any Halévy opera staged.

Not many people have. It was only natural that after his death in 1862 Halévy's operas should have gradually given way to new works by younger composers, among them his former Conservatoire students Gounod, Bizet and Saint-Saëns. Only *La Juive* held on in Paris until a storehouse fire in 1893 destroyed its lavish scenery. A Covent Garden scenery which claimed to be the most magnificent in Europe was destroyed by fire even earlier. Twentieth-century revivals include *La Juive* by the Paris Opéra in 1933 and by Maggio Musicale Fiorentino in 1960. In 1973 it had two concert performances, one in Frankfurt and one at the Royal Festival Hall in London; there was also a performance in 1974 by the Nottingham University Opera Group. *L'Eclair* was revived in Germany in a German translation. Not enough to re-establish Halévy as the household name he was until the turn of the century.

My own interest in his music was indirectly due to my American stepmother who, for my ninth birthday, had ordered from New York a child's clockwork record player complete with Yankee Doodle Went to Town. My father tactfully brought home from the local music store a 78 rpm record which had a sweet voiced girl called Lakmé Delibes singing on the one side, and a distraught lady called La Juive Rachel Halévy pouring her heart out on the other. The clockwork mechanism was not powerful enough to cope with a full-size record and usually ground to a halt long before Rachel did. When I graduated to the use of a more sophisticated record player I got hold of whatever was available on the old Odeon, Decca and CBS labels – bass Cesare Siepi singing Cardinal Brogni's aria *Si la rigueur*, tenors René Verdière and Tony Poncet singing Elazar's *Dieu que ma voix tremblante*, Caruso singing Elazar's *Rachel, quand du Seigneur la grâce tutelaire* accompanied on the piano, soprano Jane Rhodes singing Rachel's aria *Il va venir*.

For an opera to be properly appreciated it has to be seen as well as heard. When treating Halévy's work I therefore had to find a way of introducing and arousing interest in operas which, at the time of writing, do not feature on any known current repertoire, and are only scantily represented in record catalogues. A solution was suggested by the practice prevalent in Halévy's time.

In order to acquaint and familiarise the public with a new opera, editors of nineteenth-century quality periodicals allowed their reviewers yards of print space. Sometimes no less than three weekly instalments, of some two thousand words each, would be devoted to a single new work. The first would introduce it and recount the plot in great detail act by act. The next two would discuss the music, painting a word picture of an andantino in a minor key or an unusual percussive accompaniment, explaining why it was effective or faulty. It was not an easy undertaking. Reviewers did not have the benefit of a score; hand copied scores were not available, while printed ones would be published only long after opening night. Some cautiously prefaced their pronouncements with 'as far as one can judge by one single hearing.' The conscientious did not go into print until they had seen and heard the opera in question a second time.

Berlioz and Wagner were wizards of the word picture. Other distinguished reviewers of the time were Théophile Gautier,

Blanchard, Catelin, Fiorentino, Monnais, G. Bénédit. Their vivid and erudite accounts of plot and music helped readers see and hear in their mind a distraught Ginevra groping through the streets of a plague-ridden Florence, a repentant she-devil dying while a ruined castle goes up in flames, a tense Lyonel, blinded by lightning, waiting for the last stroke of eight to remove his bandages and know whether his eyesight has been restored. What they did for audiences of their own times they may well do again for present-day readers, introducing them to music which was once all the rage in the western world.

Painting a word picture was one way of popularising a new opera. Publishing easy arrangements of operatic highlights for the use of amateurs was another. Such arrangements were the 19th-century equivalent of today's record industry, the precursors of today's hit tunes. It was taken for granted that educated people could play the piano, sing, perhaps even form a trio or a quartet. Music publishers would acquire the publishing rights of an opera and commission easy arrangements of best tunes, mostly for voice and piano, sometimes for strings, more rarely for wind and brass. During his meagre Paris years in the early 1840's Wagner made arrangements of *La Juive*, *La Reine de Chypre* and *Le Guitarrero* by Halévy and *La Favorita* by Donizetti. Without always seeing what was on offer at the Paris venues, without having to wait for the Paris successes to be produced in the provinces, the public became familiar with the All-Time Greats and Forty Best Melodies of the day.

In our own time the record industry has taken over from the arrangers of the past, though in the case of Halévy not enough to do him justice. There have been several recordings of highlights and selected acts from *La Juive* as well as a complete recording on cassette and CD. There is at least one non-commercial recording of his most popular opera comique. By the time this is read more new recordings may be available, illustrating his versatility and his gift for melody and orchestration.

Halévy lived during one of the most eventful periods of French history, witnessing the fall of Napoleon, the rise and decline of constitutional monarchy, the re-emergence and demise of a new wave of Republicanism, the establishment of the Second Empire under Louis Napoleon. Far from living in an ivory tower he took part in what was happening around him, finding time for causes he believed in. As a musician his life reflected what a reviewer called 'the seven stations of the cross' meted out to a young generation of French-born composers. Like many of his co-evals he experienced the frustrations of a budding musician, the envy of colleagues, the hypocrisy of reviewers, the backbiting and scandal-mongering of the profession.

Born when emancipation was opening new doors to French Jews yet at the same time enticing them to total assimilation, he followed the golden path. Without being an observant Jew he was proud of his ancestral heritage, moving confidently in a gentile ambiance. He was affable and peace-loving, ambitious without being disloyal. He was erudite, a good writer, an engaging public speaker. Above all he was a composer of opera, that magic spectacle which brought together music, dance and painting, which drew on the joint talents of great artists and craftsmen, which used the most sophisticated of stage machinery. At a time which saw the ascendance in Paris of French-born composers like Boieldieu, Hérold, Auber and Adam over their Italian contemporaries, he was the acknowledged leader of the nascent French school of his generation.

FROMENTAL HALEVY

1

BORN IN FRANCE

*F*RANCE, IN COMMON WITH MOST European countries since the Middle Ages, found it expedient from time to time to expel her Jews who, notwithstanding, persistently infiltrated back. In 1394 they were expelled by Charles VI, better remembered as the king stricken by madness, who in Shakespeare's *King Henry the Fifth* was the loser of the battle of Agincourt, and who some four hundred and fifty years later was the subject of a patriotic French opera by the Jewish composer Fromental Halévy. The last time Jews were expelled from France was in 1615, by Marie de Medici, Queen Regent during the minority of Louis XIII. Again they crept back. From then on their presence was tolerated except in certain towns, including Paris, where they were denied the right of residence.

Louis XIV was reputed to be well disposed towards them. The story goes that in 1657, after he had won a battle near the town of Metz, he was prevailed upon to honour the local Jewish community with a visit to the synagogue. When he arrived with the royal retinue two rabbis came out to welcome him, holding up the scrolls of the law wrapped in velvet richly embroidered with gold and silver thread, calling the blessing of God upon His Majesty.

'Are you the rabbis of this synagogue?' His Majesty enquired.

'We are, Sire.'

'Are you sure you are?'

1

Both rabbis assured His Majesty that there was no doubt about their Rabbinical status.

'How dare you call yourselves rabbis of a synagogue in a French town without a Royal Appointment?' His Majesty bawled. 'This is insubordination.'

The terrified rabbis nearly dropped the scrolls of the law, went down on their knees and begged for mercy. Louis XIV graciously granted the royal pardon, confirmed the kneelers as Rabbis by Appointment to His Majesty the King of France, and the Jewish community of Metz flourished ever since, none deterred by the occasional persecution or execution of coreligionists called Moshe, or Levy, or Halévy.

Most of the Metz Jews had crossed over illegally from Germany, some having started from Poland. The only languages they used were Yiddish and Hebrew; Yiddish for everyday life, Hebrew for prayers and religious studies. As yet no attempt was made to learn French. They continued to follow the traditional Jewish occupations which had been imposed upon them by the circumstances of history – peddling, selling on credit and money lending which, when transacted on a large scale, came to be known as banking. Gradually they moved further inland, settling in nearby Lorraine. In 1715 one Samuel Levy, Rabbi of the Metz Jewish community, became Court Banker to the Duke of Lorraine. A few years later he went bankrupt and took himself off to Paris. He had just begun to prosper again when the police caught up with him and threw him into the Bastille, together with another Jewish banker, to serve a seven-year sentence. In no time the two prisoners arranged to be provided with Kosher food, were allowed to say their daily prayers and celebrate the Sabbath in style.

Officially Jews had no right of residence in Paris but the French police, with the exception of a rare perfunctory raid, turned a blind eye to their presence. By 1789 the Jewish community in Paris numbered about 500 people out of a total of 40,000 in the whole of France, all basking in the promise of tolerance heralded by the Revolution. On 27 September 1791 the National Assembly, under the seal of Louis XVI, gave them full civil rights. On 22 August 1795, long after Louis XVI had been guillotined and the First Republic proclaimed, the law was reaffirmed and extended. After years of illicit infiltration and life lived in perpetual apprehension, the Jews of France were full French citizens, free to practise their religion and take up any craft or profession they wished to follow.

At the time of the 1795 re-affirmation of full rights of citizenship and freedom of religion, there was a German Jew living in Metz, who had either smuggled himself into France a few years earlier, or had just recently arrived. Born in 1760 in the prosperous culture-loving Jewish community of Furth, not far from Nürenberg, he had been given the Hebrew names of Elyahu Halfon Levy; in France the first became Elie, the second was dropped while the third was kept. Levy however was not a surname but just another forename, bestowed on male infants in addition to other forenames to denote their descent from the tribe of Levy, whose members were by birthright the exclusive instrumentalists and choristers of the ancient Temple of Jerusalem.

From his native Furth Elie Levy had brought a taste and aptitude for study. Not only was he a Talmudic and Biblical scholar, but also a linguist, counting among his languages his native Yiddish and German as well as excellent French, Hebrew, Aramaic, some Greek and a smattering of classical Arabic.

It was probably the local matchmaker who arranged a marriage between the respected though impecunious scholar of Metz and young Julie Meyer from the small Jewish community of Lorraine. Mlle Meyer's parents must have crossed over illegally from Germany, but she herself was born in France, in the village of Malzeville, near Nancy. They married c.1798, the bride just over seventeen, the bridegroom nearly thirty-eight. Shortly after the marriage the couple bade farewell to family and friends and went to Paris to seek their fortune in the brave new world that was opening up before them.

By then Paris Jews had left peddling behind, becoming shoe-makers, jewellers, engravers, embroiderers. Some were teachers of Hebrew and religious studies, while the astute and worldly went into commerce and banking. Although they had become conversant with French, they still preferred to live among themselves, congregating in Le Marais, in the vicinity of the local synagogue, the centre of their religious, social and cultural life. No exception to the rule, Elie Levy and Julie found a modest accommodation among their coreligionists in what was then rue

3

Neuves-des-Maturins, and it was there that on 27 May 1799 the future composer Jacques-François-Fromental-Elie Halévy was born. Some six months later, on 9 November 1799, Napoleon staged his *coup d' état* and was made First Consul. The Reign of Terror with its fierce anti-clerical notions and its closure of religious institutions of all denominations was over. Synagogues could be reopened.

A firm believer in emancipation, Elie Levy preached at all times the French version of the slogan of the Jewish Enlightenment: *Tiens au pays et conserve ta foi*, freely translatable as Be Loyal to Your Country and True to the Faith of Your Fathers. Thus, when the Peace Treaty of Amiens was concluded on 27 March 1802 between Napoleon, Great Britain, Spain and Holland, he demonstrated his combination of French patriotism and traditional Jewishness by composing a dual language poem to celebrate the event, causing it to be sung in Hebrew and read out in French at the synagogue of rue Saint-Avoye. Fromental, still under three, would have clung to his father during the ceremony while his mother, pregnant for the third time, would have watched from the Women's Gallery.

On his arrival in Paris Elie Levy tried his hand at commerce, promptly losing all the money his wife had brought him as a dowry. From then on he eked out a living from small administrative tasks within the Jewish community, by preference devoting himself to scholarly pursuits. He edited the distinguished but short-lived periodical *L'Israëlite français* founded by Chief Rabbi Abraham de Cologna, started working on a Hebrew-French dictionary, wrote a treatise on the fables of Aesop which he compared with those of King Solomon. His thoughts on Jewish education were assembled and published in a text book entitled *Instructions réligieuses et morales à l'usage de la jeunesse israëlite* subtitled in Hebrew *Limudey Dat U-mussar*, with Mosaic and Talmudic injunctions rendered in their original Hebrew, explained and interpreted in French. When, under Napoleon, a Central Jewish Consistory was established, he translated into French loyal poems of praise written in abstruse Biblical Hebrew by community rabbis for State occasions; and an outstanding translator he was too.

There was no poverty in the household, but money was scarce. Young Julie, who during the first eight years of their marriage gave birth to five children – son, daughter, second son and two more daughters – was a loyal helpmate, probably finding time to accept the odd embroidery job to supplement the family income.

For the basic education of his children Elie Levy relied on custom. At a time when there were no Jewish schools as yet for either boys or girls, girls were taught whatever their mothers could teach them: boys were sent to a *heder*, a day school attached to a synagogue, where they were taught to read and write Classical Hebrew and, in the case of Fromental and his younger brother Léon, also the rudiments of French grammar. Fromental retained enough of his early learning to set to music at various stages in his career some psalms in the original Hebrew; his brother Léon, three years his junior, mainly recalled being rapped on the knuckles when he was inattentive or failed to satisfy the criteria set by the *melamed*, the *heder* teacher.

After the *heder* Fromental was sent to a French boarding school which took day pupils, run by a Monsieur Gazot who was both Headmaster and Latin Master. The curriculum was demanding: French essay writing, the classics, Latin. All of seven, Fromental was top of the class in Latin and the Headmaster, to show his approbation, invited him to his home to meet his family. There was a teenage son there, a music student at the Paris Conservatoire, who was told to look after the visitor. François-Felix took the child to his room and played the piano to him. For Fromental, who had never seen one before, it was a revelation. He touched it, tried it and astounded his host with his extraordinary ability to retain and reproduce passages he had only just heard.

The following morning he mentioned his experience to a classmate of his. The classmate, son of a German-born piano maker called Roller, invited his friend to his home, led him through the ground floor to the back of the house and showed him into a huge cavernous hall where several pianos were stored. That evening Fromental informed his father that he wanted to learn to play the piano. Papa Elie did not demur and in due course a small harpsichord was delivered. By then the family had moved to what was rue Michel-Lepelletier to accommodate the growing number of children. A small two-storey house, it was sparsely furnished with some bedding, two walnut tables covered with paper tablecloths, one white and one ruled, books and writing materials. The place of honour was given to the harpsichord.

At Fromental's day school music was taught by François-Felix, the Headmaster's teenage son, who had already won the first prize for fugue and counterpoint at the Paris Conservatoire and who was teaching younger students the art of *solfège* – ear training and sight reading. In 1809, having taught Fromental for a couple of years at school, he enrolled him as a student in his class at the Conservatoire. Fromental was just over nine. He was enrolled by his recently acquired surname of Halévy.

Historically, Jews in France had no surnames. They were known as Jacob Samuel son of Abraham Moshe or, if they had the right to do so by virtue of their descent from the ancient tribe of Levy, as Jacob Samuel Levy son of Abraham Moshe Levy. It was rather confusing and from an administrative point of view highly unsatisfactory. On 20 July 1808 Napoleon, by then Emperor and much concerned with law and order within his empire, issued the following decree:

> Napoleon, Emperor of the French, King of Italy and Defender of the Rhine Confederation:
>
> On the recommendation of our Minister of the Interior, and having considered the matter in the State Council, we order that:
>
> Para 1: Those subjects of our Empire who are of the Jewish faith, and who until now have not adopted a surname, or a fixed first name, shall now be required to select one within three months of the proclamation of this order, and make it known by declaration before the State Civil Authorities at the relevant place of residence . . .
>
> Para 3: No surname shall be admitted if it is taken from the Old Testament, or if it is the name of the village of the applicant's residence.[1]

Some French Jews had anticipated the 1808 decree and had been able to register a Biblical forename as a surname. Those who had not, like Elie Levy and most of the Jewish community in France, started looking for a suitable alternative. Elie would not brook a French gentile name like Michelet or Beaulieu which were adopted by some of his coreligionists. He wanted a Hebrew surname, preferably one which would be reminiscent of his traditional forename. Scholar that he was, he recalled Yehuda

Halévy, a famous 13-century Jewish poet who lived in Muslim Spain and wrote beautiful Hebrew poems expressing his longing for Zion. Halévy, as distinct from Levy, was not an Old Testament name; it conformed to the new French law while satisfying Elie's Jewish loyalties.

What clinched his choice may well have been Fromental's musical promise. *Halevy* in Hebrew is a combination of the definite article *ha* and the noun *levy*, jointly meaning The Levite, a person born into a tribe which in ancient times was entitled by birthright to serve at the Temple of Jerusalem in a musical capacity. A serving Levite could be either an instrumentalist, a chorister, or a composer of hymns of praise. It was a fitting surname to bestow on a budding musician, a true descendant of the tribe of Levy, whose music would bring honour to his faith and his country.

In the autumn of 1808, before the expiration of the three-months' time limit set in the Imperial decree, Elie Levy presented himself at the Town Hall and made his choice known, filling in the particulars of the declaration along the dotted lines, so that it would have read as follows:

> Before us, Mayor of Le Marais, in the 3ᵉ arrondissement of the Municipality of Paris, there presented himself before us one Monsieur Elie who declared taking unto himself the name of Halévy as a surname, and the said person signed before us as required by law.[2]

And so it came to pass that in 1809, at the beginning of his first term at the Conservatoire, the nine-year-old Jacques-François-Fromental-Elie was registered for the beginners' solfège class of the Paris Conservatoire under his official surname of Halévy, the Levite, the musician.

2

CONSERVATOIRE AND PRIX DE ROME

*T*HE PARIS CONSERVATOIRE, UNDER its official name of *Le Conservatoire national de musique et de déclamation*, was founded in 1795, rising like a phoenix from the ashes of a music school for the National Guard, whose aim was to regale the masses with concerts of wind instruments. Organised on a national basis, it was to provide musical entertainment for public occasions as well as to be a teaching academy for all branches of music. That Fromental Halévy was admitted at the age of nine was well within the rules. Students were admitted at any age between eight and thirteen, with equal numbers of boys and girls. Girls, however, were chaperoned by their parents during lessons.

The curriculum for entrants comprised three foundation stages, the first being the solfège stage. The second was devoted to singing and playing an instrument, and the third to the theory of music and harmony. Discipline was rigorous, regular hours for practice were insisted upon, and examinations to assess progress were held twice a year, the examiners being five distinguished composers who held the rank of inspectors. Within ten years of its foundation the Conservatoire had a staff of forty and a studentship of over four hundred.

Having successfully got over the hurdle of the first three stages, young Halévy passed into the hands of some of the most illustrious composers of the day. The staff during his years at the

Conservatoire included Dutch-born Gossec (1734–1829), one of the most prolific and influential composers of 18th-century France: Méhul (1763–1817), nowadays regarded as the greatest French symphonist after Gossec and before Berlioz; Boieldieu (1775–1834) who had a remarkable gift for melody; Berton (1767–1844) who was given to setting the composition of fugues as homework; Catel (1773–1830, who had been teaching at the Conservatoire since its foundation and had published a book on harmony which remained a standard text book for many years; and Italian-born Cherubini (1760–1842), composer of masses, operas and instrumental music, the dominant figure in French musical life for more that fifty years. He would be the greatest single influence on Halévy's musical development, his mentor and his protector.

Fromental was making excellent progress and in 1814, at the age of fifteen, was made a teacher at the solfège foundation course, just like young François-Felix Gazot who had initiated him into the Conservatoire six years earlier. He was rather small for his age. 'My students are all taller than I am', he told his family. 'When I get to class they pile up scores on my piano stool so that I can comfortably reach the keys when accompanying their singing.'[1]

That same year the Allies, with Britain as Napoleon's arch enemy, had gone onto the offensive in order to topple him. On 30 March they were masters of Paris. The following afternoon, 1 April, Fromental, oblivious of the world outside, was practising as usual at his piano on the first floor when horse hooves were heard from the street below. His mother called out to him from downstairs to stop making a noise and keep the windows shut. Léon, the younger and less obedient of the two brothers, immediately ran to a window and threw it wide open to see what was going on. The shops had all closed, windows had been shuttered, doors bolted. A squadron of Cossacks was riding slowly down the street, ferocious astride their magnificent horses, their long lances held upright within touch of the two boys at the window. Suddenly the boys understood. Napoleon had been betrayed. The enemy had entered France.

It was as yet difficult to grasp the full import of what was happening. Fromental, and certainly his brother Léon, could not remember a time when Napoleon had not been Emperor. Life within the close-knit Jewish community had been punctuated by public expressions of loyalty indicated and scheduled by Napoleon's Minister of Religions. After the surrender of Madrid, in 1808, a ceremony was held at the synagogue at the rue Sainte-Avoye to celebrate the Emperor's victory and wish him a speedy return. The following year three ceremonies were held at the synagogue: the first to celebrate Napoleon's victories on the battlefields of Tann, Eckmul, Ratisbonne, Landshut and Abensberg; the second to mark the Emperor's birthday; and the third to celebrate the peace treaty between France and Austria and the anniversary of Napoleon's coronation. The birth of a son and heir to Napoleon and Empress Louise was another occasion for synagogal celebration. Elie Halévy had been much involved with these command performances, translating Rabbinical loyal addresses from Hebrew into French for the benefit of the less erudite members of the Jewish community. At home the boys would have heard their father's elegant translation of a long Hebrew poem inaugurating a synagogue in Marseilles, calling the blessing of God on Napoleon the Great, the Empress Louise and their young son and heir the King of Rome. The Emperor had always been referred to on such occasions as Napoleon the Great. Now Napoleon the Great was being ousted.

Ten days later, on 11 April 1814, he abdicated and was exiled to the island of Elba, off Italy. In May Paris welcomed its Bourbon king, Louis XVIII. The following year the Halévy family moved house to rue Sainte-Avoye so that the breadwinner would be nearer the synagogue where he was now employed as a clerk to the Central Jewish Consistory of Paris.

It would have been impossible for any Conservatoire student to have successfully passed the three-year foundation course without being bitten by the bug of ambition. The system encouraged competitiveness, and the glittering prize at the end of the road was the Prix de Rome which awarded the winner a five-year grant for the further study of composition in Italy, and an exemption from military service at home. Students who failed first time were encouraged to attempt again and again, until they passed the maximum age limit of thirty. Second and third prizes were also awarded, entitling their winners to a gold medal and a free pass to the Paris opera houses. In the professional shortspeak a first prize winner was known as '*a* Prix de Rome,' as distinct from '*the* Prix de Rome' which referred to the prize itself.

When young Fromental entered the Conservatoire the Prix de Rome for musicians was still regarded as an innovation. At its inception, under Louis XIV, it was awarded only to painters, sculptors and architects who were sent for their post-graduate study to the newly established Académie de France in Rome; hence the name. It was only in 1803 that the competition for the prize was made open to engravers and musicians as well. The first budding composer to win it was one Androt aged 20. He arrived in Rome in January 1804, caught the plague and died in August. At his obsequies a De Profundis of his own composition was performed. The following year the prize was left in abeyance as no musician had been able to satisfy the examination board.

Halévy made his first attempt to win the Prix de Rome in 1816, when he was only seventeen. Obviously he lacked maturity, but so did the other competitors; for the third time since its introduction some thirteen years earlier no first prize was awarded. A second prize was cold comfort. Halévy went back to his composition classes with Cherubini and the following year had another go. Second prize again; the real prize was awarded to Batton (1798–1856) whose future compositions made little impact on French musical life. Thoroughly chastised, Halévy let a full academic year pass by without putting his name down for a third attempt.

The rules of the competition had not much changed since they were first set down in 1803. It was held on the premises of the Institute of France, the overall authority which handed out the prizes to winners from the five categories under its aegis: painters, sculptors, engravers, architects and musicians. For the music competition there were two stages, the preliminary and the final. The first required the competitors to compose a fugue; Halévy was fairly competent at counterpoint but Berlioz, who was destined to fail five times, later said that making competitors write a four-part fugue was not the best way to find out who could compose a large-scale work for voice and orchestra.

The ability to write a work for voice and orchestra was precisely what the examiners were looking for. The five or six students who had passed through to the final stage were required to write a cantata on a set text, for one, two or three voices, with orchestral accompaniment. The poems that had been specially commissioned for the purpose and read out to them were mostly couched in hackneyed style. Text in hand, each competitor would be led to a small cell provided with a piano, where he was incarcerated for the duration; three such cells, at the Institute of France, are still visible under the library rafters, graffiti and all. The time allowed was three weeks, but those who finished earlier were allowed to leave. All competitors had to pay 6 francs a day for board and lodgings and 12 francs for the hire of a piano. The Conservatoire contributed 50 francs towards costs, but those who stayed the full three-week course were heavily out of pocket.

The daily routine never changed. Twice a day, at eleven in the morning and six in the evening, the cells were unlocked, the inmates let out and allowed to meet over a communal meal. Security was strict. Letters, documents, books, change of clothes were meticulously searched to prevent concealed advice being smuggled in. Oddly enough, every evening from six to eight visitors were allowed into the courtyard of the Institute, participating in the evening meal and joining in an unsupervised conversation, during which any amount of musical consultation could have taken place.

In those early days the jury consisted of representatives of all the five categories which formed the Institute of France. In other words, most of the adjudicators were not musicians who knew what they liked, but engravers, sculptors, painters and architects who liked what they knew or, as often as not, whom they knew. The five or six cantatas were performed one after the other. There was no orchestra; what the jury heard was a piano reduction accompanying the singers. Before the final voting there was much canvassing and lobbying, after which the elderly usher passed the urn round for the jury to drop their ballot papers into. On prize-giving day the winning cantata was restored to its original glory and, for the first time, heard as scored.

In 1819 Halévy entered the competition for the third time. The poem commissioned was called *Herminie*, though not the same *Herminie* which was selected six year earlier. This time he was awarded the coveted Prix de Rome, though only as a joint winner with one Massin-Turina. The rejoicing in the Halévy family was muted. Mme Halévy had just died.

Julie Halévy was only thirty-eight when she died. The cause of death was given by her family as chest trouble, presumably tuberculosis, a fatal disease in those days. What may have aggravated her condition was overwork and a strong maternal instinct which drove her to deprive herself for the sake of her family. Elie Halévy was devastated, unable to cope with the responsibility of looking after four children whose ages ranged from seventeen downwards, while the eldest, who was twenty, was about to go away for five years. Fromental had been contributing to the family income ever since he started teaching solfège at the Conservatoire at the age of fifteen and Elie came to the conclusion that his earnings could not be spared. Father and son held a consultation, as a result of which it was decided that Fromental would apply to the Conservatoire for leave to defer his grant by a year as well as for a curtailment of his away-from-Paris stay from five years to four.

Accordingly Fromental wrote to the Conservatoire authorities informing them that his mother had just died and that he was working on an opéra comique. 'I hope to see it performed in a few months' time,' he wrote, 'and, if successful, it should enable me to provide for my family while I am away.'[2]

The application was studied with astonishment and disapproval – it was unprecedented. Obviously strings had to be pulled and Halévy *père* found access to the very man whose intervention could tip the balance in his son's favour. He was Baron Antoine-Isaac Silvestre de Sacy (1758–1838), one of the most distinguished orientalists of the day, a scholar showered with honours, a *grand officier* of the Légion d'Honneur, the second highest of the five ranks constituting the order founded by Napoleon; and a professing Jew to boot. Elie Halévy, no mean scholar himself, approached him through their common interest and explained the problem. Baron de Sacy dropped a word in the right ear and the application was approved, however grudgingly:

> Young musicians are awarded a grant to Rome to study music and improve their work, and it would matter little to the cause of art if Monsieur Halévy's work does not get produced. However, one can only applaud the pious sentiments which had prompted the young man's application, considering that his father has just lost his helpmate.[3]

With the grant deferred for a year, the term abroad reduced from five years to four and the fifth year's grant still payable when he was back in Paris, Halévy directed his efforts towards finding a theatre which would put on his first opera comique. He had made some influential contacts and on 20 December 1819 wrote to Baron d'Est, Royal Superintendant of Entertainment Expenditure, as follows:

> Sir, you have kindly promised me your support and guidance in the first steps of my theatrical career. Having full trust in your kindness I am asking you today to be good enough to take an interest in a work written, if I may say so, under your auspices. My music for *Les Deux pavillons* is finished. Monsieur Cherubini my teacher has kindly gone over it and given me advice which I have attentively followed. I would now like to offer it to the members of the Society of the Opéra-Comique Theatre for their approval, and I take the liberty of asking you to be so kind as to ask them to grant me an interview. I hope you will treat my request favourably adding this mark of goodwill to all the other kindnesses with which you have honoured me until now.[4]

It was a young man's letter, obsequious, stilted, probably drafted by his father and neatly copied out like a schoolboy's prize homework. Never again would Halévy write another like it. With age and success his letters would become matter-of-fact, crisp, sometimes even humorous, while his handwriting, invariably neat, would grow minute and loopy to the point of illegibility.

Les Deux pavillons was never performed but the extra year in Paris gained by the deferment of the grant was not wasted. Within months of his unsuccessful application to the Opéra-Comique Halévy was commissioned to write a vocal score of an entirely different kind and was able to experience the tremendous elation of a young composer hearing his work performed in public for the first time in his life.

3

DE PROFUNDIS

*A*T ELEVEN O'CLOCK ON THE night of 13 February 1820 the Duc de Berry was leaving the Paris Opéra with the Duchess on his arm, about to hand her into their carriage. It was carnival time; Mardi Gras revellers were milling in the streets; someone bumped hard into him and ran away. Instinctively he put his hand to his chest, felt the handle of a knife protruding and pulled it out. A stream of blood gushed out. 'I've been stabbed,' he cried. 'I'm a dead man.' His aides gave chase and caught up with the attacker who had collided with a fruit barrow and was being held fast by an irate barrow boy. The Duke was rushed to his home and in the small hours of the morning died in the arms of his pregnant wife. 'I forgive him,' were his reputed last words. It was a political murder.

Duc Charles-Ferdinand de Berry was born in 1778 and, as nephew of the guillotined king Louis XVI, sought refuge in England. In London he married a Miss Anna Brown, had two daughters by her and arranged for the marriage to be annulled as soon as he heard that an uncle of his, brother of the guillotined king, had been restored to the throne as Louis XVIII. He returned to Paris to be welcomed and acknowledged as heir presumptive. By way of preparation for future grandeur he married the eldest daughter of the King of Naples.

In Versailles, in 1783, a boy was born to a poor family who grew up to be a saddler and a fervent admirer of Napoleon. The disgrace of the abdication made Louvel shed tears of rage and vow to avenge Napoleon by exterminating the entire Bourbon family. His hit list included Louis XVIII, the Duc de Valmy and Count d'Artois. In the meantime he went to Elba to work in Napoleon's stables as a saddler, returned to France during the Hundred Days and was present at Waterloo. Back in Paris he became master saddler in Louis XVIII's stables to be nearer his main target, but never managed to get anywhere near the King. One day he heard from the grooms that the Duc de Berry had returned from England. It was then he added the Duke's name to his hit list and decided he would be his first victim, presumably because of all the surviving Bourbons the Duke was the least protected by a bodyguard.

Louvel had no clear plan of action and perhaps was not bright enough to think of one. For the next four years he just walked about the streets of Paris, frequenting places where he hoped he was likely to catch a glimpse of his quarry. When he was arrested he offered no resistance and readily admitted the stabbing.

His mild manner puzzled his interrogators who immediately suspected that he was only a simpleton in the service of an international plot. England was a prime suspect; so were Austria, Spain, the Bonapartist party. Louvel kept insisting he had no accomplices. Courteous and patient, he informed his interrogators that since Louis XVI had been legally tried and guillotined, no brother or relative of his had any right to rule France. During the trial he conceded that stabbing a man to death was a horrible thing to do, but it was the only possible way to punish those who had betrayed the nation. Asked what he would have done had he not been caught he answered without hesitation that he would have proceeded to kill the next Bourbon until they would have all been wiped off the face of the earth. The Defence pleaded insanity. The Prosecution demanded the death sentence. He was guillotined on 7 June 1820.

Even before the trial got under way an order was issued by the Minister of Religions to all denominations to hold a commemorative service for his Royal Highness the late Duc de Berry, heir presumptive to the throne of France. Fromental Halévy immediately wrote to the authorities of the synagogue at rue Sainte-Avoye suggesting that he would like to compose a vocal work for the occasion.

A commissioned work was basically alien to synagogal liturgy which had been handed down from generation to generation. At the same time it was not as alien to current synagogal practice as it would have been when Fromental was a child. New elements had already begun to infiltrate into the traditional service. Halévy could remember that those command celebrations in honour of Napoleon, in which his father had been involved as a translator, had been followed by organised music. At first there was no more than a children's choir responding to the cantor; admittedly without training or use of sheet music, but a choir all the same. Then two harps were introduced. When the peace treaty between France and Austria was celebrated a Hebrew song of praise was composed along the lines of a Te deum. Recent cantors were trained musicians, well versed in western secular music. Last but not least, a music committee had been formed to supervise and direct the growing fusion between traditional liturgy and modern vocal music 'crafted' like secular music.

Halévy's qualifications for what he proposed to do were impeccable. Not only was he a Prix de Rome, but he had had a traditional Jewish upbringing and was the son of one of the pillars of the Paris Jewish community, a scholar much involved with past command ceremonies held at the rue Sainte-Avoye synagogue and an employee in the service of the Paris Jewish consistory. If there were other candidates for the commission Halévy easily outshone them. The Committee considered the nature of his proposed work and commissioned it.

What he produced was a *Marche Funèbre et De Profundis*, for three voices and an orchestra. For text he used the Hebrew words of Psalm 130, preparing an Italian translation as well. The vocal parts were divided between two tenors and a *basse-taille* – a voice whose range is between a bass and a baritone. The solos were written for Israel Lovy, an outstanding cantor whose rendering of the Hebrew song *Lecha Dodi* during the Friday night service attracted crowds of music-loving gentiles from the aristocratic Faubourg Saint-Germain, to the annoyance of the Jewish regulars; there were only 107 seats for men and 85 for women in the synagogue, at that time the largest and most prestigious in Paris. To satisfy his gentile admirers Lovy gave a recital in the foyer of the Théâtre-Italien.

There was obviously no shortage of proficient Jewish musi-

17

cians about. The work called for first and second violins, violas, cellos, double basses; first and second flutes, oboes, first and second clarinets, first and second bassoons; first and second horns tuned to D and F, tenor, alto and bass trombones; muted kettledrums tuned to F and D, a bass drum, and a piano. The *Marche funèbre* was marked Andante Maestoso, with a profusion of ff and pp. The *De Profundis* gave a phonetic transcription of the Hebrew verses following the Sephardi (Spanish Jewish) tradition of rendering a guttural *a* as *ang*.

The Duc de Berry died on 14 February; the ministerial order to commemorate him would have been issued a week or so later; the performance, before a mixed audience of Jews and gentiles at the overcrowded rue Sainte-Avoye synagogue, was held on 24 March. The speed of composition and the ability to organise, supervise, coach and insist on a performance conforming to his instructions became the hallmark of the young composer. The work was published by Ignace Pleyel and is nowadays presumed the first professionally 'crafted' synagogal music to be published in France in the 19th century. It was a trail blazer.

The 24 March 1820 was a great day in the history of synagogal music in France, and a great day for Fromental Halévy who, still under twenty-one, was already a performed and published composer. He dedicated this first fruit of his talent to the mentor who would remain a lifelong friend and whom he loved like a father – Luigi Cherubini.

4

VILLA MEDICI

*I*T WAS CUSTOMARY FOR WINNERS of the five categories of the Prix de Rome, ceremoniously awarded in October, to set out for Italy in January of the following year. Painter, sculptor, architect, engraver and composer would make a party of five, or more if there were joint winners, and hire a coach to take them all the way. It was an arduous economy class travel for students on a tight budget; no change of horses, indifferent inns. It took a long time to get across France, over the Alps, and down to Northern Italy. For Halévy, setting out in January 1821, it was his first view of foreign parts. In the diary he started keeping he recorded his first impressions.

> The first thing that strikes a visitor on his arrival in Italy is the extreme superstitiousness and corruption of the people. No true religion, no morals, no sense of honour. That's what the people of Rome are like, and particularly the people of Naples. Lots of priests, monks, Madonnas, crosses in every street corner, indulgences attached to the worship of the Madonna – that is the state of the people. As soon as you cross the Alps French morals disappear. It is mainly in Rome and Naples that we can observe the true Italian character. Earlier on, from the Alps as far as Rome, French mores have permeated Italian mores and been absorbed into them, but as for the rest of Italy the Italian traits manifest themselves very strongly.[1]

Once in Rome the new arrivals made for the Villa Medici, their home for the next few years, where they reported to the director and were shown to their quarters. Although the Academy of France in Rome had been functioning since 1666, the Villa Medici was acquired only in 1803, a sixteenth-century palace on Monte Pincio, commanding magnificent views over gardens, pine woods and the bustling life in the city below. Much refurbished, it provided studios for artists, practice rooms for musicians, individual though mostly small bedrooms, and a library which would invariably close at three in the afternoon.

Life at the Academy of France in Rome had originally been strictly regulated, with early morning bell, prayers, and curfew. During the revolution students dragged the statue of Louis XVI into the coal cellar. Laureates whose journey from Paris was postponed for a couple of years arrived when normality was restored, together with wives and children they had acquired, installing themselves on the premises as of right, brats and all. By Halévy's time a happier and more sensible way of life had evolved. During the day some students would work, others would lounge; in the evening they would get together, strum guitars, sing popular songs. Second and third years would await with curiosity the arrival of the new batch from Paris, when initiation rites would be indulged in. Halévy was solemnly told he would have to spend a night in the Jewish quarter, but was disabused before he had a chance to set out.

Monsieur Tavenin, the current director of the Academy of France at the Villa Medici, had a superb apartment at his disposal where once a week he held open house for students and important guests who might be useful contacts in the future. Students were free to plan their work or leisure as they pleased, but once a year they were required to send back to Paris a sample of their progress, whether a painting, a drawing, an engraving, a sculpture or a piece of music. Halévy was assiduous. During the years of his grant he sent to Paris the requisite number of compositions, three in all. As was the custom they were performed, though not in full, at one of the seasonal Conservatoire concerts, then consigned to oblivion.

While Rome was a good centre for artists to explore and seek inspiration, it was hardly a place to inspire musicians arriving from Paris, the music powerhouse of the age. A scathing description of the Roman musical scene was given by the Irish novelist Lady Morgan who attended some performances shortly before Halévy's arrival.

> The Roman theatres are dark, dirty and paltry in their decoration; but what is infinitely worse, they are so offensive to the senses, so disgusting in the details of their arrangements, that to particularize would be impossible; suffice it to say that the corridors of the Argentina Theatre [which in 1816 gave the first performance of Rossini's *Almaviva*, later to be renamed *Il Barbiere di Siviglia*] exemplify the nastiness of the Roman habits and manners . . .[2]

Of the actual standard of performance, having seen Rossini's recent opera *Otello*, she opined that the opera in Rome was just about tolerable, except that when it was not, the audience was prohibited from showing displeasure.

> On the first murmur of disapproval, the offender is seized by the police or guards with which theatres are filled . . . and is carried to the Piazza Navona, where he is mounted in a sort of stocks and flogged. He is then carried back and placed in his seat to enjoy the rest of the opera, with what appetite he may.[3]

She went on to describe further unacceptable practices during a performance at the Teatro della Pace of Rossini's *Mosè in Egitto*.

> Teatro della Pace is smoky and time-stricken . . . The audience was composed of what an English government newspaper would call wretches, ruffians, the scum of society – the people . . . Every box was crowded. The *trasteverini* [people from Trastevere, a poor quarter of Rome] were numerous . . . They shouted, screamed and mingled their *bravos* and *bravissimos* with *gran bella cosa, cosa superba, cosa stupenda*. Meanwhile the most amiable familiarity subsisted between that part of the audience nearest to the stage, and the performers. The prompter, with his head popped over the stage lights, talked to the girls in the pit, the violincello flirted with a handsome *trasteverina* in the boxes; and a lady in the stage-box blew out the lamp lighter's candle as often as he attempted to light it, to the infinite amusement of the audience, who loudly applauded her dexterity. With an economy duly practised at Rome by all classes, the musicians, when they had done playing between the several acts, extinguished their candles, put them in their pockets and joined the audience in the front of the house. In justice to La Pace Theatre it must not be concealed that the same economical custom prevails in many theatres, not of the first rate, throughout Italy.[4]

Musical life in Rome being what it was, prize winners were not slow to make their disappointment known. Complaints reaching Paris about the unsuitability of Rome for sophisticated budding composers partly accounted for the inclusion of Germany in the study tour. Moreover, the curriculum allowed students, with the director's permission, to absent themselves from the Villa Medici for indefinite periods in order to visit other centres of Italian music, like Naples, Venice, Bologna, Ferrara, or Milan. Halévy's diary shows that he made ample use of that provision. In May 1821 he set out with two friends on a musical pilgrimage. They stayed the night at a Capuchin monastery where each was given a small clean cell and offered breakfast at five in the morning. From there they went on to Palestrina, birthplace of Giovanni Pierluigi Palestrina, (c.1525–1594) the study of whose works was high on the first year curriculum.

Further entries in 1821 and 1822 mention more trips, some by coach, to Naples, Vesuvius, Eboli. His travelling companions may well have been other music Prix de Rome laureates whose stay overlapped with his; his co-winner Massin-Turina, of whom Léon Halévy mischievously said that he stayed on in Italy to become 'profoundly unknown'; Le Borne (1820), Rifaut (1821), Le Bourgeois (1822). In Naples they had a meal which he described as delicious; away from paternal supervision he was no longer worried about dietary laws, enjoying what fare he was offered at the Villa Medici, a monastery, or a wayside inn. On a bright January morning he picked up shells on the beach.

The travelling party to Vesuvius included ladies, a fact recorded in his diary with the cryptic remark 'among whom was my lady friend.'[5] Equally cryptic is an entry addressed to a young woman. 'After our conversation you must have been less cheerful. I said to you hard things which must have upset you.'[6] The young woman as well as her mother were both married, and it is not clear whether they had been playing him up or whether he was offering unsolicited advice on their marital problems from the vantage point of a twenty-two year old bachelor. He accused them both of flirtatiousness. Elsewhere in his diary he drew three identical profiles of a woman, most unprepossessing to look at unless he was a poor artist, with the words *que l'amour* written next to them three times; perhaps a shorthand way of saying 'There is nothing but love.'

Keen on familiarising himself with the Eternal City he had drawn up a list of historical sites to be visited and sometimes went sightseeing on his own. On one such occasion he had an experience which he recorded in his diary at unusual length.

He had set out from the Villa Medici intending to visit the Capitol, a good walking distance away, but lost his way in a maze of streets and alleyways. He asked where he was and a kind passer-by told him he was in the 'ghetto.' The conversation was held in Italian; the curriculum required students to be proficient in the language by the end of their first year.

'What is a *ghetto*?' Halévy asked.

'It is the quarter of the Jews.'

'Jews?'

'Yes, they live within this enclosure. Those are their houses. At the end of this small square you will see a house somewhat bigger than the others. That is their place of worship . . .'

'This aroused my curiosity,' the diary goes on. 'I knew there were Jews in Rome but had not heard anything about them. I decided to make use of the opportunity that chance had put my way.'

He went on as directed, entered the synagogue and found it full of men, their heads covered, praying. 'I don't know why I was moved,' he recorded. 'Perhaps it was the sight of those unfortunates worshipping the same God that their forefathers did five thousand years ago.'

For someone who had been traditionally brought up within the Jewish community of Paris and who had recently had a De Profundis in Hebrew performed in a Paris synagogue, the above dialogue and description read like a conscious attempt to distance himself from his origins. This was not the case. Halévy had been born into an emancipated Jewish community. In Paris, in spite of a serious regression during Louis XVIII's reign, Jews were not segregated; some, like his benefactor the Orientalist Baron Antoine-Isaac Silvestre de Sacy, had risen to the highest honours. He himself had competed at the Conservatoire with no sense of racial or religious discrimination. If most of his coreligionists lived in Le Marais, it was from choice, not coercion. The concept of a *ghetto* – an Italian word – as a Jewish quarter separated by gated walls from the Christian section of a town was surely new to him; hence his compassion for 'those unfortunates' whose like he had not seen in his native France.

After prayers he got into conversation with the men round him and was invited to someone's house for the ritual Seder meal in the evening; he had not realised it was the eve of Passover. 'You will have to go through some filthy streets,' his host said apologetically. 'We no longer live in Jerusalem. We live as aliens among people who just tolerate us.'

In the evening Halévy made his way to his host's house through the ghetto maze. 'The houses were small, dilapidated, ill-lit, full of women and children, their clothes attesting to their poverty.' He found the house, as mean as any other in the narrow street, climbed a tortuous staircase. Indoors it was well appointed and elegant, the large dining table covered with a richly embroidered silk tablecloth. He was introduced in order of precedence to his host's mother, wife, five children and other Jewish guests. 'Monsieur is a stranger whom I met at the synagogue,' the host said to his family. The table had already been set with unleavened bread and other prescribed dishes. The host read the *Haggadah*, the ritual commemoration of the Exodus of the Children of Israel from Egypt. He had a strange oriental name and had been to France and England. Halévy brought the conversation round to the topic that intrigued him most – the ghetto. The first ghetto had been established in Rome in the sixteenth century, following a bull issued by Pope Paul V, with walls and gates that were locked at night and on some Christian holidays as well. 'This is the new Roman ghetto,' his host concluded.[7]

Halévy was studiously making notes for composition. An incomplete opera plot with English names like Mr Darcombe, his daughter Laura and her governess Mrs Aubrey is faintly reminiscent of the English background of his 1839 opéra comique *Le Shérif*. Melodies neatly written on hand-ruled staves suggest diligence. Marks were given to singers he heard either in Rome or in Naples, mostly in Rossini operas. Benedetti was no more than a big man who sang *basse-taille* [range between bass and baritone]; Ambrogi, who also sang *basse-taille*, had a good voice; David put much expression into his singing; Nozzari was an excellent musician as well as an excellent teacher.

He made good use of the official encouragement to students to visit music centres other than Rome by staying in Naples, where

Rossini had been writing his best Italian operas for the Teatro San Carlo. Not only did he meet Rossini but he composed music for three ballets which were performed at the San Carlo and favourably received, or so he wrote to his family. He also composed three canzonetti in the Neapolitan style, dedicating them to the eldest of his sisters.

The last phase of his Prix de Rome was spent, as laid down in the curriculum, in Germany; his diary is silent on this phase. There is no record of his attending opera performances in Berlin where society ladies were known to applaud like men, unlike their Paris counterparts who expressed their approval in a more feminine way. During his German stay he composed an overture, set a psalm to music for orchestra and two choirs, and sketched the finale of a grand opera in the Italian style. The operatic climax occurred when the hero, Marco Curzio, threw himself in full view of friends and foes into an abyss to placate the vengeful gods for an offence given to them by someone else. Plot and music, as described in a letter to his brother Léon, already heralded the dramatic elements, the dazzling spectacle and the theme of self-sacrifice that would inform the grand operas of his middle years like *La Juive*, *La Reine de Chypre* and *Charles VI*.

His return journey included a stop in Vienna, where Prix de Rome students had a benevolent protector in the person of Mozart's rival Salieri, Court Kapellmeister and tutor by correspondence to the Paris Conservatoire. Hérold, an earlier Prix de Rome winner, had been introduced to and affably received by Beethoven; he had been too scared to use a letter of introduction in his possession. 'I saw him at somebody's house,' Hérold recorded. 'He refused to play and the host did not insist because everybody knows Beethoven would not play even for the Emperor of Morocco if he does not feel so inclined.'[8] Halévy fared better. He was introduced to Beethoven when the latter was working on his Choral Symphony and actually called on him. The impact of that meeting is not known. An undated entry in Halévy's diary made in Vienna does not refer to it, while Léon, writing after Halévy's death, did not go beyond stating that young Fromental was allowed to visit Beethoven 'several times.'

5

FIRST STEPS IN PARIS

*I*T WAS A HAPPY FAMILY REUNION. Father, brother and sisters embraced the victor of Rome, marvelled at his robust and manly appearance, made plans for the future. Halévy went to the Conservatoire to pay his respects to Cherubini who in 1822 was appointed its director, and was given back his teaching post at the solfège class. One of the first things that Cherubini had done as director was to arrange a separate entrance for girl students; presumably they were harassed by male colleagues. It is interesting to note that although the Conservatoire had been co-educational since its foundation in 1795, no woman was awarded the Prix de Rome until 1913, when Lily Boulanger was a co-winner. The proposition of incarcerating female students in cells during the competition and, if winners, sending them to the Villa Medici to live in what was to all intents and purposes a boys' boarding school, was unquestionably impractical.

Halévy was confident of a quick success. A returning Prix de Rome laureate could expect to have his first work performed under the aegis of the Academy of Fine Arts, one of the five Academies that constituted the Institute of France. Article 25 of its constitution provided that 'each returning laureate shall receive from the Music Faculty of the Academy of Fine Arts a dramatic work, either modern or from the ancient repertoire, to be set to music. This work shall, under the aegis of the authorities, be put on at one of the theatres of the capital, or at one of the main cities of the realm.'[1] Halévy applied for a text from the ancient repertoire and composed *Pygmalion*, a one-act opera.

When no theatre showed interest in a young man's first opera, he wrote through intermediaries to Viscount Sostène de la Rochefoucault, Director of the Academy of Fine Arts, asking his help to 'overcome the countless obstacles confronting young composers on the threshold of their careers notwithstanding the intended protection offered by a solicitous Academy.'[2] *Pygmalion* went into rehearsal at the Opéra but was eventually shelved all the same. *Erostrate*, a three-act opera, fared no better. That was a double disappointment since brother Léon had had a hand in the libretto.

Gradually it dawned on Halévy that the award of the Prix de Rome, years of post-graduate work abroad, and Article 25 were no guarantee of success. The innocent hopeful, wrote a near contemporary, 'submits his work to a theatre director who tries to wriggle out of his obligation by saying that the libretto is poor. Some five or six years later, provided the composer has been persistent, made a nuisance of himself and refused to take no for an answer, the director puts it on, but sees to it that it has only three performances, shoddily executed at that. The young composer – no longer so young – goes back to giving private music lessons, writing love-songs, dance music, transcriptions and piano reductions. He ends where he had started.'[3]

There were no miraculous exceptions to the pattern. Hérold had had to wait four years before his first opera was put on. Halévy had to wait seven. 'A lesser man, a less gifted composer, a person with less self-confidence, would have retreated into silence,'[4] wrote a friend recalling the early years. Halévy bore his disappointments with fortitude, drawing on an inner source of dogged perseverance that would keep him going for the rest of his life.

In the meantime the family left the squalid old house near the local synagogue and moved into the more salubrious rue de la Jussiènne. Alas, for the eldest of the three sisters who since the mother's death had been looking after old Elie, brother Léon and the two younger sisters, the move came too late. She died in 1824 at the age of twenty-three. Elie was also failing. He died in 1826, aged sixty-six, comforted by the news that Fromental had just been appointed *chef du chant* at the Théâtre-Italien. The entire Jewish community of Paris followed his coffin to its last resting place.

It was imperative to get away from a house where two deaths had occurred within two years of each other. Fromental and Léon, with their younger sisters Flore and Melanie, moved into the fourth floor of an elegant apartment-house in rue Montholon. The brothers were the breadwinners, Fromental coaching and Léon writing, while the sisters kept house and were hostesses to a growing number of neighbours. The floor below was occupied by the distinguished architect Le Bas with his wife and daughter, and soon the four Halévys and Mlle Le Bas were making music together. When the Le Bas family moved out their apartment was taken by an old friend of Elie Halévy, a Monsieur Rodrigues of Bordeaux, whose son Olinde became a well-known philosopher. Another Rodrigues branch, the brothers Edouard and Henri, also occupied an apartment in the block, and so did two Pereira brothers. It was a colony of affluent, gifted and ambitious young people most of whom were, like the Halévys, Jewish by birth but no longer orthodox. In some cases social calls matured into matrimony. In due course a Pereira would marry a Rodrigues girl, as would Fromental Halévy though not until many years later, when he had fifteen operas to his credit.

His first opera to be performed was *L'Artisan*, a one-act opera comique to words by Saint-Georges, with whom he would collaborate for many years to come. The story unfolds in a shipyard at the port of Antibes. Justin, a skilled carpenter of unknown parentage, has been brought up by a kind woman together with her daughter Louise. A naval officer comes ashore, informs Justin that he is his long-lost cousin and that a rich inheritance awaits him in Paris provided he goes to the capital and marries an heiress. Louise, in desperation, accepts an offer of marriage from the middle-aged foreman of the shipyard. Justin declares that he does not want money, he wants to go on being an artisan. He renounces his inheritance in favour of his cousin the naval officer, though not the title of Baron; rank in the make-believe world of the opéra comique was considered desirable, if not frankly mandatory. The foreman concedes that he is too old to take a young girl for a wife, the Baron artisan and Louise get married and everybody is happy. The dialogue is conducted in what is meant to be the working-class dialect of Antibes, a pleasant departure from the laboured poetic style of the lyric theatre of the time.

L'Artisan was put on at the Opéra-Comique on 30 January 1827 and failed to make an impact. A tactful friend said that the story was not interesting, and that the music reflected the story. The critics were less tactful and the audience was sparse. Halévy's first operatic work to reach the stage was taken off after fourteen performances, never to be revived.

With that perseverance which would brook no failure, he commissioned another libretto from Saint-Georges, collaborating on the music with Rifaut, a Prix de Rome winner of a recent vintage. *Le Roi et le batelier* was another one-act opéra comique which was bravely put on by the Opéra-Comique only ten months after the cool reception of *L'Artisan*. Like *L'Artisan* it was written in what was meant to be the local dialect of the simple people.

The story is set on the banks of the Seine in the spring of 1594, when Henri IV laid siege to Paris to assert his right to be king of France. In the opera he tries to do so by peaceful means. The oarsman Claude rows him every night to the other bank, taking him for a Parisian soldier. The 'soldier' assures him that provisions are going to be smuggled into Paris to relieve the famine, and that the signal for the loyal smugglers is the song *Vive Henri IV*. There is an exchange of necessary but harmless firing, Claude sings the password song, a flotilla of small boats is let through, the besieged are grateful. The King, now in his true identity, leads a peaceful army into Paris.

Le Roi et le batelier was premiered on 8 November 1827, a birthday tribute to Charles X, father of the murdered Duc de Berry, who had succeeded to the throne of France some three years earlier. Certainly the portrayal of Henri IV as the peace-loving benefactor of the besieged Parisians was worked in with a purpose. Again the plot was unremarkable and the music likewise. After thirteen performances it was taken off.

Barely a year later Halévy was ready with *Clari*, based on a popular novella of the time; it had already been set to music by Henry Bishop in London to an English libretto by J.H. Payne, and put on at Covent Garden on 8 May 1823 under the title of *Clari* or the *Maid of Milan*. Halévy's *Clari* had an Italian libretto by the exiled Florentine poet Giannone and was put on at the Théâtre-Italien on 19 December 1928 with La Malibran in the title role.

The commission was an achievement in itself, partly due to the fact that the composer had been a *chef du chant* at the Théâtre-Italien for the past three years and had neglected no opportunity to put himself forward. The Italian exiles who filled the theatre liked the work and the reviewers praised the able scoring by a French composer of Italian folk tunes and rhythms. Indeed it was no pastiche. Halévy had put to good use what he had absorbed in Italy, when complying with the Prix de Rome curriculum requiring students to compose a vocal work against an Italian background with a set Italian text, and to go round collecting folk tunes and prefacing the collection with a learned essay.

In the event *Clari* was his worst failure so far. In spite of Malibran's drawing power it was taken off after six performances. Of Bishop's English *Clari* at least one song has achieved immortality: Home Sweet Home.

The following year, after seven years of rejections, lukewarm reviews and poor houses, Halévy picked up a witty libretto dealing with a topical subject, and at long last made a breakthrough. It was *Le Dilettante d'Avignon.*

To understand its popularity it is necessary to take account of the uninterrupted and unchallenged domination of Italian opera in Paris. Starting early in the eighteenth century with Pergolesi, the Théâtre-Italien went on to produce Italian operas by Gluck, Cimarosa, Mozart, Paër, Spontini, Rossini, Donizetti. Napoleon believed that Italian music would regenerate French music and imported the best of Italian talent. While in Dresden in 1806 he saw the opera *Achille* by Court Kappellmeister Paër and heard Madame Paër sing with her partner Brizzi.

> 'Mme Paër,' Napoleon said after the performance. 'You are a beautiful singer. What is your fee?'
> 'Fifteen thousand francs, Sire.'
> 'You will be paid thirty thousand. Monsier Brizzi, you will be paid the same.'
> "But Sire, we have a contract to sing in Dresden.'
> 'Regard the affair as settled. Talleyrand will arrange it through the diplomatic channels.'[5]

That same evening Napoleon ordered his aides to persuade Paër to move to Paris. The composer was abducted and kept incommunicado until the following morning, when the King of Saxony graciously agreed to declare his contract null and void. In due course Paër was appointed the director of the Théâtre-Italien.

It was inevitable that the preferential status of Italian opera in Paris should be resented by a growing number of French composers. François-Benoit Hoffman was a much sought after librettist who, on his death in April 1828, left behind an incomplete libretto satirising the cult of Italian music in France. The brothers Halévy sensed that the time was ripe for such a satire. Léon cleared the right to rework the libretto provided Hoffman's name should precede his on programmes and printed text, and Fromental started to compose.

Le Dilettante d'Avignon, a one-act opéra comique, is set in a small opera house at Avignon, whose director is deaf to any music unless it is Italian. In fact he is deaf to any kind of music. He has just dismissed a company of French singers and engaged an Italian one instead, little suspecting that they are the same singers now sporting Italian names. An audition cum rehearsal is called. The opera director explains his attitude: 'I wish there was a prohibition on singing in any language other than Italian. French words are barbarous, they degrade the melody. I can't stand them any more. I'm going to speak Italian.'[6]

A delightful comic situation is created when the opera director, whose Italian is non-existent, interviews the French singers whose Italian is based on Italian arias.

'What is your genre,' the director asks one of the singers.

'I only know two genres,' replies the singer, 'the good and the bad.. The good is the one that draws the public, the bad is the other.'

The satire is lent further topicality by the French *chef du chant*, a Prix de Rome winner, who has recently returned from the Villa Medici and 'gives singing lessons while waiting to be allowed to compose operas.' He is known to the director by the Italian name of Imbroglio.

There is a learned argument between director and company about a 'duet for three,' and how to sing while riding a horse on land and water. Love interest is provided by the director's daughter who is in league with her sweetheart, the so-called

Imbroglio. In the end all is revealed; the opera director lends an ear to the wise words of the male singer, whom he now realises is the French leader of a French company. 'Both genres are good,' says the singer referring to the Italian and the French. 'Instead of arguing about their respective merits it would be wiser to take from one what is reasonable, and from the other what is graceful.' There is general jubilation, and the final chorus is a hymn of praise to both genres:

> *Honneur, honneur au génie*
> *Ou de France ou d'Italie.*
> *Honneur, honneur au génie,*
> *Au talent point de patrie.*

Le Dilettante d'Avignon was premiered at the Opéra-Comique on 7 November 1829. The critics liked the satire, lavished praise on the witty use of solos and ensembles. *Le Journal des débats* could not help pointing out that for a composer who barely a year earlier had won acclaim for *Clari*, an opera in the Italian language put on by the Théâtre-Italien, Halévy was something of a turncoat. Then it gave praise. 'The introduction to the new opera is original and well crafted, and the duet for three voices shows talent . . . The chorus *Vive l'Italie* was greeted with outbursts of enthusiasm and had to be repeated. It is skillfully written; the modulation, the details – all deserve praise.'[7] Obviously the anonymous reviewer was an inveterate admirer of Italian opera, for he wistfully added: 'Without being as important a work as *Clari*, *Le Dilettante d'Avignon* does honour to Monsieur Halévy. It is a total success.'[8]

And so it was. The music publisher Schlesinger bought the publishing rights and within days of the premiere had piano reductions of the most popular sections ready for sale. It was kept on the repertoire for many seasons and had 119 performances. In years to come it would be referred to as 'Halévy's first masterpiece.'[9]

The person who had used his influence more than most to pave the way for Halévy was Cherubini, once his composition teacher and now his protector. He would have put in a good word for his former student when the latter offered his first works to the Opéra-Comique, or *Clari* to the Théâtre-Italien. He would certainly have recommended him in 1829 for the post of a second *chef du chant* at the Opéra, to be held jointly with Hérold. After the death of both his parents the Cherubini house became Halévy's second home. He visited without ceremony, used the intimate form of address – *tu* – with the composer's son Salvador, treated Mme Cherubini with filial affection and was on friendly terms with the two married daughters. Soon he was acting as Cherubini's personal secretary. It was from the Cherubini home that he wrote a chatty letter to Salvador who was touring Egypt with a brother-in-law.

> 7 May 1829
>
> I am writing to you *tête à tête* with your mother. It is nine o'clock in the evening. A single lamp sheds a mysterious light on the bedroom where the scene unfolds. Your mother is resting in bed while I am writing. But do not worry. It is just a cold she had caught while bidding goodbye to Mme de Salin . . .
>
> The weather has been appalling, rain, wind, here and there a touch of sun, which peeps out only to be missed all the more. April was as cold as November. We kept singing 'Pretty month of May, Why have you gone away?' Well, May came back, the leaves came with it, but no sun or warmth . . .
>
> This year's Conservatoire concerts were even more successful than last year's. The final concert was held last Sunday. Distinguished audience, much applause, two Beethoven symphonies, a lovely motet by your father. The Duchesse de Berry was there [Halévy was in her good books since his De Profundis for her late husband] . . .
>
> At the concert before last we heard a Credo and something else by your father's colleague Le Sueur [music co-director with Cherubini at the Tuileries Chapel and teacher of composition at the Conservatoire]. I wish you had been there, dear Salvador, you would have been able to tell us whether this music might have pleased Egypt, for here in Paris it made a ridiculous impression. The audience laughed, the orchestra had to laugh willy-nilly, everybody laughed except the composer who, by way of consolation, had himself ennobled and now has a coat of arms . . . [10]

He gave Salvador news of forthcoming opera productions and the latest of the Paris horror stories; a society lady had been murdered in broad daylight by a gentleman who then blew his brains out. He facetiously rebuked his friend for being an unreliable correspondent.

Haven't you been writing to me? To me, who must have some Egyptian blood running in my veins considering that my ancestors had made a long stay in that ancient country? It may not be impossible that one of my great-great-grandfathers sacrificed to Baal and fornicated with a pretty Egyptian lass; for all we know I may be related to some mummy you have seen . . .[11]

He ended with news about the two married sisters one of whom happened to call on her mother while he was writing his letter, about the little nephew, the grandmother – his entire extended family. 'Your mother and your sister,' he signed off merrily, 'desire me to inform you that I am the most detestable man on earth and that you wouldn't know me when you come back.'[12] It was probably a family joke about his growing self-assertion and his confident expectations of success.

What is striking about this long high-spirited letter is that although it was written in May 1829, when he was already working on *Le Dilettante d'Avingon*, Halévy made no mention of it. It was his way. His extant letters to his many correspondents deal with everyday arrangements, administrative questions, and never discuss his musical views. His reticence about his work may have been due to an instinct that warns a composer or a writer not to talk his work out of himself; his views would be amply and elegantly expounded in his future lectures and books.

The year 1829 was a turning point in his career. After the Piccinis, Sichinis, Spontinis, Cherubinis, Rossinis and Bellinis of the Paris opera, *Le Dilettante d'Avignon* established Fromental Halévy as a French composer, the youngest of the French school which already boasted Boieldieu, Auber and Hérold.

6

EBB AND FLOW

*F*OR HALEVY 1830 WAS THE YEAR of the three first nights; for France it was the year of the three glorious days.

When Louis XVIII died in 1824 he was peacefully succeeded by his sixty-six year old brother the Count d'Artois, father of the murdered Duke de Berry, who ascended the throne as Charles X. The policies of this new Bourbon monarch did not go far enough for a new generation of liberty-conscious Frenchmen. He tried to strengthen his position by going to the country, only to be proved unpopular when the ballot papers gave the Republicans a landslide victory. He dissolved the new Chamber before it had a chance to convene, and the liberal press reacted by calling on the people to fight for their rights. On 27 July 1830 the shops of Paris remained closed, barricades were put up, demonstrations were held. Bourgeois, workers, war veterans, students and defecting riot troops marched together in the streets waving the Tricolor, chanting the Marseillaise. By the end of three glorious days, *les trois glorieuses*, Charles X abdicated in favour of his fifty-seven year old nephew Louis Philippe d'Orléans, who had been promoted by his followers as the best possible of all possible constitutional kings. He chose to be crowned not as King of France like his predecessors but as King of the French by the Will of the People. He was the Citizen King.

During this turbulent and exciting year Halévy wrote three

new works and had them performed to audiences intoxicated with the promise of liberty, seeking in a world of fantasy a few hours' respite from political tension. The first of the three was a new departure for him – orchestral music set to a story without words. It was an adaptation by Eugène Scribe of the famous eighteenth-century novel *Manon Lescaut* by Abbé Prévost. On the hoardings it was described as *ballet pantomime* in three acts.

The story is set in the eighteenth century and begins outside the Paris Opéra. The Chevalier des Grieux is incurably smitten with pretty Manon who, unlike the Abbé Prévost Manon, is guileless, naive, childlike, innocent of the ways of the wicked world. She asks Des Grieux to buy her a lovely cloak she has just seen in a shop window; that it is beyond his means she can no more grasp than a child asking her *Maman* to buy her a dress like the one the princess has. She pouts so prettily that he spends his last franc on it then hurries off to a recruiting centre to enlist as a soldier so that he can go on supporting her.

While waiting for his return she struts about happily, admiring herself in the new cloak. The Marquis de Greville passes by, pays her a few compliments and offers to show her round the opera house. She follows him for just a quick look.

Des Grieux returns and gathers from passers-by that the young lady in the pretty cloak has been escorted into the opera building by the Marquis. He rushes inside to seek revenge. The Marquis who is now also his Colonel puts him under arrest for desertion.

The Marquis installs Manon in a sumptuous apartment and threatens to send Des Grieux to the wars if she does not yield to his will. She drives him out. Des Grieux finds a way in and love is restored. The Marquis returns. In the duel that ensues Des Grieux wounds him and runs away.

Manon has been exiled to the colonies and assigned to a group of women convicts whose job is to mend sails. The overseer importunes her. Her only friend is a young Indian serving a life sentence in this eighteenth-century version of a labour camp.

Des Grieux has been looking for Manon ever since his escape from Paris. He has joined up as a sailor and at long last traces her to the convicts' camp. They declare undying love and manage to escape with the young Indian's help, though not before Des Grieux has been badly wounded by a guard's bullet. They wander in the desert, dying of thirst and exhaustion, sealing their love with a symbolic ceremony of marriage. The Governor catches up with them – he is a sadder and wiser Marquis de Greville. He pardons the lovers and wishes them to be married. It is too late. Manon is dead, the dying Des Grieux faints over her body.

There are two versions as to the date of the first night. One, in the published text of the story, gives it as 30 April 1830, with music by Halévy and words by a mysterious 'M'; the other, in Soubie's *Soixante-sept ans de l'Opéra*, gives it as 3 May 1830 mentioning the librettists as Scribe and Aumer. Whichever date it was *Manon Lescaut* was just the sort of sweetener the Paris audiences needed in the stressful days which preceded the July revolution, a tear-jerker to make them forget the grievances of the moment. In its first two years it was performed thirty-nine times. In its third it had eight more performances.

On 27 May 1830, while *Manon Lescaut* was having good houses at the Opéra, the Opéra-Comique put on a one-acter which Halévy had written in collaboration with one Ruolz, to words by Fulgence. Why Halévy should have chosen to collaborate with Henri de Ruolz who was a research chemist with musical ambitions is not clear, except that they had fallen into a jolly, school-boyish kind of friendship. They addressed each other in the familiar form – *tu* – and Halévy was forever trying to drag Ruolz out of his laboratory to attend small gatherings held at his rue Montholon apartment. The following high-spirited note probably dates from that time:

> My emollient friend, my soluble Henri, my fluid Ruolz, do you remember you promised to come and see me this evening, Tuesday? I forgot to remind you yesterday that I am expecting you, but not at eleven o'clock at night as is your wont. Shun your habit of reacting like an imponderable gas and come like the others at nine. I would love you for it. Goodbye. Farewell. I weep, I dissolve in tears, I lose weight, I swoon, I evaporate. Goodbye for ever. I explode, brrr . . . [1]

The fruit of their jolly collaboration, under the title of *Attendre et courir*, was taken off after six performances. A few years later Ruolz succeeded in having a two-act opera of his own performed at the Opéra. It sank without trace. He re-immured himself in his laboratory and in due course patented a process of gilding metals.

The third Halévy work of 1830 was also a one-acter, set to words by Saint-Yves who in years to come would establish himself as a distinguished librettist. The story is set in a busy hotel in Berlin and provides some amusing complications. Baron Valhen, Gustave, Springler, Monsieur and Mme Olivier and young Eveline try to solve them with duets, trios and quartets, – and when they find the happy answer they join forces in a cheerful finale. *La Langue musicale* was put on at the Opéra-Comique on 11 December 1830 and restored Halévy's credit by having thirty performances, running well into the following year.

By then his name had been on the hoardings virtually non stop for four years and Paris audiences had come to expect a new offering from his pen at least once a year. Royalties however were still meagre. It was then that the Citizen King Louis Philippe was reported to favour the Republican notion that the Paris Opéra should no longer enjoy the subsidy granted to it by Napoleon some twenty years earlier. He was considering withdrawing it.

For Hérold and Halévy whose main regular source of income was their work as respectively first and second *chef du chant* at the subsidised Opéra, the fear of losing their livelihood was unnerving. On 24 March 1831 Hérold appealed to the new Opéra director Dr L. Veron for clarification and help:

> Dear Director,
> May I intrude on you for a moment? Alarming rumours are rife about impending changes; may I beg you, Sir, to stand by me should things come to such a pass? I acquit myself of my duty with a dedication that nobody can doubt. I love my work; I have tried to prove it. I would be most distressed to see myself removed from a theatre to which I have devoted all my affection. I beg of you, Sir, to take heed of the supplication of a musician who will always be deeply grateful to you.[1]

Five months later the rumours became fact when Louis Philippe withdrew the Opéra subsidy decreed by Napoleon. Veron economised by dismissing some of the orchestra players and increasing the work load of those who were retained. Hérold started proceedings disputing Veron's right to dismiss him; it was a test case. The upshot was that both *chefs du chant* were kept on. At this difficult stage in the finances of the Opéra, Veron and Halévy entered into an agreement on *La Tentation*, a ballet-opera based on the story of the temptation of Saint Anthony.

By its very nature a ballet-opera was a combination of dancing and singing, with ballet dancers doubling up for singers in the leading parts. Team work was of the essence. Thus the operatic sections were composed by Halévy to words by Cave and Coralli while the ballet music was a collaboration between himself and C. Gide who was familiar with ballet exigencies. As soon as the work was sufficiently advanced Veron scheduled it for rehearsals. Later he admitted that his decision had been prompted by the need to choose the lesser of two evils. The cholera had been raging in Paris for some time. The opera's best singers – Nourrit, Levasseur and Mme Damoreau – had taken three months' leave of absence to escape the epidemic and sing in London. A show of song and dance was less of a financial risk than a full-scale grand opera performed by singers of the second rank. In the event Veron's decision paid off handsomely.

The story of *La Tentation* begins in a hermitage in an eastern desert. The hermit blesses a young couple and during the wedding festivities laments his renunciation of married love. Outside a storm is brewing. When Marie, a lost pilgrim, seeks refuge in the hermitage, he becomes amorous. She repels his advances and calls on the Madonna for help. A thunderclap. The hermit is struck by lightning. He recovers, remembers that he has succumbed to temptation and runs away.

The scene changes to a volcano. A meeting of devils and fallen angels decides to create a temptress who would claim the soul of the hermit. Into a huge cauldron are thrown all the well-tried ingredients of devilry: a black cat, a monkey, a white-tailed eagle, rat poison, venomous reptiles. While the concoction is simmering, the assembly intones blood-curdling sounds, the real music of hell. A gong is beaten slowly, once, twice, thrice. The cooked dish emerges. General consternation. It is an ugly little monster that would not tempt the most passionate of warriors, let alone a saintly soul. Back to square one. Mark II is Miranda, a beautiful young girl clad like Lady Godiva.

The next scene takes place outside a castle. Miranda, now wearing something less scanty than just her long hair, invites the hermit in. Something in her stirs. She kneels down and tries to pray. A thunderbolt. The castle goes up in flames.

The hermit and Miranda are miraculously transported to a Sultan's harem, where they are surrounded by all the splendours of the Orient. The Sultan chooses Miranda for his bed that night. Both she and the hermit try to knife him and are condemned to death. Miranda throws herself from the harem turret into the sea; the hermit dives in after her.

Back at the hermitage Marie is drawing water from the well, sees Miranda's reflection in the water and offers her a cross. The devils hold an orgy. The hermit is going out of his mind, speaking words of love to trees and monsters. A court of devils condemns Miranda to death. There is a pitched battle between devils and angels. The angels win, the souls of Miranda and the hermit enter heaven as saints.

La Tentation had been lovingly choreographed for a little-known young dancer who had been spotted by the keen-eyed Opéra director himself. Mlle Duvernay was temptation incarnate – young, innocent looking, helpless, and ravishing with it. After the rather mixed reception of the first night Veron decided to drop the ugly monster scene and allow the ravishing Miranda to emerge from the cauldron first time round. No sooner had he made his decision known than a crowd of irate English balleto-manes besieged his office at the Opéra and induced him to put out notices assuring the public that the cauldron scene would be restored and performed in its entirety.

That Mlle Duvernay had become the idol of Paris was unquestionable. Every night there were frenzied shouts of *bravo* from the stalls, boxes, pit and gallery after a *pas de deux* in which a male devil was initiating her into devilish practices. The rousing score had its fair share of *bravos*, but it was obvious that the crowds queued up for the temptress. *La Tentation* opened at the Opéra on 20 June 1832 and was included in the repertoire for the next six years, culminating in well over a hundred performances. In years to come this ballet-opera would be rated as one of the highlights of Dr Veron's four years' directorship of the Opéra.

Of the few who did not like it the twenty-one year old Frederic Chopin, a recent arrival in Paris, was the most dismissive. 'La *Tentation* [the temptation],' he wrote on 2 August 1832 to the young pianist Ferdinand Hiller in Frankfurt, 'did not tempt any person of taste; it is as uninteresting as it is out of touch with the spirit of the century – rather like your German cooking.'[2]

In 1833 Halévy was ready with his annual offering in the form of a slight one-acter which had the benefit of two librettists, P.F.A. Carmouche and de Courcy. The story of *Les Souvenirs de Lafleur* takes place on the estate of Monsieur de Vallonne, who has put his young nephew Adrien under house arrest to make him study for the diplomatic service exams. Adrien has no intention of wasting his youth on the diplomatic service and informs his uncle that he is in love with his pretty cousin. Uncle promptly forbids him to see her.

Adrien chats with old Lafleur, his uncle's faithful servant, and gathers that in his youth Uncle was quite a lad. Lafleur would not betray any confidence, but by some transparent ruse he manages to acquaint Adrien with two of his uncle's youthful exploits. One was a sale of trees from the estate forest to a timber merchant, which made his fortune, and the other was the visit of a sweetheart who penetrated the chateau by disguising herself as a dairy maid. Adrien uses both exploits as a blueprint. He sells trees to a timber merchant for a good price, and asks his pretty cousin, disguised as a dairy maid, to marry him. Uncle is about to explode, but when Lafleur reminds him that Adrien has only followed in his footsteps he is mollified, accepts the marriage and keeps Lafleur in his service.

Halévy had composed *Les Souvenirs de Lafleur* as a vehicle for the singer Jean-Blaise Martin (1768–1837), a bass with an unusually flexible voice, who at the beginning of his career had neglected no opportunity to show off his *fioritura*. Musicians of the day were fond of recalling how the composer Grétry, after the performance of his opera *The Judgment of Midas*, said to young Martin: 'Lovely singing, but what a pity you left out the grand aria.'

'I assure you I sang it all,' said the surprised Martin.

'In that case, my good friend, you have embellished it so much I failed to recognise it.'

Martin matured into one of the best basses of the Opéra-Comique, retiring at the age of fifty-five. Some ten years later he made a comeback in the title role of Halévy's *Les Souvenirs de Lafleur*, astounding critics and audiences with the perfectly preserved purity and range of his voice. The first night at the Opéra-

Comique, on 4 March 1833, drew guffaws of delight and admiration from old fans and curious newcomers; the opera looked set for a long box office success. Unfortunately Martin's stay was short – he was after all in his sixty-fifth year – and when he left there was no-one else who could breathe life into a thin plot framed in unremarkable music. After his farewell performance the opera was taken off. He died four years later, honoured and lamented.

1833 ended with a work which was conceived as an act of friendship and brought in its wake a glittering offer. It was a completion of *Ludovic*, an opéra comique left unfinished by the untimely death of Halévy's colleague Hérold.

Ferdinand Hérold (1791–1833) had walked the *via dolorosa* that most Prix de Rome laureates were destined to follow: a hopeful return to Paris, knocking on closed doors, several years' wait for the performance of a first opera, living on teaching and coaching. He was a little apprehensive when Halévy was appointed second *chef du chant* at the Opéra where he had been first for some time, but he soon realised that his rival, far from aspiring to supplant him, was co-operative, friendly, devoid of any desire to advance himself by malice or intrigue. Soon he was relying on the younger man to stand in for him at short notice when tuberculosis made him miss his scheduled coaching sessions at the Opéra or when he was engrossed in composition. This happened quite often in 1832, when he was working on his opera *Le Pré aux clercs*. A day before the first night he sent a note requesting the usual favour:

> My dear Halévy,
> Tomorrow is the fatal day. I will therefore have to miss my turn at the Opera tonight. My apologies for my long absences; it will not happen again for a long time.[3]

Halévy stood in for him. The following night, 15 December, *Le Pré aux clercs* opened to be acclaimed as a masterpiece. Five weeks later Hérold was dead.

He had left an unfinished score for a two-act opéra comique called *Ludovic* to words by Saint-Georges. The first act had had a great deal of work put into it while the second had only been sketched. Halévy worked with his usual speed and within four months of Hérold's death the new opera opened to a full house of habitués, wondering what a Hérold-Halévy posthumous collaboration would yield.

Ludovic of the story is a hot-blooded Corsican who manages Francesca's farm in a village near Rome. He is in love with her. Francesca wishes to marry her cousin Gregorio so that he would be entitled to the married man's exemption from conscription to the papal army. Ludovic is mad with jealousy. Fearing his violence, the couple pretend that it is Francesca's confidante that Gregorio is actually going to marry. When the truth comes out Ludovic fires a shot at Francesca, runs away and becomes a wanted criminal.

Time passes. Francesca with her arm in a pretty sling now realises the extent of Ludovic's love for her and decides to save him. Cousin Gregorio, who in the meantime has been called up, finds in himself qualities of bravery and generosity and helps his rival to hide. A series of police raids, ambushes and near misses ends with a declaration of love and a pardon from the authorities. Everybody is happy.

Ludovic was put on at the Opéra-Comique on 16 May 1833 and by the end of the following year had achieved seventy performances. A quartet that Halévy wrote for the first act, for Francesca, her confidante, Ludovic and Gregorio was one of the highlights of the work and had to be repeated at each performance. The posthumous collaboration was a tremendous success.

In spite of the success, or perhaps because he realised how fickle success was, Halévy kept up the more secure rewards of a composer's life. In 1827 he became professor of harmony at the Conservatoire; in 1833 a professor of fugue and counterpoint which led to a collaboration with Cherubini on the *Art of the Fugue*. In 1834 he succeeded the late Hérold as first *chef du chant* at the Opéra. In years to come his punishing extra compositional schedule would include joining the editorial board of the *Revue et gazette musicale*, essay writing, lecturing, administrating, chairing committees.

While still working on *Ludovic* a significant change occurred in his home life. His beloved brother Léon, a Greek scholar and a successful writer, had long felt that his Jewish religion was an obstacle to an academic career and discreetly converted to Catholicism. His act, though not the reasoning behind it, was not an isolated case; emancipation and assimilation led many Jews to seek new truths. Rabbi Deutz, principal of a Jewish school, took holy orders; Théodore Ratisbonne became a Catholic and founded the missionary order of Notre Dame de Sion while his brother Marie-Alphonse, Brother Marie after his conversion, founded an ecumenical centre in Jerusalem.

The academic wall breached, Léon was appointed a joint professor of literature at the *Ecole polytechnique* and a consultant to the Department of Historical Monuments. In 1832, in his thirtieth year, he married Mlle Le Bas whom he had known since the four young Halévys moved into their rue Montholon apartment. After the wedding he settled with her in the spacious grace-and-favour quarters of his father-in-law architect Le Bas, designer of Notre Dame de Lorette and member of the Academy of Fine Arts.

Conversion, marriage and move did not weaken the strong bond between brothers and sisters; a time would come when the extended family would live together again under the same roof. For the time being Fromental, a bachelor of thirty-three, stayed on at rue Montholon, with Flore and Melanie keeping house for him and lovingly basking in his glory. Neither sister ever married.

7

LA JUIVE

*I*N EIGHTEENTH-CENTURY FRANCE
opéra comique meant a comic opera with spoken dialogue; by the
19th century it had come to mean any opera with spoken dialogue, whether comic or not. Most composers did not work
exclusively in one genre or the other. The factor deciding their
choice was primarily the quality of plot and libretto.

From his very first attempt at operatic composition Halévy had
given much time and thought to finding a good librettist,
someone who would be a dramatist as well as a poet; for the
libretto had to be in verse and was referred to as a poem. On the
published text the poet's name – or poets' if there were more than
one – would take precedence over the composer's. If an opera
was a success, the poem would be praised as an inspiration to
great music; if it was indifferent, critics would point out that the
basic fault lay with the uninspiring text. 'Halévy had stumbled on
a poor poem and the authors dragged him down with them,' was
a characteristic comment by the critic Fiorentino.[1]

It was Hérold's demise that indirectly renewed Halévy's connection with one of the most sought-after librettists of the day.
After the critical acclaim and financial success of *Ludovic*, the
Opéra director Dr Veron sat up and took notice. There was his
own *chef du chant* whom he had dismissed as a lightweight
composer revealing depth and a fine sense of drama. Without
wasting time he commissioned him to compose a grand opera to a

libretto by Scribe, to all intents and purposes the reigning librettist of the Paris Opéra. That in itself was a signal honour.

Eugène Scribe (1791–1861) was one of the leading French dramatists of the day, who applied the principle of the well made play to librettos. Whether writing for an opéra comique or a grand opera, he brought together most of the dramatic elements that characterised the romantic novels of the time: contrasting emotions, passionate love, intrigue, religious or political conflicts. He set his plots in medieval or Renaissance times, taking liberties with historical events but using them to great effect. His stories were peopled with titled persons, or persons ending by discovering their birthright to a title. There would be abundant scope for pageantry, crowd scenes, processions, magnificent indoor and outdoor scenery.

Halévy had come into contact with him as early as 1830, when he composed the music for *Manon Lescaut*, a ballet without words which Scribe and Aumer adapted from Abbé Prévost's novel. Since then their professional relations had progressed no further. Scribe was grand, condescending, fawned upon, courteously inaccessible; certainly not someone a youngish composer who had never composed a grand opera would dare suggest ideas to. He was excited, apprehensive, agonising over what kind of plot Scribe would come up with. Scribe came up with *La Juive*.

His choice of period and plot must have been influenced by an awareness that he was writing for a Jewish composer who should be stirred and inspired by his people's tragic history. Jewish history had the true elements of great drama: persecution, self-sacrifice, revenge. There had always been a conflict between loyalty to the ancient faith and the instinct to survive by embracing Christianity, between the love of a chaste Jewish girl for a gentile and the dogma of both religions condemning such love as mortal sin. Perhaps Scribe remembered that Rossini had put such a conflict to good use in *Moïse*, the French version of *Mosè in Egitto*. His own chosen period was the Middle Ages. After he had worked out the story and disposition of the main scenes he summoned Halévy to Montalais, his summer residence near Meudon.

'It was a fine summer evening [in 1833] in the park of Montalais,' Halévy recalled many years later, 'when Scribe first told me his story of *La Juive*. I was deeply moved. I shall always remember this talk which is linked with one of the most interesting periods of my life as a composer.'[2]

As usual Scribe had based his story on historical events. His Cardinal Jean-François Brogni was a real character, born about 1342 to peasant stock in the village of Brogni near Geneva. In due course he became a cardinal in the papal court of John XXIII. When the King of Naples sacked Rome Brogni drove him out. King Sigismund, Emperor of the Romans, fresh from his victory over the army of the Bohemian reformer John Huss, urged Pope John XXIII to convoke the Council of Constanz in order to resolve claims to the papacy made by several rival Popes. The Council opened in November 1414 and Cardinal Brogni presided over fourteen of its sessions.

Of this intricate papal history *La Juive* retains only three facts: the sack of Rome, referred to in retrospect; the presence at Constance of Cardinal Brogni; and the celebration of Emperor Sigismund's victory over the Hussites. The rest is pure Scribe.

The story takes place in 1414 in the city of Constance in Switzerland. The curtain in Act I rises on a large square, with a church on the right, a jeweller's workshop on the left, and a fountain in the middle. It is a public holiday, dedicated to thanksgiving for Emperor Sigismund's victory over the heretic Hussites. The church portals are wide open to allow the overflow of the congregation to kneel on the steps outside. In the workshop Elazar the Jew urges his assistants to carry on working. 'What sort of place is it where people work on a public holiday?'[3] the celebrants ask suspiciously. Rachel, Elazar's daughter, pushes her father into the back room to avoid attention. A cloaked stranger approaches the shop. A Guards officer scrutinizes him, recognises him with surprise and salutes. The stranger, who is Prince Leopold in disguise, orders him to keep his mouth shut.

The Grand Provost arrives with the town criers, proclaiming the imminent return from the battlefield of Prince Leopold who has vanquished the heretics. There will be a triumphal procession, the Emperor will distribute largesse, the fountain in the square will flow with wine instead of water. The hammering in the jeweller's shop must be silenced.

'How dare you work on a public holiday?' he shouts when Elazar and Rachel are brought before him.

'Why not? I am not of your faith. The God of Jacob allows me to work.'

'You hate our laws.'

'Why shouldn't I? Your laws sent my sons to the stake. They died stretching their hands out to me.'

'You will follow them, and so shall your daughter.'

Just as the Grand Provost's men are about to lead the offenders away Cardinal Brogni appears.

'Where are you taking them?' the Cardinal enquires.

'They are Jews, sentenced to death.'

'What is their offence?'

'Profaning our feast-day with work.'

'What is your name?' the Cardinal asks the Jew.

'Elazar.'

'This name is not unfamiliar to me. I have heard it before.'

'So you have. It was a long time ago. In Rome. You were not a man of God then. You had a wife whom you dearly loved.'

'Respect the grief of a bereaved husband and father. The enemy came through the city gates and burnt my palace over my wife and our infant daughter. God gave me strength. I offered Him my vows. I am His servant, His minister, His priest.'

'To persecute us?'

'To save your souls.'

'Have you forgotten that in Rome, when you were a Magistrate, you sent me into exile?'

'You had been found guilty of usury. The Court demanded the death sentence. I commuted it to exile. I saved your life. Today I shall save it again.'

'May it please Your Eminence,' the Grand Provost intervenes. 'It is too risky to pardon him.'

'God is merciful,' says the Cardinal. 'Elazar, you are free.' He holds out his hand. 'Let us be friends, brother. If I have offended against you I beg your forgiveness.'

'Never. Never shall I forgive the hated Christians,' Elazar mutters as he returns with Rachel to his workshop. Brogni sings one of the best known bass arias of Act I – *Si la rigueur*:

> If the bitterness of vengeance
> Makes them hate your sacred laws,
> Let forgiveness and clemency, oh Lord,
> Bring them back to you.

CARDINAL BROGNI: MUSIC OF *SI LA RIGUEUR*

The crowd disperses. Prince Leopold, still disguised, sings a love song. Rachel recognises the voice of her long-absent sweetheart, the itinerant Jewish artist Samuel, and joyfully sings back from the balcony. She goes down to greet him outside the shop where they re-affirm their love. She invites him to the Seder, the Passover rite commemorating the liberation of the Children of Israel from bondage in Egypt. The church bells start ringing, the crowd returns to the square, the chorus sings a drinking song, the fountain flows with wine.

Elazar and Rachel come out of their house and get pushed and jostled until they have their backs to the church wall. The Grand Provost seizes his opportunity:

'What, a Jew seeking refuge in our church? Let's do what our Lord Jesus did in the Temple of Jerusalem. Throw out all the tradesmen from the House of God.'

49

LEOPOLD SAVING RACHEL & ELAZAR FROM THE MOB

ELAZAR PRESIDING OVER SEDER CELEBRATION

'To the lake! To the lake!' the incited mob chants. Father and daughter are forcefully separated. Rachel sees Leopold returning.

'Samuel, run for your life. They will kill you too.'

Leopold draws his sword. The crowd retreats. As soldiers rush in the mob starts chanting again: 'To the lake!' Again the officer recognises Leopold and orders everybody back. The crowd is puzzled; so is Rachel. On a sign from Leopold the officer escorts father and daughter safely back to their home. The crowd sings its astonishment.

Now the triumphal procession approaches: trumpeters, standard bearers, crossbowmen, members of the various guilds, magistrates, archers, men-at-arms, heralds, cardinals, bell ringers, Cardinal Brogni's halberdiers, members of the Council, pages, clerics. Cardinal Brogni rides in on his horse escorted by his gentlemen and pages. The Emperor's halberdiers march in, followed by heralds carrying the imperial standards. Finally the imperial pages clear the way for Emperor Sigismund mounted on his horse, surrounded by his gentlemen and hussars, followed by princes of the empire. A fanfare is sounded, the church organ booms. The splendour and magnificence of the procession bring down the curtain on Act I with a rousing chorus: '*Gloire. Honneur à l'empéreur. Gloire à l'empéreur.*'

Act II takes place in Elazar's house. It is Seder night, relatives have gathered to celebrate the Passover. Elazar leads a chorus asking God to conceal their rites from hostile eyes: 'If there is a traitor amongst us, let God strike him dead.' He hands round the traditional unleavened bread. 'All of you, children of Moses, partake of this unleavened bread, consecrated with my own hands.' Prince Leopold, Samuel to his hosts, does not know what to do with it and surreptitiously drops it on the floor. Rachel is horrified. Elazar now sings one of the moving tenor arias of the opera – *Que ma voix tremblante*:

> God, let my trembling voice
> Rise to Heaven.
> Stretch your powerful hand
> To your unhappy children.
> Your people are oppressed
> And Zion, from its grave
> Implores your favour,

Rising towards you,
Begging life
From its wrathful father.

ELAZAR: MUSIC OF *QUE MA VOIX TREMBLANTE*

There are loud knocks on the door. All appurtenances of the Seder festivity are hastily concealed, the guests disappear, Leopold hides behind his easel and brushes. In comes Princess Eudoxie, the Emperor's niece and Prince Leopold's wife. She buys from Elazar a precious jewel and orders him to deliver it to the palace the following morning with her name and her husband's engraved on it. Elazar charges her an exorbitant price and bursts into song about the pleasure of cheating the hated Christians – *Oh quel plaisir, quel plaisir de tromper les Chrétiens.*

After the Princess leaves, Leopold emerges from behind his easel and persuades Rachel to see him alone later that night. A beautiful and sensitive aria expresses her qualms at agreeing to a clandestine meeting, which gradually give way to the intoxication of love – *Il va venir*.

RACHEL: MUSIC OF *IL VA VENIR*

Leopold confesses he is a Christian and begs her to run away with him. Elazar storms in and threatens to kill him. Rachel pleads with him to spare both her sweetheart and herself – *Pour moi, pour moi, mon père*. Elazar fights back his hatred of the Christians for the love of his daughter and says he will marry them himself.

'Kneel down,' he orders the couple. 'I am a priest according to the laws of my people. Let me hear your marriage vows; and his too.'

'Never,' says Leopold.

'What are you saying?' Rachel and Elazar are flabbergasted.

'I can't marry you. I love you more than ever but this marriage is a crime, it is blasphemy. Don't ask questions. I must go. Goodbye, Rachel, forever.'

The curtain goes down on Act II with Elazar's aria of unleashed hatred erupting like a volcano.

Act III is set in the imperial gardens, beautifully laid out with trees, bushes, flower beds and romantic paths. Servants are putting the finishing touches to tables set with gold and silver plate, cut flowers and candles. The second great spectacle of the opera is taking place. The Emperor walks in with his retinue, ladies and gentlemen in court dress, prelates, princes, officers, magistrates. Leopold, the victorious Commander just back from the battlefield, beautifully arrayed as Prince of the Empire, takes precedence over all. Four stewards on horseback bring in the main dish of the feast, *le plat d'honneur*. The gathering awaits the highlight of the feast – Princess Eudoxie decorating the victor with the precious jewel she bought the night before from Elazar.

Elazar and Rachel are ushered in to deliver the jewel as ordered. They recognise Prince Leopold as their Samuel of yesterday. Rachel, mad with jealousy and humiliation, declares before the imperial assembly that she and the Prince are lovers.

To grasp the enormity of the crime one must recall that in the Middle Ages a Christian in love with a Jewish girl was as abhorrent to the Church as a Jewish girl in love with a Christian was to Jewish law. When a Jewish girl followed a Christian lover she was considered dead and her father would mourn her death for seven days. The medieval Church did not play about with symbolism; it imposed a real death sentence on both Christian and Jewess and, for good measure, on those who aided and abetted them. Cardinal Brogni, who in *La Juive* is the embodiment of ecclesiastical law, makes no allowances for rank or power. Prince, Jewess and Jew have sinned against Christianity and all three shall pay the penalty. The deep bass voice booms:

CARDINAL BROGNI KNEELING BEFORE ELAZAR

You three who are united by a horrible alliance
Let you be cursed.
It is the Almighty Himself
Who through me rejects you and bans you.

Turning to Leopold, the Cardinal pronounces on him the greatest penalty of the Roman church, excommunication – *L'anathème*:

Let our church close its doors to you,
Let Christians all over the world avoid you.
Cursed on earth and cursed in Heaven,
No burial place and no prayer said over your corpse.

Prince Leopold is made to surrender his sword and the curtain falls as all three are led out to prison.

Act IV takes place in Rachel's prison cell. Princess Eudoxie has come to beg the Jewess to spare Leopold's life by retracting her accusation. Rachel tells the Princess that she has loved the Prince in all innocence, and Eudoxie answers that she too has loved him from the bottom of a true heart. The two women, both betrayed, sing a duet of their love for the same man, Eudoxie pleading with Rachel to listen to her sorrowful voice – *Que ma voix plaintive*.

Rachel unbends. 'Let no one say that a Jewess has not shown charity to a Christian.' She calls for the Cardinal, retracts her accusation and causes Leopold's death sentence to be commuted to lifelong exile. Her own sentence is unaltered. The Cardinal is mysteriously drawn to her by pity. He goes to Elazar and tells him that if Rachel embraces Christianity both their lives will be spared. Elazar rejects the offer. The Cardinal, moved by something stronger than himself, kneels down to the Jew to beg for the life of a Jewish girl. Elazar taunts him. 'If I can face the stake I can surely face your tears.' As Brogni rises heavily to his feet Elazar cruelly adds: 'Do you remember how your palace was burnt during the sack of Rome with your wife and little daughter?' Brogni groans with pain. 'Well,' says Elazar, 'The little girl did not perish. She was saved by a Jew, by one of those hated Jews.' It is of course Elazar who has saved the Cardinal's little daughter from the flames, escaped with her to Constance, and brought her up as his beloved Jewish daughter Rachel. In spite of Brogni's pleading he reveals nothing.

Alone in his cell Elazar is beset by remorse. 'In my hatred for the Christians and my desire for vengeance I now destroy my daughter.' He sings that heart-rending aria, the showpiece of tenors of all times, the one with which Caruso would move his audiences, many generations later – *Rachel, quand du Seigneur la grâce tutelaire*:

> Rachel, when the Lord entrusted
> Your cradle to my hands
> I pledged my entire life to your happiness,
> And it is I who now deliver you to the executioner.
> I hear a voice calling to me: I am young, I want to live,
> Dear father, spare your child.
> Oh Rachel, it is I, your loving father,
> Who delivers you to the executioner.

ELAZAR: MUSIC OF *QUAND DU SEIGNEUR*

About to save Rachel's life by informing the Cardinal that she is his own daughter, Elazar hears the crowd outside the prison baying for blood. His moment of weakness is over. Rachel is Jewish, she shall never be one of them. He and she will die the death of martyrs. The curtain goes down as he is taken out to the place of execution.

Act V returns to the city square, which has already been prepared for the spectacle of death, with a cauldron of boiling oil at the ready. The blood-thirsty crowd sings lustily of punishment, pleasure and the glory of God. Rachel clings fearfully to her father. Cardinal Brogni begs Elazar to tell him where he would find the Jew who saved his daughter's life in Rome. Elazar refuses. 'It is time,' says the executioner. Elazar can bear it no longer. 'Stop, stop,' he calls out. 'Just one word.' Turning to Rachel he says: 'I am going to die. Do you want to live?'

'What for? To love? To suffer even more?'

'No, to be raised to the highest rank.'

'How?'

'Just a drop of water on your brow.'

'I a Christian? Let us go. The flames are awaiting us.'

'Their God calls you.'

Rachel sings the answer that has made her the pride and glory of the Jewish people all over the world. 'And ours awaits me. I choose death. I run towards martyrdom.'

As the monks sing and pray to God to be merciful to the sinners Cardinal Brogni begs Elazar for the last time:

'My daughter whom the Jews saved from the flames – is she still alive?'

Elazar watches Rachel being led up the scaffolding from where she will be thrown into the boiling cauldron.

'She is.'

'Oh Lord, where is she then?'

'There,' shrieks Elazar as Rachel is thrown in.

Brogni falls to his knees and buries his face in his hands. Elazar proudly mounts the scaffolding to his death. The monks sing piously: 'It is all over, we have taken our revenge on the Jews.' Nine bars from the orchestra – curtain.

The labour pains of *La Juive* had been severe; not because Halévy was awed by the grandiose project, but because the story had fired his imagination as no story ever had. It was as if he had seen a revelation; he was coming face to face with his heritage, his people, their martyrdom through the ages. Like the prophet Jeremiah he carried the word in his heart, it was like a burning fire in his bones. Ideas teemed in his head, his source of creativity was inexhaustible, gushing out, overflowing. He worked at home, in his studio at the Opera, at friends' houses in the country. He was in a trance; his sisters and brother anxiously watched him neglect himself, succumb to stress, drive himself ill. He had started working on the score sometime in the late summer of 1833; by the first week in October 1834 the opera was in rehearsal.

The leading singers had been selected while the composition was in progress. The part of Leopold had originally been offered to the tenor Nourrit who delicately pointed out that Leopold was a superficial character and that he, Nourrit, would much rather tackle the formidable part of Elazar. Halévy was taken aback. Tenors were supposed to be heart-throbs, not wizened old men. Elazar was definitely a mature bass. Nourrit turned on the charm and Halévy allowed himself to be persuaded. As he was working on Elazar's arias he discovered that a tenor voice was lending the part shades he had not visualised before. He was so taken with Nourrit's involvement that he did not flinch when the latter suggested a radical change in the score.

Apart from being a beautiful and intelligent tenor, Nourrit was also a professor of singing at the Conservatoire, something of a poet, with a keen eye to dramatic development. He suggested that instead of bringing the curtain down on Act IV with a finale, as was the convention, Halévy should end it with a solo for Elazar, to bring out the loving father side of his character. He offered to write the words himself. 'He wanted to choose the most sonorous syllables, those kindest to his voice,'[4] Halévy recalled. He negotiated the proposition with Scribe who graciously gave his consent. The result was *Rachel, quand du seigneur la grâce tutelaire*, the aria that never fails to clutch at the heart strings wherever it is performed.

Leopold's part was given to the tenor Lafont and that of Princess Eudoxie to the veteran soprano Mme Dorus-Gras. The excellent bass Levasseur was Cardinal Brogni, and the soprano Mlle Falcon, a former student of Nourrit's, sang Rachel. Although still young she was already suffering from the throat disease that would force her to retire within two or three years. After the dress rehearsal her voice gave up and for the next fifteen days director and composer called on her every morning to enquire whether she would be able to sing the following evening. The public was getting restive.

In his creative fever Halévy had allowed the horn of plenty to overflow and his completed score ran to five and a half hours. During the final rehearsals a full half-hour was lopped off, the overture was dropped altogether. At long last all obstacles were overcome. On 23 February 1835, a few hours before curtain rise, he dashed off a note to G. Monnais who was on the staff of *La Revue et gazette musicale* although they had only met once.

> Dear Monsieur Monnais, I have not been able to find the time to see you this morning as I had hoped to do. I am counting on your benevolence of which you have already given me ample proof. Please support me tonight with your hands and your pen.[5]

It was now up to the audience and the rest of the musical press.

8

COOLNESS INTO ADULATION

*I*N VIEW OF THE FACT THAT AS from its first performance on 23 February 1835 until its original scenery was consumed by fire in 1893 *La Juive* was shown at the Paris Opéra 550 times, that it was the mainstay of French provincial theatres for more than fifty years, that it was performed in translation in Europe, Tsarist Russia and America and was a vehicle for the greatest opera singers of their generation – it is interesting to note that its initial reception by the Paris critics was far from enthusiastic. In fact it was cool, condescending, with more than a touch of sneering.

This initial coolness was due to several causes, foremost among them an over-zealous publicity campaign. Right from the start of rehearsals in October 1834, a good five months before its opening, the Opéra director Dr Veron kept feeding the press with stories of scenic splendour, authentic costumes, cost of production. There was hardly a Paris paper which did not regale its readers with details of armoury and live horses on stage. One worked out the cost to the Opéra of having the fountain flow with wine every night, while others published 'reliable figures' revealing an overall production cost of 100,000 francs, 150,000 francs, 170,000 francs . . . Reviewers tended to scoff even before they heard a single note.

The second cause went far deeper. *La Juive* was a startling, abrasive title. Jews in France, perhaps to distance themselves from a word that had undesirable undercurrents, called themselves Israelites. Elie Halévy had published a periodical called *L'Israëlite français*; Léon Halévy described his brother and himself as born into an Israelite family; the official Jewish authority in Paris was called the Israelite Consistory. Now here was an opera that restored a word which had been tacitly shelved to avoid unpleasant associations, flaunting it in its very title. French critics felt out of their depth, uneasy about possible racial and religious sensitivities; Elazar's character invited comparison with Shylock. One had to tread gently. Only *La Quotidienne* had no qualms. On 27 February 1835 it came out with a pseudo-analysis of Jewish history, reviving old prejudices and innuendos.

> In order to grasp the interest of the subject we have to hark back to the religious ideas which preoccupied Christianity at the beginning of the 15th century. All over Europe the Jews were the victims of social repugnance. Put outside civilization by custom and law, this nation was forced to exist by following reprehensible occupations. With no political life open to them, the Jews confined their ambition to finance. They prospered and became rich by secret negotiations and disgraceful transactions of money, precious stones, gold and silver. In this way they amassed immense wealth which they withdrew from circulation and enjoyed in private until angry people and greedy rulers deprived them of it. Persecutions started; their gold was confiscated while the state turned a deaf ear to their complaints. It is one of those Jews, who became rich through his skill as goldsmith and jeweller, whom the composer chose for his hero.[1]

The third cause of critical reservation was bound up with Halévy's personality. 'Halévy has never put himself under the patronage of any of those grand string-pullers,' Nourrit wrote to a friend in Le Havre about a month after opening night. 'He is modest, and because he does not go about proclaiming himself the best of the lot, he is treated like a little boy.'[2]

That condescending 'little boy' attitude found expression in *Le Courrier français* of 27 February, four days after opening night:

> Let us consider the work of this young composer, Fromental Halévy, whose heart must have beaten faster every time he picked up his pen and approached his piano thinking of the task which had been assigned to him and which he was trying to accomplish. Write a five-act opera after Rossini, Meyerbeer, Auber! What a test! Well, Monsieur Halévy acquitted himself quite satisfactorily; without equalling

these masters he placed himself at an honourable distance behind them.[3]

Of those who insinuated that the lavish production was designed to conceal the paucity of the music, *La Revue des Deux Mondes* was perhaps the most virulent:

> We are so sorry for Monsieur Halévy. His music must have got buried under all those helmets, cuirasses and chains of mail; for it is impossible to take seriously these massed voices and instruments which for five and a half hours on the clock accompany songs written in the style of Rossini, Auber and Meyerbeer.[4]

The same reviewer had recently slashed Bellini's *I Puritani*. Now he declared himself ready to shower him with flowers. 'It is however sad,' he concluded, 'to rehabilitate a mediocre work only because an even worse one has recently emerged.[5]

Le Constitutionnel of 25 February followed the trend, grudgingly conceding that the music had some merit:

> Monsieur Halévy probably finds it regrettable that all those excellent things which abound in his score are locked in battle with scenic luxury . . . His style, learned, correct, grave in its harmonies, sober in its ornamentation, well crafted rather than inspired where melody is concerned, risks appearing somewhat severe and reserved in the midst of this orgy of scenery, costumes, horses and emperors. Had the visual sphere been less dazzling, the audience would have listened more attentively to the music, and recognised its merits one by one, step by step.[6]

One of Halévy's most impressive effects in Act I was achieved by an organ played off-stage when the congregation outside the church was singing a Te Deum. Thirty-two year old Berlioz disparagingly suggested that the use of an organ in opera had become mandatory after Meyerbeer's *Robert-le-diable* four years earlier. In his delightfully wicked style he wrote in *Le Rénovateur* of 1 March:

> So now the public is captivated by a duet of organ and flageolet, combining the infinitely grand, noble and religious with the infinitely small, petty and dance-like . . . As for *La Juive*, in spite of all the efforts made to stop us hearing the music, in spite of the jangle of armoury, the sound of horses' hooves, the tumult of the crowd, the volleys of bells and cannons, dancing, loaded tables and fountains

flowing with wine – in spite of all this anti-musical din at the Royal Academy of Music [the original name of the Paris Opéra] one could still catch in mid-flight some of the composer's inspirations.[7]

He ended his review with the much quoted word *misérable*, an adjective which, depending on context, may mean worthless as well as wretched in a compassionate sense. Berlioz's *misérable* when read in context may well have been a grudging expression of commiseration for a fellow composer who had been ill served by over-zealous producers:

> Let us do justice to the efforts of the singers whose task is to make us appreciate the few scenes where the iron-clad infantry and the gold-encrusted cavalry were kind enough to leave the field free to that wretched music.[8]

Alone among the Paris weeklies *La Revue et gazette musicale* mentioned the word 'masterpiece.' It was hardly surprising considering that its founder and proprietor was the music publisher Schlesinger, who had paid Halévy 30,000 francs for the publishing rights of the score and was having copies of the libretto sold at the entrance of the Opéra for a franc a piece. In its issue of 1 March an anonymous reviewer declared:

> The music of this vast and beautiful opera is without doubt M. Halévy's masterpiece. It is beautiful on more than one plane; it is beautiful in its form and thought; beautiful in its originality and maturity; beautiful in its scenic expression; beautiful in its melodies, harmonies and orchestration . . . The aria *Si la rigueur* [Cardinal Brogni's in the first act] reminds one by its majestic simplicity of Mozart's most beautiful inspirations in *The Magic Flute*. It is particularly in the second act that the composer's genius shows its greatness and pathos. No more horses, cuirassiers, bells, cannons, fountains flowing with wine to distract attention. It was passion, pure passion, without any superfluous ornamentation.[9]

Most critics, even those who discerned the merits of the score behind the bells and cannons, were wary of praising a newcomer to grand opera. 'A dazzling new talent invites resistance,' explained the *Journal de Paris* four weeks after opening night. 'Critics prefer to dole out their praises one by one and point out a composer's gradual development rather than lay themselves open to ridicule by turning out to be false prophets.'[10]

So they confined themselves to telling the story of the opera, reserving musical judgment on the excuse that it was impossible to do justice to the work after one hearing. It was as if they were waiting for a lead. The lead came loud and clear from *vox populi*. 'Never have I seen such audience involvement at the Opera, such universal enthusiasm,'[11] reported Schlesinger's reviewer after the first night. The crowds kept flocking in, applauding, raving, spreading the word, sometimes queuing up seven or eight hours for a ticket. *Le Ménestrel* was among the first to eschew the facile digs at equestrian pageantry, and on 1 March published a more considered view:

> It is on Shakespeare's Shylock and Walter Scott's Rebecca that Scribe has modelled his characters of Elazar and Rachel. It is to that double inspiration that the poem of *La Juive* owes its most dramatic elements . . . M. Halévy's score, like all great operas, needs to be heard several times to be fully appreciated. But as from today it can be stated that it is a remarkable work which contains many first-class beauties. There are many arias full of melody and feeling spread throughout the work, but it is mainly the orchestration and the ensembles which show how the composer has developed . . . The work has already been cut to reasonable proportions and is bound to have a long run.[12]

Reviewers were beginning to eat their words. Halévy may have found some solace in the grudging retraction of *Le Courrier français* of 9 March:

> The music of *La Juive* grows on public opinion as did *Robert-le-diable* and many other works, today famous, on first hearing hardly recognised. Having heard this beautiful, great, learned music we find we can hardly ever go out of the Opéra without having discovered yet another gem we had not noticed before. That is why we shall wait a while before formulating our exact opinion of this great work by Monsieur Halévy, a young composer who has joined the ranks of the Masters and who has lived up to his promise. Preparations are already in hand for producing *La Juive* in Rouen and Brussels.[13]

Perhaps the most professional and objective judgment of *La Juive* came from Nourrit, the handsome young tenor who did not flinch from making himself up as a wrinkled old Jew, who contributed to the libretto one of its most moving verses, and who knew the score inside out. In his letter of 27 March to his friend in Le Havre he wrote:

> Halévy is neither a Rossini nor a Meyerbeer; but after these great

masters he is today the only young composer who offers most hope. A good half of *La Juive* can stand comparison with countless works considered good, while many operas of the second rank would gladly be rated as good as the other half.[14]

The public kept flocking in if only to see the marvels of the production. Good seats were expensive. Jules Offenbach, a German-born Jewish lad of sixteen struggling to earn a living in Paris as a cellist, decided to approach Halévy for a complimentary ticket. It was not as cheeky as all that; Halévy had already noticed him in the small orchestra of the Opéra-Comique during a rehearsal of his forthcoming *L'Eclair*. One free evening young Offenbach posted himself in the forecourt of the Opéra and after an hour's wait saw Monsieur Halévy arrive. He stopped him and asked whether he could get him in free. Halévy, wary after the mixed reviews, pointedly asked: 'Do you want to see well or hear well?'

'Above all I want to hear well, Maestro,' young Offenbach replied.

'Then come with me.'

They settled down in a box in the upper circle where every note of the 'magnificent score' made its full impact. When recalling this first hearing some twenty years later Offenbach referred to *La Juive* as a masterpiece.[15]

The two criteria against which a new musical work was measured were harmony and melody. Shaken out of their initial caution by consistent public enthusiasm, reviewers made use of their press tickets to give the opera a second and third hearing. In due course they gave praise to Halévy's innovative orchestration and his gift for melody. The Bolero woven into the festivities in the imperial gardens in Act III was pointed out as further indication of his keen ear for folk tunes, noticed in *Clari* seven years earlier. No mention however was made of his use, in the Seder night prayer at the beginning of Act II, of the responsorial pattern preserved in traditional Jewish chants and psalmody.

Changes of cast allowed critics to offer fresh analyses of the score and draw attention to musical gems glittering under the cuirasses. In 1837 the original Elazar, the sensitive Nourrit, given to depression and paranoia, left the Opéra while the original Rachel, the unsurpassable Mlle Falcon, retired because of her

TENOR ADOLPHE NOURRIT

incurable throat disease. The part of Elazar was taken over by Duprez, whose interpretation totally eclipsed Nourrit's. Rachel was briefly sung by Mlle Nathan, who like Mlle Falcon was Jewish, then by Mme Stoltz. The writer and poet Théophile Gautier wrote:

> The score, we can now say, has placed Halévy at the top rung of contemporary composers; large in the ensembles, finished and spirited in all details, it is a work written by the hand of a master. Scholarly as well as dramatic, the orchestration is as clear as it is well crafted.[16]

Berlioz, immovable, found fault with the score. Some ten years earlier valve trumpets and valve horns were introduced into France, valves having the advantage of facilitating the use of chromatic phrases and giving composer and player greater flexibility. While Berlioz was among the first to use a valve trumpet in the overture to *Les Francs-juges* in 1826 and *Waverley* in 1827–8, Halévy was the first to use the valve horn, scoring *La Juive* for two valve horns as well as for two ordinary ones. Berlioz damned him with faint praise:

> The orchestration has an originality which captures attention without ever straining it, and a colouring which is in perfect harmony with the religious, passionate and austere character of the subject. The horns are used with skill, testifying to the composer's predilection for them; he has obviously given much thought as to when to use them and the style proper to them. I regret however that he has made such frequent use of the valve horn whose timbre lacks the melancholic nobility of the ordinary horn . . . I also think he made too much use of the ophicleide [precursor of the tuba], bass drum, massed brass.[17]

Another change of cast in June 1840 was reviewed in *La Revue et gazette musicale* by G. Bénédit:

> *La Juive*, shown 98 times in Paris, has for the past five years made the fortunes of all our provincial theatres. There is hardly a town of any size that is not familiar with the beauty of this wonderful music, surely one of the most beautiful of our time.[18]

Bénédit described the scene when Elazar was prepared to suppress his hatred for the Christians and allow Rachel to marry a gentile, only to hear Leopold say 'Never.'

> Never . . . At this word hate, anger, rage and fanaticism reawaken horribly in the heart of the old Jew, and from that violent shock all the

SOPRANO CORNELIE FALCON

unleashed passions burst out as if from a volcanic crater; this long menacing phrase in E minor bursts out, erupts, dominates the tumult of the orchestra, swooping over the ensemble like fire over the head of a monument. This is grand and sublime. There is in it a spark of genius sufficient to establish the reputation of twenty composers.[19]

Wagner too reviewed *La Juive* at great length. In view of his virulent attack on Jewish musicians in his essay *Das Judenthum in der Musik* published in 1850 and again, in a revised form in 1869, it is of particular interest to recall what he wrote and said about it. He was a relative latecomer to Halévy's music; it was mainly during his stay in Paris from late 1839 to 1842 that he got to know it, earning a precarious living from piano and instrumental arrangements of some of Halévy's operas for Schlesinger's publishing house. He attended several performances of *La Juive* and was once amazed to see Duprez's Elazar, when running away from the mob at the end of Act I, address the audience with shouts and broad pathos instead of singing in tempo. He was even more amazed to see Halévy directing him from the wings and later hear him candidly admit that the cast liked it better that way because it was more effective.

That bizarre little episode did not prejudice Wagner against *La Juive*. In early 1842 he published three very long articles in *La Revue et gazette musicale*, giving a German eye's view of Halévy's work and its contribution to the French musical scene:

> Nothing could have been better suited to his kind of talent than the subject of *La Juive*. One might almost say that a sort of fatality guided him to this libretto, predestined to stimulate his every force. In *La Juive* his true vocation manifested itself by many striking and undeniable proofs, like the writing of music that issues from the innermost depths of human nature . . .
>
> In attempting to define his music our first duty is to sound its depth; there lies its point of departure, that is where he took his view of the art of music. I am not talking about a transitory passion; I speak of that strong emotion, incisive and profound, quickening and convulsing the moral world of every age. This is what constitutes the magic element in the score of *La Juive* . . . This is what gives life to every figure appearing in this terrible drama, and this is what guided the composer to preserve aesthetic unity amid the most violent contrasts . . .
>
> The external music of *La Juive*, if I may call it so, is in keeping with

the primary internal concept; the common and the trivial have no place in it. Conceived as a whole, the work is fashioned to the tiniest detail with the utmost care. The various sections of the scenic scheme are welded to each other; in this respect Halévy markedly and happily differs from other opera composers of our age . . . He keeps his dignity as dramatic composer. Moreover, his fecundity goes into a variety of dramatic rhythms, particularly noticeable in the orchestral accompaniment . . . But what strikes us above all as worthy of admiration is that Halévy has succeeded in stamping on his score the seal of the epoch . . .

How did he achieve this effect? That is a mystery whose key may be found in the mode of his production. He might be classified as belonging to the Historic School, had it not been for the constituent elements of his mode which tally with the Romantic School . . . Abruptly breaking away from Auber's system, Halévy boldly sprang out of the rut of conventional turns and rhythms to enter a career of free, unconfined creativity, recognising no other law than that of truth. He needed to be very confident of his strength and the resources of his talent to walk away from the trodden track which would have led him to quicker popularity. He needed to have unshakeable faith in the power of truth and give it all the concentrated energy of his talent . . .

Contemporary young composers have strayed into other paths. Laxity and indolence led most of them towards mannerism, making them insensitive to the influence of Halévy's brilliant energy that has sped French grand opera along a new road.[20]

The suggestion that Wagner praised Halévy because his articles had been commissioned by Schlesinger, the composer's publisher who had a vested interest in *La Juive*, is belied by his recurrent favourable references to the opera long after both publisher and composer were dead. In the diary she kept of her husband's last years, Cosima Wagner recorded that he kept a score of *La Juive* handy and every now and then would reach out for it and call his visitors' attention to some particular quality he admired in it. He would mention it over a Sunday lunch, pore over it after dinner, contrast it with Goldmark's *Die Königin von Saba* which he had seen in Vienna in 1875. During his stay in Italy, already a sick man, he saw it for the last time at the San Carlo Theatre in Naples and again praised it to his visitors, saying that it was full of verve and refinement, not in the least Jewish . . .

In 1855 *La Juive* celebrated its twentieth anniversary on stage. On 11 March *La Revue et gazette musicale*, no longer under the proprietorial eye of Schlesinger who had retired and returned to his native Germany, came out with an emotional tribute from a reviewer who had followed the fortunes of the opera from its earliest days:

> Twenty years! For a work of the theatre it is like a hundred years. How many works die during such a long span of time? Equally, for those works which survive, what proof of vigour, what intimation of immortality! *La Juive* has survived and grown whether continuously performed or whether allowed to rest before being put on again. Among famous revivals one will never forget Duprez who stamped the role of Elazar with something so new, so original, that he completely effaced the still fresh memory of Nourrit . . . In the role of Rachel Mlle Falcon has remained superior to all those who followed her. But masterpieces do not depend for their success on the skill of their interpreters. *La Juive* has had its good days and its bad days; it had unequal voices and styles; but it is still *La Juive*, and its resplendent crown has not lost a single jewel.[21]

This is perhaps the right moment to anticipate an event which took place after Halévy's death on 17 March 1862. Some two and a half months later, on Wednesday 28 May, a commemorative gala performance of *La Juive* was held at the Opéra. After the second act the curtain went up to reveal his bust, sculpted and donated by his widow, which had been lowered from the flies. The five main singers, the Elazar, Rachel, Brogni, Eudoxie and Leopold of the day, each took off their laurels and placed them on the sculpted head. More laurels were flung from the boxes; there was a standing ovation for a full ten minutes. Some time later the four short streets which surround the Opéra building were renamed; two after Gluck and Auber and two after Scribe who had died in 1861, and Halévy. There they are to this day, rue Scribe and rue Halévy, commemorating the librettist and composer who between them had given the Opéra one of the most enduring successes in its history.

9

L'ECLAIR

*E*VER SINCE THE GREAT SUCCESS
of *Ludovic* in 1833 Halévy was continually harassed by various
calls on his time which kept distracting him from his work. In
1834, already in the throes of *La Juive*, he was one of six
composers who had been commissioned to write *Six galops brillans*
for the Opéra balls of that year, the other five being Auber,
Boieldieu, Carafa, Henry Herz and Labarre. For the newly-
launched *Revue et gazette musicale* he contributed on 9 March of
that year an article on *Les Canons de Cherubini*. He would no more
decline an invitation to write a piece of incidental music or an
article than a commission for a new opera; it was evidence of
growing recognition, an honour.

One honour he particularly aspired to, along with many other
musicians, artists, writers, architects, scientists, philosophers and
the like, was to be elected to the Institute of France through one
of its five academies. Each academy had forty life members; on
the death of an incumbent an election to fill the vacancy would be
held, preceded by the customary excitement of lobbying and
string-pulling.

The Academy of Fine Arts divided its forty seats among
fourteen painters, eight sculptors, eight architects, four
engravers and six musicians. When François-Adrien Boieldieu,
composer of *La Dame blanche* and *Le Calif de Bagdad*, died on 8
October 1834, Halévy had high hopes of succeeding him. In fact

Boieldieu himself had indicated him as his successor. The grateful heir presumptive, as a tribute to the deceased and a reminder to the living of his own merit, speedily wrote three commemorative articles which were published in *La Revue et gazette musicale* on 12, 19 and 26 October. Old Cherubini for his part spared no effort to pave the way for his protégé. His fellow academicians were persuaded to put back the election by six months as a token of respect for the defunct, while the inner circle was told that rehearsals for *La Juive* had just begun and that in six months' time, after the undoubted triumph of the opera, its composer would be a most distinguished addition to the Academy. Six months later, in February 1835, *La Juive* was performed and the election duly held. Halévy was defeated by the sixty-five year old Antoine Reicha, composer of many operas and author of a popular teaching manual. Either Cherubini's tactics had antagonised his fellow academicians, or the initial reviews of *La Juive* made them cautious; or perhaps they genuinely wished to honour an elderly composer who had been contributing to Paris musical life for many years.

For Halévy the defeat was a hard blow; he put a brave face on it and immersed himself in his next self-imposed assignment. This was *L'Eclair*, a three-act opera comique to words by Saint-Georges and Planard, which had been rejected by Rossini and Adam; it had the disadvantage of a tiny cast – two sopranos and two tenors; no alto, no bass, no chorus.

Jules-Henri Vernoy de Saint-Georges, like Scribe, was one of the most prolific librettists of his time and, again like Scribe, often worked with collaborators to keep up with demand. He had the advantage of being a competent musician who played several instruments. One evening, at a *salon* recital, he listened stoney-faced to a German flautist play a difficult work. 'I can play it as well as he does,' he informed the gathering. A servant was instructed to fetch a whip with an ivory handle. Saint-Georges, dandified and heavily perfumed as usual, played the whip without missing a note, producing sounds which were 'nearly melodious,'[1] as a gossip columnist later reported. He had already written for Halévy the librettos of *L'Artisan* and *Le Roi et le batelier*, two ephemeral operas comiques performed in 1827; and he was the librettist of Hérold's *Ludovic*, which Halévy posthumously completed to great acclaim.

The story of *L'Eclair* takes place in a beautiful house by the sea, somewhere near Boston, USA. The owner is eighteen-year old Henriette who is visited by her Boston sister, a merry widow by the name of Mme Darbel.

George is a young Englishman down from Oxford, visiting his uncle in Boston. He is the conventional French idea of an Oxford grad — aristocratic, phlegmatic, imperturbable, but not a bad chap at heart. Uncle is a Dubliner, a naturalised American, a successful doctor and a friend of the sisters. He is often referred to but never seen or heard, a convenient ploy which helps to drive the story forward. On his orders George is staying with the sisters with a view to marrying either the one or the other. While he is having his dinner on the veranda, an American Marines officer by the name of Lyonel stops for a chat before going to the beach for some leisurely fishing. A thunderstorm breaks out. Lyonel is struck by a flash of lightning and goes blind. Henriette rushes out and drags him to the safety of her home. Mme Darbel goes back to Boston, George stays on and decides to marry Henriette.

Three months later Mme Darbel comes down for another visit. George is surprised to learn from her that nurse and patient have fallen in love. He paces up and down, ponders the situation as he has been taught to do in his philosophy class at Oxford, and transfers his favour to Mme Darbel.

It is time to remove the bandages from the patient's eyes. The treatment has been successful. For the first time in his life Lyonel sees the two sisters whom until now he has only known by their names; one is beautiful, the other plain. He kneels before the beautiful one: 'Henriette,' he says adoringly to Mme Darbel. The real Henriette faints. The following morning she disappears, nobly ceding Lyonel to her sister and ordering them to marry. George, with a philosophical shrug, reverts to his original decision to marry Henriette if she ever returns.

Forty days later, believing herself immune to unrequited love, Henriette returns home only to hear that her order has been disobeyed. She and Lyonel fall into each other's arms and George, the phlegmatic, unromantic and naively self-complacent Oxford graduate, again bestows his hand on Mme Darbel.

L'Eclair opened at the Opéra-Comique on 16 December 1835. Young Offenbach, playing his cello nightly as a member of the orchestra, called it a masterpiece of harmonic and melodic inventiveness. *La Revue et gazette musicale* of 20 December could not have been more pleasing:

> For the past three years the Opéra-Comique has not had anything comparable to the success of *L'Eclair*. Words, music, male and female cast, production – everything has succeeded beyond all expectations and hopes. Without taking a rest after his hard labour over the vast and demanding score of *La Juive*, Monsieur Halévy has undertaken, as if he were playing a game, a musical *tour de force*, the very idea of which had frightened off the most intrepid: an opera in three acts, with only four singers and no choir. He emerged from this trial with unequalled ease, grace and vigour.[2]

A few years later, on the occasion of a change of cast the same periodical published a longer appreciation by its regular reviewer Henri Blanchard:

> Three acts without a bass and choruses do not leave much scope for musical development; what the composer did was a *tour de force*. Deprived of a bass voice and choir he drove the work forward more nimbly than ever . . . This is not the traditional sort of music which pleases by offering easily memorisable tunes. It is innovative, original, eminently distinguished; it is sprightly and attractive, blazing a new trail, audacious as well as graceful, knocking on the doors of the future with lively, rich, animated, powerful orchestration, one that has nothing in common with that brass band sound which has been grandiloquently described as Modern Instrumentation.
>
> I cannot go into a detailed analysis of Monsieur Halévy's score because its originality, richness and variety loom large from every section of the orchestra. It is a drama, a many-voiced musical comedy, radiating life and youth. Suffice it to recall the thunderstorm which brings down the curtain on Act One. Usually the music of a storm is sacrosanct, all pervasive; here it is subordinate to the person who is on stage, speaking in a daze. What we hear is a subdued storm; but what novel and gripping effects enter into this mezzo-tint. One could say, and do forgive the pun, that *L'Eclair* [the Lightning] lit up the path of the young French School . . . [3]

After the rave reviews of *L'Eclair* and the triumph of *La Juive* Halévy was the only composer with two successful operas running in Paris simultaneously, one at the Opéra, the other at the Opéra-Comique. Like *La Juive*, *L'Eclair* was kept in the repertory, scoring over two hundred performances up to the composer's death in 1862 and another hundred after it. It was shown in the provinces, in Europe, in America. 'It is particularly appreciated by the American public for two reasons,' explained a news item. 'First because of its charming music and secondly because the story takes place in the United States. As far as the spectators are concerned it is a family affair or at least a national afffair.'[4] Only England turned a deaf ear; poking fun at an Oxford graduate was not quite the thing.

Success bred its own irritations. The publishing rights of *L'Eclair* had been offered to Schlesinger for what seemed a reasonable price at the time of the preliminary negotiations. On 20 December 1835, four days after the tremendous success of its opening, Halévy asked him to review the original terms; of all his correspondents Schlesinger was the only one with whom he did not mince his words. He wrote that he had discussed the matter with his librettists, the co-holders of the copyright, whose attitude was that Schlesinger was at liberty to publish the music if he so wished, but certainly not the words, which were theirs. 'I am offered 12,000 francs for the score,' Halévy bargained. 'There are two publishers who are prepared to pay me this sum; others have made equally good offers. Monsieur de Saint-Georges and Monsieur de Planard know that. What will become of me if they think I have arranged with you to defraud them? Or if I feel that they harbour such a thought against me?'[5] Obviously a compromise formula agreeable to all parties was reached, for Halévy continued to have his work published by Schlesinger until the latter's retirement and return to his native Germany in 1846.

With all this unprecedented success Halévy held on to his regular post as *chef du chant* at the Opéra. To friends who tried to persuade him to give it up and stop driving himself so hard he made the lame excuse that it gave him a respite from composition. That it did not; what it did give him was a position of strength from which to offer new works to the Opéra or the Opéra-Comique. For that position of strength he was prepared to put up with a great deal – call rehearsals, attend performances, schedule and re-schedule programmes, find an understudy in the nick of time, soothe frayed tempers, stoop to quasi-domestic duties. Thus, on 24 April 1835, when already the acclaimed composer of *La Juive*, he wrote with trepidation to Dr Veron, the

Opéra Director who behind his back was known as the Opéra Dictator:

> I take the liberty of asking the Director to order that the regular delivery of firewood be strictly adhered to. The theatre, the artists' dressing rooms and the rehearsal hall are poorly heated and there is no firewood anywhere. The singers all come to me to complain; all I can do is refer them to the Director while pointing out to him that the lack of fire has caused colds and can disrupt work.[6]

Stage accidents were also left to the *chef du chant* to cope with. During a performance of Meyerbeer's *Robert-le-Diable* Nourrit was knocked unconscious by heavy rigging dropping from the flies at the beginning of Act IV. Halévy, in attendance as usual, pounced on the tenor Lafont – Leopold in *La Juive* – who had just walked into the auditorium and persuaded him to step into the part.

Standing up for overworked singers was another of his concerns. Mlle Falcon, bravely singing in spite of her throat trouble, wrote pleadingly: 'Maestro, I hardly need to tell you how tired I am. I should like to take advantage of *La Juive* not being performed on Monday to take a much-needed rest . . . I will be ready to sing again on Wednesday. If Dr Veron tries to make me sing tomorrow as well . . . [in a different opera] I shall be more annoyed with him than I would dare tell him to his face, and still not sing.'[7]

His duties did not become any lighter when the brilliant architect-producer Duponchel took over as the Opéra Director after Dr Veron had moved on. 'My dear Nourrit,' he wrote in haste, 'instead of singing *La Juive* on Saturday would you be able to sing Friday? Am writing on behalf of Director Duponchel who is ill in bed and in difficulties. Your devoted friend F. Halévy. N.B. My dear Adolphe, you know I will gladly commit murder just to please you.'[8]

Fellow composers who had an opera in rehearsal could also be difficult. He had to carry out their instructions, run errands for them, and never take offence. Meyerbeer, whose *Robert-le-Diable* had been the pride of the Opéra since its opening in 1831 until the advent of *La Juive*, had to be treated with kid gloves. On 12 June 1835 he sent Halévy detailed instructions for calling a rehearsal of *Les Huguenots* which, although outwardly courteous, read like an order-of-the-day issued by a superior to an underling:

> Dear and illustrious colleague,
>
> I am indisposed and cannot go out this evening. Monsieur Duponchel promised to ask you to call on me so that we can make arrangements for tomorrow's rehearsal which is of special importance as M. Scribe will attend it. Perhaps he has not seen you today and forgot all about it.
>
> Be kind enough, *cher Maître*, to convene all the big and small parts as well as the men's choir at 12.30 for 12.45 at the choir rehearsal hall in order to rehearse the individual parts and choruses of Act I. An hour earlier, that is at 1130, I would like the women's choir to be convened and Mme [Dorus-]Gras and Mlle Flecheux called so as to go through Mme Gras's aria in Act II. I will also go through the women's choruses in Act III as I have some comments to make in this section.
>
> May I also ask you, *cher Maître*, to send a note to M. Pape [the piano maker] asking him to see that the piano for tomorrow's choir rehearsal is in better shape than the one he sent us last time, which was untuned. I apologise, *cher Maître*, for inconveniencing you with all these details.[9]

Just before sending the missive off Meyerbeer remembered another little inconveniencing detail. 'Saturday evening,' he hastily added. 'Please be kind enough to notify M. Habeneck of our rehearsal tomorrow.' François-Antoine Habeneck was the conductor.

Les Huguenots was a resounding success, destined to achieve one thousand performances, but Nourrit, who sang the part of Raoul to Mme Dorus-Gras's Valentine, was increasingly suffering from sudden loss of voice which nobody as yet associated with paranoia. Cajoling, rearranging and even cancelling a performance were the responsibility of the *chef du chant*. On one occasion Rossini's *Guillaume Tell* was at risk. 'Dear Adolphe, I have earmarked Lafont to sing Guillaume if your damned hoarseness makes it impossible for you to keep the promise of the posters,' he wrote in a note urgently dispatched by messenger. 'Do consider, dear friend, singing even as you are, with an announcement to the audience.'[10] The messenger brought back a verbal refusal. Halévy dispatched another urgent note:

> Dear friend, before putting out a No Performance Tonight notice to the public I want to ask you again whether, after an announcement to

the audience, you would agree to sing in *Les Huguenots* instead. Do forgive me, dear friend . . . Had I been Director in my own right (God forbid) I would not harass you so; I have to carry out the instructions of another and, before sacrificing takings which are not mine to sacrifice, I have to do my best to save them . . . I await your final decision. Please answer in writing.[11]

The stressful life of a *chef du chant* was taking its toll; the two-year interval between *L'Eclair* and the next opera was unusually long by Halévy's record. It was however a period of accruing honours. Before 1835 was out he was created Knight of the *Légion d'Honneur* – later he would be elevated to the rank of Commander – joining the illustrious galaxy of Rossini, Auber and Meyerbeer. On 28 May 1936 Reicha died, vacating the seat in the Institute of France which he had held for less than a year. This time Halévy was elected without much ado, succeeding him on 2 July; close friends claimed that he never got over the humiliation of his original defeat, and that to the end of his life he regarded himself as Boieldieu's direct successor, pretending to himself that the Reicha interregnum had never happened.

He was further honoured by his position at the Opéra, where he became Director Duponchel's right hand man, his deputy in all but name. In 1837, to facilitate planning meetings, a commodious grace-and-favour apartment at the Opéra building was put at his disposal. It was one of several which were allocated to distinguished personalities in order of precedence. The main one was occupied by Director Duponchel, his wife and their baby. Mme Duponchel's establishment consisted of a stableful of horses, a formidable dog, groom, coachman, valet, hairdresser, chambermaid and cook. Halévy, still a bachelor, invited his brother Léon to share with him. 'The two households of the two Halévy brothers,' an Opéra dresser recorded in her diary, 'consist of Monsieur Fromental, his two sisters, Monsieur Léon, his wife and their little boy, two servants and a lackey. They occupy an apartment of sixteen rooms of which fourteen are on one level.'[12] The little boy was Ludovic, later a successful librettist, born in the lucky year of *Ludovic*. His sister, born a few years later, was named Valentine.

It would have been unnatural for so swift a rise not to cause envy; but while colleagues were courteous to the point of fawning, the ubiquitous Opéra dresser gave vent to her feelings, perhaps her inherited prejudice, in her diary. The frequent planning meetings between Duponchel and Halévy, which were often attended by Léon, she referred to as *The Sanhedrin*, the seventy-one strong assembly of Jewish scholars convened by Napoleon in 1807, named after the Supreme Council of the Jews during the period of the Second Temple in Jerusalem.

Socially Halévy was much in demand. Meyerbeer invited him to an all-male party which included pianist Moscheles, actor Duprez, director Duponchel, conductor Habeneck and Herr Kuster, Intendant of the Munich theatres. Liszt, on a visit from Geneva, accepted his invitation to give a recital in his grandiose Opera apartment. Chopin invited him to dinner, which he charmingly and regretfully declined:

> I am obliged to give up the pleasure of dining with you tonight. A rather acute sore throat which has not let go of me this past fortnight has become even worse since yesterday and forces me, on doctor's orders, to eat little and speak even less, two things which are rather distressing at table. These two privations upset me only because they prevent me from joining Liszt, yourself and your other friends some of whom, I hope, are also mine. Please apologise to them on my behalf and accept, my dear good Chopin, my cordial wishes.[13]

At the height of his success he sent the autograph scores of his greatest triumphs to the father figure he would never forget. 'Please accept, my good and beloved Master,' he wrote to Cherubini in the accompanying note, 'these two scores of *La Juive* and *L'Eclair* and accept again the expression of the profound and everlasting gratitude of someone who will always love you like a son. F. Halévy.'[14]

His loyalty to Cherubini led to a contretemps with Berlioz which the latter would never forget. In the autumn of 1837 Berlioz's *Requiem* was due to be performed in the chapel of Les Invalides to commemorate the death of a French general in Algeria. Cherubini felt that one of his own masses should have been selected for the occasion and Halévy volunteered to have a word with the influential editor of *Le Journal des débats*. He had not expected to see Berlioz esconced in the editorial office; the latter had just been accepted as the paper's music critic. Halévy changed gear. He explained that Cherubini was hurt and that the ribbon of a Commander of the *Légion d'Honneur* would make up for the slight to his honour. The upshot was that the *Requiem* was performed as planned, Cherubini was awarded his decoration and Berlioz went on to review Halévy's work for the next twenty years, sometimes favourably, more often dismissively, always wittily.

L'Eclair, like *La Juive*, withstood the test of time. When it was revived in the spring of 1857 *La Revue et gazette musicale* regarded it as a classic.

Among the operas which have been in repertory for twenty five years few can claim the undisputed right to be revived as deservedly as *L'Eclair*. Charming, sprightly and interesting, its score gracious and dramatic in turn, containing beauties of the first order, crafted with skill that defies all comparison – these are the characteristics which have assured the brilliant success of this work and will continue to guarantee it to the end of time. M. Halévy has had many successes on the stage of the Opéra Comique, but none was as complete and as well deserved. The distinguished composer has never shown himself a greater master of melody, more elegant and at the same time more natural, than he has in this work. It was first performed on 16 December 1835, and it seems as if it were only yesterday. Surely that is the test of a work of genius, an evergreen which defies time's fell hand and the vagaries of fashion.[15]

10

LEADER OF THE FRENCH SCHOOL

*H*ALEVY'S NEXT OPERA WAS ANOTHER collaboration with Eugène Scribe, who set the plot in plague-stricken Florence, between the autumn of 1552 and the spring of 1553.

Guido et Ginevra, subtitled the Plague of Florence, opens deceptively pleasantly with a pastoral ball. Ginevra, the daughter of the Duke of Tuscany attends it dressed as a shepherdess. The sculptor Guido, who has never moved in ducal circles, takes her for his social equal and is about to declare his love when she is set upon by brigands. He throws himself into the fray while the ducal guard whisks her away to safety.

A marriage of convenience has been arranged between Ginevra and Manfredi, the depraved Duke of Ferrara. His jealous mistress pays the ever-handy brigands to kill the bride. During the wedding ceremony a poisoned veil is thrown over her head and her women scream that she has been struck down by the plague. Everybody flees in panic. Guido, who has been invited to sketch and sculpt, has recognised his lost shepherdess. He mournfully watches her body being lowered into the church vaults and is then driven out.

The cool air of the vaults revives Ginevra. When the brigands steal in to strip her of her jewellery they are petrified by the sight of a spectre walking about. Clad in her white funeral robe she gropes her way through the streets of Florence into her husband's palace; he is celebrating widowhood with his reconciled mistress. Both sinners are struck down by the plague. Spectre-like Ginevra floats to her father's palace, finds it deserted and drops on the stairs, about to die in a snow storm. Guido finds her and carries her away.

It is spring. The Duke of Tuscany is touring his domains, distributing largesse to the survivors of the plague. At a small village in the Apennines he discovers his daughter alive and well together with her rescuer. Guido movingly pleads for her hand in marriage and the old Duke, deviating from operatic conven-tion which allows a titled lady to marry a commoner only if he turns out to be a scion of a noble house or has noble rank conferred upon him, gives the couple his blessing.

As was his practice, Halévy had been composing the solo arias with certain singers in mind. Nourrit, his first choice for the part of Guido, was already learning the part at the piano when the shadow of a rival fell across his path.

The trouble had started when Director Duponchel, to pre-empt cancellations due to Nourrit's recurring indisposition, began looking for a second leading tenor. He and Halévy audi-tioned Gilbert Duprez, recently returned from a successful sea-son in Italy, and were immediately captivated. At first Nourrit was agreeable to sharing the work and the honours, but soon he began to suspect that he was being edged out. One evening Duponchel popped into his dressing room shortly before the curtain was due to rise on Auber's *La Muette de Portici* and found him in good voice and high spirits. Half an hour later he was handed a note from his *chef du chant* alerting him that Nourrit had developed a sore throat and that the understudy would step in. For the next three mornings Duponchel called on Nourrit in person to see how he was getting on. On the fourth he sent his deputy to assess the situation.

'Is Nourrit any better?' he enquired on Halévy's return.

'He is, Monsieur le Directeur, but . . . '

'But what?'

'He's gone mad.'

Out came the story which grew more melodramatic in the telling. Nouritt, minutes before the curtain was due to rise, was told that Duprez was sitting in the front row of the stalls. 'The thought that his rival was going to hear him and judge him made

Nourrit lose his head, his voice and his courage, none of which he has recovered.'[1] After his breakdown the part of Guido was assigned to Duprez. Nourrit left the Opéra as soon as his contract permitted, went to Italy, became deeply depressed and in Naples committed suicide by throwing himself out of his hotel window. He was only thirty-five.

A few days before opening night with Duprez in the lead, tenor and composer exchanged urgent notes about a sartorial problem. Duprez wanted to know whether Guido should wear plain black like an artist or a richly embroidered costume like a nobleman. Obviously the choice was up to him, not to the artistic director. Halévy suggested plain black for opening night, reserving judgment until seeing how it fitted in with other singers' costumes, 'Above all,' he wrote, 'sing, my dear Duprez, as only you can sing. If I were you I wouldn't bother about the rest . . . '

He himself was beset by a similar problem. 'Now I want your advice,' he continued. 'Should I wear the Institute costume or plain black?'[2] The gala dress of members of the Institute of France consisted of a calf-length black coat with green embroidery, worn over short culottes and black leggings. For Halévy, who became a member only two years earlier and as yet had had few occasions to display his uniform in public, it was a matter of great importance; a wrong choice could suggest disrespect for the Institute to which he had the honour to belong or, conversely, sheer ostentation.

Guido et Ginevra was premiered at the Opéra on 5 March 1838. The press took the new work very seriously and Berlioz devoted to it no less than three articles in *La Revue et gazette musicale*. The first, on 11 March, gave a general impression:

> It is unanimously agreed that Monsieur Scribe's libretto is one of the finest he has ever written. Composers are not always lucky in their librettists but we trust M. Halévy will not disagree with us when we say that this time the musician has every right to be satisfied.[3]

He enumerated the gems of the opera: Guido's love song, Ginevra's aria, the duet of the jealous mistress and the hired brigand, Guido's 'sublime aria' on Ginevra's tomb, the chorus *Vive la peste*, 'one of the finest pieces Halévy has ever written,' the duet of Guido and Ginevra, the prayer to the Madonna, and the concluding trio during which Guido addresses the Duke of

Tuscany and claims the right to his daughter's hand, a moving plea, superbly sung by Duprez, which never failed to bring the house down.

In the second article, on 18 March, Berlioz declared that 'the score is a worthy sibling to *La Juive* and *L'Eclair*'[4] and in his third, on 1 April, he continued:

> The score of *Guido et Ginevra* adds a beautiful jewel to M. Halévy's crown. Placed on the borders of the Italian and German schools he worthily continues the great tradition of Méhul, Lesueur and Cherubini, revitalising it by drawing on new sources, and rising as its glorious representative.'[5]

Unlike Berlioz, the poet and writer Théophile Gautier began his review with a disparaging remark about Scribe, 'the certified purveyor of all sorts of dramatic provisions,' whose vault scene was 'similar' to Shakespeare's Romeo and Juliet. Of the composer he wrote as follows:

> Halévy is a mature talent arrived at its apogee. His reputation is made, he has taken his place at the head of the French school – all he need do is take care to keep it. Brilliant imagination, profound knowledge of his craft, perfect mastery of orchestral resources, exquisite taste in his choice of instruments, horror of the vulgar, delicacy and distinction in his melodies – these are the eminent qualities which we pointed out in *La Juive* and which we find again, though not to the same extent, in this new work of his.'[6]

Gautier called attention to the composer's use of the relatively novel idea of a *Leitmotif* (a leading-motive) which he called the Mother-Idea.

> Guido's love song, *Hélas elle a fui comme une ombre*, sung by Duprez, is one of the most beautiful melodies Halévy has ever written. Its theme is the mother-idea of the entire score. In the course of the opera Halévy knew how to bring it back time and again with happy effect. It is melancholy, suave, sweet and naive.[7]

The thirty-three performances of *Guido et Ginevra* would have counted as a box office success but for the inevitable comparison with the extraordinary run of *La Juive* and *L'Eclair*. Long after it had been taken out of the repertory an opera goer with a selective memory and a vitriolic pen pronounced it boring and soporific.

To prove his point he embroidered on what happened one night when the friezes caught fire in mid-performance.

Fire regulations demanded the presence of municipal firemen during performance but some of them, particularly since candles were replaced by gaslight in 1831, were not as alert as they might have been and sometimes dozed off. The night of the friezes was no exception. The audience noticed nothing but director Duponchel had spied a tiny tongue of flame through his opera glasses and took charge of operations.

'Steadfast on your posts,' he ordered the walk-on parts as soon as he had alerted the firemen. 'Anyone who runs away will be fined. Five francs for those who stay put.'

The firemen wielded the hose with the utmost discretion. 'In the auditorium people realised that it was raining on stage but seeing choristers and walk-ons so calm they never suspected a thing.'

The following morning a police enquiry was held. 'How could you fall asleep with all that music going on?' the Chief Fireman was asked.

'It was stronger than me, Sir. It has never happened before.'

'What were they playing?'

'Guido, Sir.'

'Guido? Ah, mitigating circumstances. Next.'

The firemen were interviewed one by one and every one of them gave the same excuse. 'No case to answer,' the police officer decided.[8]

The opera did have some soporific passages and in due course its five acts were pruned to four. Duprez alternated triumphantly between romantic Guido and fanatic Elazar. Paris adored him; only Mère Crosnier, the Opéra concierge, referred to him to the end of her life as the Murderer of Monsieur Nourrit.

The next opera with Scribe as librettist was *Le Drapier*. Although no longer daunted by the dramatist's grand manner Halévy still addressed him in his letters with a touch of obsequiousness absent from his correspondence with other professional friends. Mostly he wrote about such mundane things as contracts, copyright, revisions, difficulties with theatre managers or publishers, but the form of address was deferential. There was no 'Dear Scribe' or 'Dear friend'; he was *Mon cher et illustre collaborateur* or *Mon cher conseilleur et collaborateur*, with *ami* tentatively thrown in as in *Mon très cher collaborateur et ami*. Many years would pass before the composer, unassuming and modest even at the height of his fame, would feel emboldened to drop formality and address his collaborator simply as *Cher ami* and send him social invitations.

Le Drapier was based on an attempt by Henri III to restore himself to the throne of France; or was it Henri IV, asked a reviewer who was not all that smitten with Scribe's way with history. The scene is set in the ancient cathedral city of Chartres. The Royalist draper of the story conspires to deliver the city into the King's hands. A poor student who is in love with the draper's daughter discovers the plot and is threatened by local anti-royalists with death unless he reveals the name of the traitor. He promises to tell all provided he can marry his sweetheart before the execution. The cathedral bells ring the death knell. This happens to be the signal for the Royalist onslaught. Chartres is conquered, the young lovers are restored into each other's arms, and in the general tumult and jubilation everybody has cause to be happy.

Le Drapier opened at the Opéra on 6 January 1840. This time Gautier, with all his admiration for the composer, could no longer contain his dislike and contempt for his librettist:

> The author of *Le Drapier* is Monsieur Scribe, an anti-poetic character if there ever was one. We are amazed that for an operatic poem one goes to someone who has no idea of the simplest rules of French versification. *Le Drapier* is guilty of disgraceful and criminal negligence on this count. The French swarms with mistakes; rhythm and metre are violated in every line, repetition of outrageous words make the sentences cumbersome. *Je t'aime* is made to rhyme with *suprême* and *moi-même* no less than twenty-seven times in the course of this three-act opera; this exceeds all bounds. We pity with all our heart composers who have to compose music to such words. It is impossible to embroider anything subtle or delicate on such a coarse canvas . . . M. Halévy did his best and fought his hardest against the poem; he has not always emerged victorious. You cannot soar to the heights with a ball and chain tied to your feet.[9]

Henri Blanchard of *La Revue et gazette musicale*, usually a great admirer of Halévy, sought refuge in generalities:

> Monsieur Halévy has not been any less successful in this work than in any of his previous ones. He is one of the two pillars on which the French school rests; the other is M. Auber. The latter has consoled us for the loss of Boieldieu; the former is a continuation of Hérold: the same finesse of melody, the same harmonic wealth with a special and most advanced knowledge of orchestration which seems inspired by the German school.[10]

But even Blanchard could not be whole-hearted about the new work.

> The overture is outstanding, as are all Halévy's overtures. If in construction and form it is not much different from any of his previous ones, it does however offer something new and original by way of modulation . . . It was unanimously applauded, and rightly so . . . The costumes were authentic and Chartres Cathedral equally so, except that it shone golden under a sun imported from Syria, or Greece or Italy . . . The performance was acceptable, perhaps even more carefully prepared than usual.[11]

Le Drapier was taken off after eight performances. Two years later Halévy gloriously redeemed himself with *La Reine de Chypre*.

For this five-act grand opera he turned to Saint-Georges, the librettist whose wit and command of stagecraft had so happily launched the opera comique *L'Eclair*. The scene was set in the fifteenth century and had some tenuous connection with the marriage of Venetian Catarina de Carnaro to Jacques de Lusignan, King of Cyprus, and her resistance to Venetian encroachment after her husband's untimely death.

The story begins in Venice. Catarina is on the point of marrying her French sweetheart Gerard when the Council of Ten orders her uncle Carnaro to marry her to the King of Cyprus to advance Venetian territorial claims to the island. She is given to understand that if she does not obey, Gerard will be killed. She sends him away minutes before the wedding, allowing him to believe that she did so to satisfy a vain ambition to be queen.

The scene shifts to Nicosia. Gerard has followed Catarina to Cyprus in order to kill her future husband. A masqued knight saves him from armed highwaymen and he swears eternal loyalty to him. During the royal wedding ceremony he realises that the knight is none other than the King. Although he stays his hand

he is arrested and condemned to death: the King, in the chivalrous tradition of a knight errant, frees him after he hears
Gerard's true story.

Two years later the Queen is pregnant, the King is dying, and
Gerard is back; he has returned to repay a debt of honour, having
heard that the King is being slowly poisoned by his Venetian
counsellor. King, Queen and Gerard are honourably reconciled.
When the treacherous counsellor warns the King that he has to
choose between giving up Cyprus or going to war against mighty
Venice, Gerard nobly says to the King: 'I will fight for you, for
your kingdom and your heir.' The counsellor is arrested and the
dying King goes out to lead his people in battle, with loyal Gerard
by his side.

La Reine de Chypre opened on 22 December 1841 and drew an
instant disgusted reaction from the novelist George Sand, a
regular opera goer and a fair amateur musician. Writing on 25
December to her good friend the painter Eugène Delacroix who
had intended to attend the premiere but decided to stay put in his
country house among his flowers and vegetables, she said: 'You
did well, old friend, not to go to the Opera. It was boring to death
in spite of the magnificence and pomp of the spectacle. I trust
your truffles gave you more musical inspiration than *La Reine de
Chypre* had given to Monsieur Halévy.'[12]

As it turned out it was another success: some 130 performances
in the course of the next fifteen years. There was however the
usual slow recognition. The custom of the time was to publish a
new score only after its first performance, not before. Critics, like
first night audiences, heard a new opera with virgin ears and
were wary of over-praising in haste; the conscientious sometimes
attended several performances before passing judgment. Thus
Berlioz attended it twice before going to press in *Le Journal des
débats:*

> There was a marked difference between the impression made on
> opening night and second night. On opening night everything in the
> score seemed dull, confused, vague; on the second night listeners
> who had been left cold and rather dissatisfied were able to discern
> many outstanding ideas and beautiful numbers which they had not
> noticed before. M. Halévy's music is not the kind you can relish and
> appreciate on first hearing; it has intimate and complex beauties

within a form which lacks neither grandeur nor spontaneity. You get to admire and live it only after attentive examination.

First let us thank the composer for his current method of orchestration. We see it as the beginning of a reaction against the school of Noise For All Occasions. The first act is free until the finale of trombones and bass drums. You can breathe, you feel relaxed with this disencumbered orchestra which will thunder all the louder when the time comes to release its lightning. In the following acts M. Halévy uses the brass for arias and dances sung by the choir; the feast turns into an orgy and violent clamours are not out of place. A happy effect.[13]

Théophile Gautier wrote: 'As far as one can judge such a vast work on the strength of two or three hearings it seems that the melodies are somewhat pale, but the harmony is rich, elegant, worthy of a great master. The orchestration is inventive and most original.[14]

And *La Revue et gazette musicale*:

True to his habit, his spirit or should one say his genius, M. Halévy has produced a complex work; not the sort of music one can understand right away and weary of soon after. One needs to have intelligent experience and a trained ear to understand the secrets of the harmony and orchestration, to grasp all the ingenuity, wealth and distinction of his musical thinking.[15]

Wagner had the advantage over his fellow critics in that he had ample opportunity to familiarise himself with the score before writing about it. He had arrived in Paris in the autumn of 1839 and for two and a half years, while unsuccessfully trying to interest the Opera in his work, eked out a living from piano and instrumental arrangements of other composers' operas, including *La Reine de Chypre*. 'Making arrangements of Halévy's score,' he later recalled, 'was far and away more interesting a piece of hack-work than the shameful labour I had spent on Donizetti's *La Favorita* . . . I was sincerely rejoiced to see his better side again. I had taken a great liking to him from the time of *La Juive* and had a very high opinion of his masterly talent.'[16]

By the time he was commissioned to write four articles for *La Revue et gazette musicale* he was probably more familiar with the opera than most. Familiarity combined with virtually unlimited print-space enabled him to discuss aspects which more restricted fellow critics could not. One he particularly approved of was Halévy's ability to characterise each location with a different musical colouring – one for Venice, another one for Nicosia.

Outwardly Halévy's opera consists of two distinct parts determined by the scene of the action. The difference of location has never been more important than it is in this drama, where both action and form are painted with local colour. If you lend but half an ear to Halévy's accents you will understand how he expresses each different location by means of sound. He has surpassed the poet.

We are in Venice, in the midst of palaces and canals . . . For nobility and charm nothing equals the loveliness of Gerard's and Catarina's duet . . . Charming and tender, clear and immediately understandable, it is still free of mannerism and those hackneyd ploys with which popularity-seeking composers nowadays garnish this kind of melody . . .

The beginning of the second act, which depicts the romantic side of Venice, is one of the most original conceptions ever penned by Halévy. The insistent monotonous pizzicato of the cellos and the dreamy harmonies of the wind section combine with the gondoliers' chorus to form an irresistible whole. It has a grand and naive simplicity whose effect is magical. Those barcarolles with their new rhythms and melodramatic harmonies which flourish in our operas whenever the scene is set in Italy are as nothing in comparison with this chorus, where for the first time the unsophisticated nature of those sons of the Chioggia who ply the canals of Venice is revealed in all its truth . . .

The third act transforms us to a different location and displays the different musical characterisation I referred to earlier. . . The joyous chorus of the Cypriot lords *Buvnos à Chypre* teems with vibrant melody, bubbles with carefree gaiety . . .

The fourth act displays extraordinary magnificence and splendour . . . It reflects the joyous transports of a people that sees in its young Queen a promise of peace and happiness . . . But it is the prayer *Divine providence* that gives the scene the last individual touch; the very first bars of the tenor conjure up a vision of those processions we sometimes see crossing fields with crosses and banners. Serenity is combined with religious fervour.

What shall I say of the fifth act, where poet and musician seem to have reached the most marvellous effect of their respective arts? It would be impossible to find anything more touching and nobly pathetic. Catarina's aria sung at the King's deathbed and his own reply spring from the innermost depths of the human heart; no words can describe the heart-rending grief here depicted . . . However, the most sublime number of the entire score is the quartet *En cet instant suprême*. Here, more than anywhere else, Halévy's talent shines in all its individuality; the grandiose is joined with the terrible, an elegiac melancholy envelops the scene like a funeral veil. It has the clarity and simplicity which are the hallmark of great masters.[17]

In his memoirs Wagner described the circumstances of his first meeting with Halévy. He had sent him his piano arrangements of *La Reine de Chypre* and was expecting some slight modifications which would make them easier to play. Halévy however had many calls on his time and, anxious as he was to do everything for everybody, often fell behind with his commitments. The printing was put back time and again and Schlesinger, afraid of missing a golden opportunity to sell sheet music while the opera was at the height of its popularity, accused the composer of 'incorrigible laziness.' He persuaded Wagner to call on him early in the morning at his elegant apartment in the Opéra building and force him to sit down and make the necessary modifications in his presence.

'The first time I reached his house,' Wagner recalled, 'was at about ten in the morning. I found him just out of bed and he informed me that he really must have breakfast first. I accepted his invitation and sat down with him to a somewhat luxurious meal. My conversation seemed to appeal to him but friends came in, Schlesinger among them, who burst into a fury at not finding him at work on the proofs he regarded as so important. Halévy remained quite unmoved.'[18] The visitor formed the impression that his host was 'good hearted and really unassuming,'[19] as well as 'frank and honest, not a sly, calculating blackguard like Meyerbeer.'[20]

From his recollections quite an endearing picture emerges of Halévy and his habits at the time. The late rising was presumably due to the nightly vigil at the Opera necessitated by the continuing success of *La Reine de Chypre*. The morning was set aside for receiving callers, dispensing hospitality, holding lively discussions. That was the time of day when he was at his most relaxed. He talked without bitterness of recent failures and claimed he could not understand why his latest opera was so popular. It was probably 'engineered' by Schlesinger, he joked, just to give him no peace. A few words to Wagner in German, a knowledgeable contribution to any topic under discussion — he fully lived up to his reputation as one of the most erudite composers of the day.

What puzzled the twenty-nine year old visitor, still at the lower rungs of the ladder, was the older man's apparent indifference to success. Wagner was perhaps too young and certainly too differently constituted to appreciate that it was not indifference; it was guardedness born out of twenty years of ups and downs, resignation to what life held in store for him and, above all, true humility that no glittering success could ever efface.

11

OPERAS COMIQUES

SINCE HIS SPECTACULAR SUCCESS in 1835 with both grand opera and opéra comique, Halévy moved between the two genres as circumstances dictated. His first opéra comique after *L'Eclair* was *Les Treize* in 1839, followed by *Le Shérif* the same year and *Le Guitarrero* in 1841, all wholly or partly penned by Scribe.

The text of *Les Treize* was of the kind that made Théophile Gautier cry out in the manner of Shakespeare's Richard the Third: 'A libretto! A libretto! My kingdom for a libretto!'[1] Busy Scribe collaborated on it with one Duport, who had already had a hand in an unperformed Halévy opéra comique called *Yella*. Between them they concocted a three-act text which was as near a farce as was permissible without losing it the right to be called an opéra comique.

The story is set at an inn near Naples. An Austrian Field-Marshal by the name of Odoard orders a sumptuous dinner for The Thirteen, an exclusive club of officers claiming to be irresistible to women. Odoard is expecting Isella the seamstress, whom he plans to seduce; so does Hector, who pretends to be a coachman sent to fetch her to the inn. In a delightfully contrived series of situations Hector persuades Isella that he is her long-lost brother born to a Count. Odoard reveals that when he was five and Isella still a babe-in-arms his well-born parents and her father the late Count had united them in holy matrimony. Isella

97

is charmed with her brother, her right to the title of Countess, and her reunion with a husband bestowed on her in infancy.

It is getting late; all parties are shown to their respective quarters at the inn. Gennaio, the innkeeper's son, the only one truly in love with Isella, locks the door of her room from the outside. When Odoard demands the key he is told that the brother has taken it. When Hector demands it he is told that the husband has taken it. They play dice for it. Gennaio wins and spends the night with Isella. The Irresistible Thirteen, over their sumptuous dinner, pronounce him a true winner.

Les Treize opened on 15 April 1839, easily pleasing the regular audience of the Opéra-Comique with its frivolity and sexual innuendoes. Berlioz immediately sensed 'an honourable success' and without needing to hear it a second time pronounced it 'one of the best pieces of writing by the composer of *La Juive*.' Whatever reservations he had were dipped in syrup:

> One may feel that many numbers are over-written; one could also reproach the composer with too frequent a use of boisterous orchestration in comic situations which could benefit from a milder approach. But on the whole the music is successful because it is engaging, lively, dramatic, never trivial and generally written with conscientiousness which is becoming a rarity in works of this nature.[2]

Gautier thought that 'the musical design is not neatly thought out and the phrases lack development.' He came to the conclusion that opera comique was not the right genre for the composer of *La Juive*:

> Although *Les Treize* is a success we think that Monsieur Halévy's true place is at the grand opera and that his inspirations are more tragic than comic. His true terrain is violent situations and scenes with great events.[3]

With a run of thirty-nine performances it was certainly a success and when it had exhausted its drawing power the Opéra-Comique eagerly accepted *Le Shérif*, a three-act comedy of deceptions like its predecessor. For his inspiration Scribe had drawn on a short story by Balzac.

The scene is set somewhere in London's dockland, displaying a pub frequented by sailors, a house by the river with a wrought iron gate permanently locked against burglars, and a large back garden. A dark mystery hangs over the house; things keep disappearing and the Sheriff, its much dreaded owner, is unable to catch the burglar. His pretty daughter Camille and her governess are wary of all strangers.

Edgar is a sea-captain who, when he was an anonymous young sailor, saved Camille from drowning in the river. Now he wishes to present himself and ask for her hand in marriage. The Sheriff however has promised her to Amobel, the son of the Marquess of Inverness. Edgar introduces himself into the house as Amobel; Amobel introduces himself as himself. Both are suspected of being the mysterious burglar, both are determined to solve the mystery and win Camille's hand. During a night vigil, with police force present, the burglar is caught. He is none other than the Sheriff, a sleepwalker who does not know what he is doing.

Le Shérif opened on 2 September 1839 and Berlioz, summarising the story in his review three days later, gleefully commented:

> One has to believe the evidence of one's eyes. The Sheriff has been stealing from himself. Camille begs Edgar's pardon, the sleepwalker is woken up, everything is explained except the dénouement – because the bride-to-be exits offering her right hand to Edgar and the left hand to Amobel. We are left wondering which of the two she is going to marry, unless she is going to marry both. This is surely an absurd supposition because this sort of thing is no less a hanging crime in England than it is in France. On my way out I met quite a number of people who were most anxious to be enlightened on the point.[4]

Although he had detected some over-long and rather dull passages Berlioz's final verdict was effusive:

> Never has Monsieur Halévy shown himself so abundant, so rich, and above all so original. This work has something special. It makes me feel from beginning to end that rare pleasure given to musicians by daring, innovative and well crafted compositions.[5]

For Gautier however *Le Shérif* was the clinching proof that opéra comique was not Halévy's forte:

> Monsieur Halévy has an uncontroversial and undisputed talent. He is thoroughly in command of musical syntax and writes very well; but the very earnestness of his musical craft stands in his way when he tackles an opera comique. In spite of his delightful *L'Eclair* we persist

in believing that he is more at home at rue Lepelletier [home of the Opéra] than at Place de la Bourse [home of the Opéra-Comique].[6]

Le Shérif came off after only fourteen performances, a humiliating setback for the leader of the French school. A few months later, in May 1840, the musical press carried the news that M. Halévy had given up his post as *chef du chant* at the Opéra 'in order to devote himself more freely to composition.'[7] Sixteen years at the beck and call of directors, artists and fellow composers, first at the Théâtre-Italien and then at the Opéra, had come to an end. He was quietly succeeded by his second-in-command, while the posts of third and fourth assistants were abolished.

One of the first things he did with his newly found leisure was to accept a nomination to a Commission of Enquiry consisting of painters, sculptors, architects, engravers and musicians. Its brief was to look into the unsatisfactory financial state of the Academy of France at the Villa Medici in Rome and suggest ways and means to improve it for the benefit of current and future Prix de Rome winners.

He held on to his prestigious teaching career at the Conservatoire. Professor of fugue and counterpoint since 1833, his class was always full to overflowing. His students adored him; he treated them as friends, without pomposity or condescension, to all intents and purposes as future colleagues. From time to time he had the satisfaction of seeing a student of his win a prize. Among the nine entrants to the 1840 annual fugue and counterpoint competition he had two winners: Gautier, aged 18, who was awarded second prize and Hubert, aged 27, who was awarded first prize by majority vote. First prize by unanimous vote was awarded however to a 17-year old student of Le Borne's, one César-Auguste Franck.

That year he succeeded the late Paër as professor of composition. By its very nature it was a post that would mould a future generation of composers and Halévy was concerned not to abuse the influence he wielded. Like Chopin's Warsaw teacher Elsler, he allowed his students to develop in their own way, careful not to stunt their individuality, never correcting their work in the way that Cherubini had corrected his when he was a student. 'I deal with grown-up young people who have reached the age of reason and should realise what they are after,' he explained. 'I am always ready to listen to them. I examine and correct what they bring me – overture, symphony, waltz . . . I have always made it a matter of duty not to thwart their inclinations.'[8]

Unfortunately what had started as a sound and realistic approach to the teaching of composition gradually became a conscious or unconscious excuse for taking less and less trouble over his students' work. Saint-Saëns who was his student in the early 1850's wrote many years after Halévy's death that sometimes the over-busy professor absented himself from his classes in order to have more time for his own compositions. He recalled the class as an open forum, where uninvited singers demonstrated their talent to a professor whose main object was not to give offence to anybody. 'The students attended all the same and taught each other. They were far less lenient than the master, whose great defect was over-kindness.'[9]

In 1840 however it was not music methodology which exercised Paris but the imminent return of Napoleon's ashes from Saint Helena. The press reminded those who had forgotten, or never knew, that before his death on 5 May 1822 the exile dictated a will in which he said: 'It is my wish that my ashes shall be laid to rest on the banks of the Seine among the French people whom I have loved so well.' Under the Citizen King Louis Philippe, Napoleon's dying wish was going to be granted.

Every detail of the transfer of the ashes from Saint Helena to the church of Les Invalides was meticulously planned. Once the casket reached Rouen it was to be taken to Neuilly, carried under the Arc de Triomphe and then laid to rest to the sound of Mozart's *Requiem*. The honour of composing funeral marches to accompany the long processional route was open to French-born composers only and fell to Auber, Adam and Halévy. On their suggestion the music manufacturer Schiltz developed a new model of giant trumpet – some called it giant tuba – whose sound would be loud enough to be heard in the open. He produced thirty such instruments which at a test performance at the Conservatoire concert hall were pronounced magnificently sonorous.

The three composers set to work. Five days before the procession two hundred military bandsman assembled at the Opéra for a dress rehearsal of the three funeral marches. Audience and press were present. Auber's march was described as sacred music, sad in character; Adam's was pronounced the work of a composer who knew everything there was to know about brass bands; Halévy's *Les Cendres de Napoléon* was awarded the highest marks for its gripping new rhythms, its vigorous orchestration, and the powerful effect he drew from the new trumpets, or tubas.

As the date of the ceremony approached Paris was swept by Ashes fever. Generals, admirals and veteran soldiers had their discarded uniforms ironed and their tarnished medals polished; military colleges handpicked their delegations; members of the Institute of France claimed their seats in Les Invalides along ministers and government officials. An influential friend of Chopin's sent him a complimentary ticket with a note saying that should he not be able to use it would he please return it immediately by messenger. On 15 December the massed bands played the three marches along the processional route as planned, and Mozart's *Requiem* was sung at Les Invalides by the leading soloists of the Opéra. Wagner was irreverent. Having read, like all Parisians, that the body of the deceased had not totally decomposed, he pointed out that it was hypocrisy to refer to it as Napoleon's corpse.

After commemorating the return of the ashes of his childhood hero, Halévy set to work on the third of the opéras comiques penned for him in a row by Scribe.

Le Guitarrero is based on the brief occupation of Portugal by King Philip II of Spain towards the end of the sixteenth century. In the garrison town of Sanatorem a Portuguese street guitarist called Riccardo serenades the Portuguese lady Zarah although he knows full well he has no chance with a noblewoman.

A Spanish officer called Zuniga wants to humiliate Zarah who has had the effrontery to repel his advances. He forces Riccardo to impersonate a Portuguese duke just returned from Mexico, win Zarah's heart with his serenading and marry her. After the wedding all will be revealed and the proud lady would find herself the wife of a street musician.

The deception works and the wedding is about to take place. Riccardo cannot bear to deceive the woman he loves, writes a letter of confession and awaits her verdict. Zuniga intercepts it.

Riccardo takes Zarah's unaltered attitude as proof of forgiveness and marries her. Zuniga then exposes him as a deceitful gutter snipe. Zarah is outraged, Riccardo wishes himself dead. When he hears that the real Duke of Portugal has returned to lead a revolt, he persuades a Spanish general that he is the wanted duke and is condemned to death.

His ruse is successful. The duke and his Portuguese loyalists surprise the Spaniards in a complacent mood and drive them away. Riccardo is rewarded for his loyalty and bravery with the title of Count Sanatorem. As he strums the guitar and sings a song of victory Zarah lovingly takes her place at his side.

Le Guitarrero was premiered at the Opéra-Comique on 21 January 1841. *Le Ménestrel*, cautious as usual after only one hearing, steered a safe course:

> Let us say right away that the music needs to be heard many times in order to be properly appreciated. This goes for everything M. Halévy has composed. Let us recall that *La Juive* first attracted the crowds by its dazzling scenery and costumes; now that the novelty of this splendour has worn off the crowds come for the music. We think that this is going to happen in this case too. The production, and particularly the libretto which is most interesting, will be the first to draw attention; then, little by little, the music will take over and establish the success of this work.[10]

Henri Blanchard was pleased: 'The music which M. Halévy has embroidered on this brilliant canvas is just what we are used to hear from this gifted composer; it is novel, elegant, distinguished, inspired.' He ended by calling him 'the leader of the young French school.'[11]

Berlioz was less effusive:

> The work has some similarities with *Ruy Blas* by Monsieur Victor Hugo, but such borrowing, I suppose, is permissible in a libretto . . . It seems to me though that many dramatic points are made at the expense of the music . . . Nothing is more irritating for a listener than a flow of a chorus brusquely interrupted by a letter whose contents needs to be imparted, or an explanation which one person has to give to another. Such ploys can easily be avoided in an opera comique where dialogue exists to impart what must not be sung . . .
>
> M. Halévy's style in this work is above all elegant, correct and mindful of the slightest details. Many melodies have original rhythms. I

thought the orchestration excellent, except for some trumpeting whose rhythm was banal and the effect therefore undistinguished.[12]

Wagner, like Gautier, had come to the conclusion that the composer of *La Juive* should have no truck with opéra comique. *Le Guitarrero* made him forgive Halévy his straying, though only just:

> For a number of years M. Halévy has undoubtedly been the most talented leader of the new French school. Unfortunately he came too soon to the idea of aping M. Auber by writing with the greatest and most easy going nonchalance . . . Thus it happened that the gifted creator of *La Juive* produced a string of worthless works which, to the honour of the public, all failed. *Le Drapier* was the last of them and from then on he seemed to have seen the error of his ways and pulled himself together for a brilliant comeback. This he achieved with *Le Guitarrero*.[13]

Of necessity Wagner had familiarised himself with the score through instrumental arrangements he was making for Schlesinger's publishing house. He explained what he saw as the essential difference between Halévy's music and that of other French composers:

> They have all issued from the school of opera comique; that is the source of their fluency, briskness, tendency to introduce melodic patterns of the *chanson* type, liveliness in handling the ensembles. Their music is chiefly conversation, for the most part witty, fusing together good manners and popular taste. When they expanded into grand opera they did not abandon their traditional terrain; they only widened its boundaries . . .

> Halévy is however an exception. His creative impulse made him start with grand opera; his whole nature and the powerful blend of his blood set him directly on the larger field and helped him win his battle there. Unfortunately he matured too quickly; it looked as if he had no past. To live what he had missed he stepped back into the cradle of French music . . . but in fact he was ill at ease in opera comique. To appear light and elegant he thought it necessary to grow flat and superficial; he turned volatile on principle. Alas, he carried this volatility into his old terrain; in *Guido et Ginevra* his struggle between levity and solidity is quite repellent.[14]

From his own Paris experience Wagner knew that a composer's livelihood depended on what an opera director considered good for box office success. 'Halévy has no independent means,' he wrote. 'He assures me that were he well-to-do he would write no more for the theatre but only symphonies, oratorios and so forth; at the Opéra he is a slave to the interests of the Director and singers and is compelled to write poor stuff with his eyes wide open.'[15]

Berlioz concurred. Stating that music publishers demanded from their composers jolly tunes and dances to satisfy a taste for the facile, he conceded that Halévy's temporary straying into bad ways had been caused by instructions from 'high up.'[16] Only George Sand remained unrepentant. 'Dear Pauline,' she wrote to her close friend the singer Pauline Viardot, 'I think, in fact I am sure, that the *Guitarist* you are expected to go to hear will bore you. Even if you are free you can always get out of it by saying you are not feeling well.'[17]

Le Guitarrero had fifty-nine performances in its first year, with some revivals in the next few years. It was, as Wagner had described it, a brilliant comeback, both artistically and financially.

12

A MOMENTOUS YEAR

*T*HE YEAR 1842 BEGAN WITH TWO new honours. In January Halévy was one of the first ten persons to be created Members of the Order of the Oak Crown, recently established by William II King of the Netherlands. At about the same time he was appointed adviser on the musical education of the children of the Dauphin, the Duke of Orleans. The prospect ahead was bright. A new grand opera to be called *Charles VI* was being sketched, marriage to a lady of the Rodrigues clan had been proposed and accepted. Last but not least, the octogenarian father figure Cherubini had composed a Happy New Year song.

It was a trifle; the old man, born in 1760 like Halévy's long deceased father, had been declining for several years. To the pianist Moscheles he had complained that with the exception of his directorship of the Conservatoire his musical life was over; he could not write a note; he was not strong enough to attend performances. To Halévy he admitted that he was feeling his age. 'These words,' Halévy wrote a few years later, 'so ordinary when other people say them, were painful coming from him and most distressing. For me his death began that day. Three months later he was no more.'[1]

He died on 15 March 1842 full of years and honours. At his state funeral, held the next Saturday, Auber, Halévy, Raoul Rochette, the Life Secretary of the Academy of Fine Arts and Achille Leclerc were the pall bearers. As the cortège slowly moved from faubourg Poissonière to the church of Saint-Roch, grief-stricken Halévy staggered as if unable to carry the weight of his bereavement; every drum roll of the funeral march sent a spasm of pain through his body, his eyes flowed with tears. 'At one stroke he had lost a master, a father and a friend,'[2] his brother Léon recalled. After the singing at Saint-Roch of Cherubini's D Minor Requiem Mass for male voices, the coffin was taken to the cemetery of Père Lachaise, where the speeches over the open grave were pronounced by Rochette representing the Academy of Fine Arts, Lafont representing the Théâtre Français, and Halévy representing the family.

The paternal relationship between the irascible old Italian and the suave French-born young Jew had been accepted by Cherubinis, colleagues and friends ever since it began. It was also accepted by Halévy's brother and sisters without seeing in it any disrespect for their late father. In his early youth Fromental had been a docile son, brought up to respect and accept autocratic paternal guidance; perhaps Cherubini was a transference. The relationship however had not always run smoothly. The quasi-father could be gruff, difficult, even rude, 'not the most courteous of men,'[3] as Moscheles tactfully observed. He did not spare the rod. The story went around that at the opening night of a new Halévy opera Cherubini sat stony-faced saying nothing. 'Master,' pleaded the anxious disciple, 'why don't you say something to me about my new opera?' 'Because it doesn't say anything to me,' was the answer.

The extent of his influence on Halévy's work was much discussed during the latter's lifetime. After his death Léon discreetly avoided any controversial standpoint by saying that the Master had instilled in his pupil an admiration for the lofty, a revulsion from the vulgar and the trivial. Whatever the extent of the musical influence, the love and affection between the two were indisputable. In his will Cherubini left his autograph scores *al suo caro* Halévy.

Three years after his death Halévy published the first section of what was meant to be an extensive study of the Master's life and work. The study was never finished, but even that first instalment which dealt with the young Cherubini's early steps in Italy suggested insight into his character; the character of a creative artist who was driven from within to go on composing, spurred on by success, undeterred by failure. Halévy wrote:

> Italian composers are lucky . . . No sooner is an opera produced than the Maestro ups and goes to another beautiful old city – all Italian cities are old and beautiful – and immediately sets to work on a new opera. Cherubini's inspiration, or shall we call it the febrile excitement needed to produce a work of art, the kind that is inseparable from all works of the mind, never deserted him . . . His thinking went like this. If he is successful success gallops with him and spurs him on; he is proud, he is happy, he is going to write a masterpiece. If his latest work is a disaster he finds lots of reasons to put it out of his mind; it is a beautiful day, a cool breeze caresses his face; the singers were bad; the prima donna sang out of pitch; the tenor sang his aria incorrectly; the baritone sang too low; the libretto was atrocious. And the orchestra! What an orchestra! And what a hostile audience! Lucky to be able to get out of this damned old city. That other charming city where he is now expected will be altogether different.[4]

There would have been many heart-to-heart conversations between old Master and disciple for the latter to be able to recreate the young man that Cherubini had been. But three years after his death was Halévy describing the young composer's character as he divined it under the carapace of the old man, or was he posthumously devolving on him his own experience of the relentless urge of creativity that would tolerate no resting on one's laurels, no giving up after failure? That perception of the febrile excitement inseparable from the process of creativity was surely more than insight into the psyche of a deceased composer. It was an unconscious portrait of himself.

A few months before Cherubini's death a happy Halévy told Wagner who had called to discuss piano arrangements that 'he was on the threshold of a wealthy marriage.'[5] What he did not tell Wagner was that the bride was twenty-two years old or, more plainly put, that she was twenty-one years younger than he was.

Hannah Léonie Rodrigues-Henriques came from a rich Jewish Portuguese-Spanish banking family, whose forebears settled in Bordeaux after the expulsion of the Jews from Spain in 1492. Her brother Hippolyte, a future financier and writer on comparative theology, was born there in 1812. A few years later the family moved to Paris where Hanna Léonie was born in 1820. On the death of the head of the family his widow moved with her two children to a block of apartment in rue Montholon, where other Rodriques relatives had already settled. That was in 1826, when the four Halévy brothers and sisters also settled there.

It is curious that Léon, when recalling in print the friendships that sprang up between the four young Halévys and the Rodrigueses and Pereiras of that block, never mentioned Mme Esther Rodrigues and her two children. He did mention their other female neighbour, young Mlle Le Bas, who joined their music-making and whom he later married. It would have been just as appropriate, and equally interesting, to mention that Fromental too had met his future wife during the rue Montholon period, that she was only a child of six at the time and that they continued to be neighbours until her middle teens. The silence begs the question what passed, if anything, during those years of neighbourhood, between the young widow and Léon who was quite a lad, or between her and Fromental.

It is not clear at what stage in the course of their acquaintance his interest in Léonie as a bride was roused, or to what extent he was aware of her mental instability which would require occasional retreats into a sanatorium. Diary entries made by Delacroix who became a friend of the family suggest that she had grown up in the lap of luxury, that she was a spendthrift, a compulsive collector of objets d'art, an ardent socialite and a domineering woman. Like her parents, uncles, brother, nephews and other members of the vast Rodrigues-Henriques clan, she was cultured and artistic. She was said to be a good amateur sculptor.

The wedding took place on Wednesday 27 April 1842, barely five weeks after Cherubini's funeral, with the bridegroom not yet fully recovered from his recent bereavement; the date had been set long before by the bride's mother and her relatives. It was a traditional Jewish ceremony, with the Chief Rabbi of Paris officiating, as befitted the social status of the Rodrigues-Henriques family within the Jewish community. Halévy was only four weeks short of his forty-third birthday. Strangely if not significantly, the age difference of twenty-one years between bride and bridegroom was the same as between his father and mother, the thirty-eight year old Elie having married Mlle Julie Meyer when she was just over seventeen.

Used as he was to having all his needs attended to by his capable sisters, Halévy left the running of the home to his young wife whose extravagance soon made inroads into his considerable earnings as well as into her own inherited wealth. Their apartment rapidly filled with pictures, sculptures, knick-knacks and souvenirs. Léonie kept open house. Her husband enjoyed the constant entertaining while worrying about its encroachment on his time. Not one to seek an argument with anyone, let alone with a dominating wife, he fell in with her ways.

On his appointment to the post of musical adviser to the Dauphin Duke of Orleans there was talk of his giving the Duke's young sons some personal tuition but eventually it was agreed that he would only advise on the choice of their music tutors. On 16 July 1842 the Dauphin was killed in a carriage accident. Halévy and Auber were each commissioned to compose a funeral march to accompany the coffin to its resting place. After they had accomplished their task at top speed the Palace sent word that the funeral would be held without accompanying music. The funeral march was shelved.

Another task that occupied him during the first months of his marriage was a reworking of *Guido et Ginevra* for a future revival. The Opéra Director wanted it reduced to two acts; he reduced it to four. By then it became apparent that the atmosphere at home was not conducive to work, particularly as Léonie was pregnant and demanded attention. All the same he continued to work fitfully on *Charles VI*, a five-act grand opera which would cause him much anguish and bring him further acclaim.

The year 1842 ended as propitiously as it had begun. *L'Eclair* was being revived in Paris; *La Juive* was playing to capacity audiences in Besançon, Marseilles and Rouen; *La Reine de Chypre*, completing its first-year run in Paris, was also having long runs in Bordeaux, Nîmes and Toulouse; and *Le Guitarrero* was a box office draw in Limoges, Boulogne, Metz, Rennes and Rouen. Abroad the success was equally staggering. *Le Guitarrero* was all the rage in Amsterdam, Berlin, Brussels, Dresden and Hamburg; *La Reine de Chypre* was being performed in Amsterdam, Frankfurt, Wiesbaden and Leipzig, where its success was equal to that of *La Juive*. Weimar was applauding *Guido et Ginevra*. Only London was as aloof as ever.

On 7 June 1843 Léonie gave birth to a daughter who was

named Julie-Esther-Anna. As if a baby in the house, composing, writing articles, teaching at the Conservatoire, entertaining at home and going out to friends and operas were not enough to cram his days, Halévy volunteered for the National Guard. It was a civic duty much favoured by middle-aged artists, particularly Prix de Rome winners who, exempt from military service in their youth, now wished to do their bit for the nation. The duties were not onerous and the uniform was elegant. Busy on half a dozen other fronts and never a stickler for discipline, the new volunteer played truant. He was summoned to appear before a military court and sentenced to forty-eight hours' imprisonment at *Aux Haricots*, the popular name for the clink. He was allowed as many visitors as cared to call, of whom Moscheles was one:

> I was extremely amused with my visit to Halévy who, having been guilty of some breach of duty as a National Guard, was locked up for 48 hours. Many famous painters before him must have endured the same fate in the same place, for artistic sketches and eccentric caricatures were drawn and painted on the walls. We chatted at *Aux Haricots* just as easily as we should have done in our own house; all the more so as his young wife was present.[6]

Esther, a placid four-months old baby, would have been left with a reliable wet nurse, one of a large domestic staff considered indispensable by Léonie. After her birth there was a lull. Her sister Marie-Geneviève-Raphaëlle, the second and last child, did not follow until 26 February 1949, the year in which Halévy would celebrate his fiftieth birthday. Although an elderly parent, and always busy at that, friends of the family recalled him as a loving and devoted father.

13

FROM PATRIOTISM TO MACARONI

GERMAIN AND CASIMIR DELAVIGNE were respected figures in literary Paris; Germain as a vaudeville writer, Casimir as a poet. Often they collaborated. It was to them Halévy addressed himself for the libretto of his next grand opera. Following the convention of the day they borrowed their story from history but, unlike Scribe who except for *Le Drapier* had set his plots in Constance, Florence and Portugal, or Saint-Georges who had set his in Cyprus, they set theirs staunchly on French soil; or rather soil that remained staunchly French in spite of the English encroachment after the battle of Agincourt in 1415.

Their hero was Charles VI, known to readers of Shakespeare's *King Henry the Fifth* as the vanquished French king who after Agincourt allowed dashing young Harry to say 'kiss me Kate' to his daughter. In French history he is the king who lost his mind during an expedition against the Duke of Brittany and was later betrayed by his Queen who wished to cede France to the English. In the Brothers Delavigne version his madness, the Queen's machinations and the ousting of the English are spectacularly woven into an epic of French patriotism and fight for liberty.

The story begins in a part of France occupied by the English. A rousing song, the pivot of the entire opera, is sung by a veteran soldier, with the loyal French taking it up in unison:

> France abhors slavery
> And whatever the danger
> Greater is her bravery . . .
> War on the English.
> Never in France
> Shall the English reign.

The Dauphin, banished from the Court after the Queen has denounced him to his father Charles VI as a potential parricide, is saved from danger by his sweetheart Odette, daughter of the veteran soldier. Together they return to the royal quarters to try to persuade the mad king to recall him from banishment. At first the king does not know his son; when he does he banishes him again.

On the steps of the palace everything is ready for the signing of a treaty which the Queen describes as the unification of two peoples, but which in fact confirms a small boy called the Duke of Lancaster as the future King of France. Charles VI is too feeble-minded to resist. Above the din and the hubbub Odette hears a voice:

> Save a lover who will forget,
> Who will see you die without regret,
> No grave will bear your name,
> No heart will cherish your claim.

She surrenders to her destiny and sets out to help the Dauphin assert his rights and save France: at a given moment she will sing her special song, the Dauphin will come out of hiding, reveal himself to the people and drive away the English and the treacherous Queen. The King, in a flash of sanity, burns his Act of Renunciation, then relapses into madness. The Queen sings Odette's song. The Dauphin rushes in and is immediately arrested.

The final scene takes place in the church of Saint-Denis, where the coronation of kings of France used to be held. Odette who has stealthily gone into the vaults now returns carrying high the royal standard, the oriflamme, so heavily encrusted with gold that it blazes like a flame. On seeing it Charles VI regains his sanity and majesty and dies with dignity. Odette hands the oriflamme to the Dauphin who, sword in hand, calls on his people to fight for freedom. As they sing 'Never in France shall the English reign' she dies unnoticed.

Halévy started working on the music some time in 1842, the year he lost Cherubini and married Léonie. He was tense and restless, swept hither and thither by the old febrile excitement, sometimes immersing himself in his work, sometimes recoiling with dread from the vastness of the task. When working on *La Juive* his restlessness had driven him from his Opera studio to his study at home, from one friend's place to another. With a young wife and a new-born baby such absences from home were inconceivable. There was however another reason for his inability to work consistently. At the back of his mind there lurked the fearful coincidence of Charles VI's madness and Léonie's latent imbalance. There had been no manifestation of it since their marriage, but he was well aware by now that she was highly strung and had had nervous breakdowns which had required a stay at an expensive sanatorium. In the circumstances composing music for scenes in which the poor old king fluctuated between madness and sanity was a harrowing experience.

There was a further reason to be dispirited. As adviser to the Dauphin on the musical education of his children he had occasion to discuss the opera with him before the latter's fatal accident. The plot was of great interest to the Palace and in due course it was circumspectly conveyed to M. Halévy that His Majesty was not pleased with the idea of a mad French king as the hero of an opera. 'But it is the brave Dauphin who is the hero,' Halévy reputedly answered. The Dauphin did not like the idea any more than his father did.

His death had an unexpected effect. Halévy's depression lifted, his composer's block dissolved, he picked up the work with renewed vigour, determined to do honour to the French spirit of liberty. As usual, he had earmarked the soloist of his choice, giving the title role to the tenor Duprez. Full of confidence and high spirits he invited him to a working session:

> My dear friend Duprez, if you want to be a darling please spare me a moment tomorrow Sunday at whatever time suits you in the vast stretch of the day so that I can orchestrate your aria; and if you want to be paramount chief and king of all the darlings, as you are of all the tenors, do spare me this precious time to come and work at my place. I know it is a great deal to ask you to venture out in this weather, but I

also know that you can brave rain, wind, hail and storms; you are totally waterproof. Come and see me then tomorrow, Sunday, at whatever time suits you, and bring with you – [and here the irrepressible Halévy changed into English] – *if you please, my dearest Gilbert, your music. I hope you will be kind enough etc.* Well, enough writing in English about an opera in which we are supposed to make short shrift of the English.[1]

The idea of making short shrift of the English seemed to be illtimed. Louis Philippe had been working on a rapprochement with Great Britain and had invited young Queen Victoria and Prince Albert for a visit. When rehearsals started various modifications to the text were introduced to accommodate singers, designers, producer and, for the first time in Halévy's experience, ministers of state. Taking account of political sensitivities across the Channel the cry *Guerre aux Anglais* was changed to *Guerre aux tyrants*. An official attempt to censor references to tyrants as well and introduce instead an innocuous alternative was thwarted.

Charles VI, a grand opera in five acts, opened at the Opera on 15 March 1843 and deeply impressed Henri Blanchard of *La Revue et gazette musicale*. Commenting that Odette seemed to be an earlier incarnation of Joan of Arc, he declared:

> The score is one of the most remarkable M. Halévy has ever written. If the listener does not grasp all its beauties on first hearing, he has to blame his own perception rather than the composer's whose talent is like those dense virgin forests teeming with life, difficult to penetrate but enclosing all the treasures of a strong and powerful vegetation. The overture is an artistically crafted summary of the many themes which occur in the work. The national anthem, a ballad and an original theme are felicitously interlaced. It is a lovely success which contributes to the art of music and enriches the French scene with another masterpiece.[2]

Gautier was so taken with the romance of the story that contrary to habit he told it at great length, giving it the best of his considerable narrative skill. Of the music he wrote:

> It opens with a brilliant, richly orchestrated overture, into which the patriotic refrain, the leading theme of the opera, has been cleverly woven . . . The music composed by M. Halévy for 'War on the

Tyrants', which opens and ends the work, has breadth, force and impetus, particularly in the last two lines, intoned in unison by all the voices.[3]

Berlioz was silent. The cudgels were taken up by the brothers Escudier, editors of *La France musicale*, who had started an anti *Charles VI* campaign while it was still in rehearsal. Production costs mounted to 100,000 francs, they had informed their readers, which was a wicked waste of state subsidy. While all other theatres were open on Sunday the Opéra was closed solely to accommodate a further rehearsal of an extravagant work. The Madness of Charles VI was the Madness of the Opéra; it was bound to ruin it.

Their review after opening night was in character. 'The libretto,' they wrote, 'is monotonous, flat, cold, saying nothing to the heart. At every moment vengeance returns with battles, triumphs, victims. It is tiring, irritating, and has no appeal to the public.'[4]

They were equally scathing about the music: 'Whereas Rossini finds without seeking, Halévy needs to seek for a long time before he finds. That is why one should not force his nature and make him produce, at tight intervals, ideas which can only come to him after long reflection and hard spiritual labour.'[5]

Their campaign continued unabated. They were the first to suggest that Duprez's sudden cold was due to his disinclination to continue singing the part of the Dauphin which was unworthy of his great talent, and the first to report that he had given it up altogether. When an industrial tribunal found him guilty of breach of contract they stood by him and hoped he would appeal. When he made his enforced reappearance as the Dauphin they gleefully reported that although complimentary tickets had been distributed far and wide most of the boxes were empty while the gallery and amphitheatre seats were occupied by nannies with strings of children.

After all that *Charles VI* was a hit; the masses adored its ode to liberty. It was however frowned upon by Louis Philippe's ministers who were concerned about the effect of an anti-English opera on France's diplomatic relations with Great Britain, particularly at a time when a State visit was being arranged. On 3

September, some six months after the opening of the embarrassing opera, the twenty-four year old Queen Victoria crossed the channel for the first time in her life and arrived safely at Le Tréport in Normandy on board the royal yacht *Victoria and Albert*. Louis Philippe had come out to meet her. The moment she set foot on French soil there were cries of *Vive la Reine*, and a military band struck up *God Save the Queen*. She and the Prince Consort were lavishly entertained in the nearby castle of Eu, the ancient seat of the Orleans family, with banquets and various theatricals performed by the best of Paris actors. In October Louis Philippe paid a return visit and was royally entertained at Windsor.

Obviously *Charles VI* was not the subversive opera it had been alleged to be, but apprehensive ministers were taking no chances. Any unscheduled performance, in whole or in part, was suspicious. Berlioz tells in his Memoirs how the inclusion of the offending chorus in a concert he had organised nearly landed him in trouble with the authorities.

It happened in August 1844, about a year after the successful exchange of State visits between Queen Victoria and Louis Philippe. Berlioz was organising a festival of music by contemporary composers among whom Halévy's name was conspicuous by its absence. Halévy was naturally offended and asked his publisher Schlesinger to persuade Berlioz to include something of his as well. Much against his will the latter acquiesced and added *Guerre aux tyrants* to the already published programme. During the performance the audience vociferously joined the choir to express disaffection with the government of the once popular Citizen King.

A few days later Berlioz was summoned to the headquarters of the Paris Commissioner of Police who conveyed to him the displeasure of the Minister of the Interior at the demonstration caused by a seditious piece of music which had not been included in the original programme and which was obviously sneaked in with sedition in mind. Berlioz explained that this was done at Schlesinger's insistence in order to salve Halévy's wounded pride at having been left out of a programme which represented almost every other important modern composer. He further explained that he had chosen that particular piece because it was technically undemanding. His explanation was accepted.

The story as told by Berlioz is interesting on two counts. First, it indicates that *Charles VI* had become a symbol of liberty and that its main chorus was so well known that concert goers could spontaneously sing along without the conductor turning to face them to bring them in. Secondly, it strongly suggests that Berlioz, whose programme included apart from two items of his own some ten others by such composers as Spontini, Rossini, Auber, Meyerbeer and a specially commissioned *Song of the Manufacturers* by one Meraux, had deliberately omitted anything by the Leader of the French School. In view of his high praise for *Le Shérif* and *Guido et Ginevra* or his occasional favourable comments on Halévy's orchestrations, it would appear that the omission had stemmed from personal rather than purely musical considerations. Perhaps he was paying Halévy back for his attempt a few years earlier to stop the first performance of his *Requiem* in favour of one of Cherubini's. Perhaps it was sheer malevolence.

Charles VI continued to be a box office draw until the February Revolution of 1848. When Louis Napoleon became President of the Second Republic and later Emperor Napoleon III, it was ousted by less politically associative operas. Only *Guerre aux tyrants* continued to rear its rebellious head and an 1897 recording of this marching song by the French bass Paul Aumonier (1874–1944), lovingly resuscitated by modern technique, attests to its enduring rousing power.

CHARLES VI: MUSIC OF *GUERRE AUX TYRANTS*

Never one to rest on his laurels Halévy started working on a new opera as soon as his latest one had been launched. As always there was the question of a librettist. Casimir, the younger of the two Delavigne brothers, had died, so Saint-Georges, the librettist of the successful *Reine de Chypre* was approached. This time there was no borrowing from history; the story was of innocent love and crude greed, with innocent love emerging triumphant and scooping a fortune to boot.

The plot is woven round the engaging personality of Beppo the *lazzarone*, a word describing a poor, low-born Neapolitan. *Le Lazzarone* of the title is an indolent lad who indulges in long siestas in the sunny marketplace after selling his modest daily catch of fish. When his is not busy sleeping he tells Batista the florist that he loves her and wants to marry her. Both are foundlings, but Batista has a birth certificate which she has never read because she cannot read.

Two rascals in search of instant wealth get to hear about Batistas's birth certificate and find out that she is a rich heiress. They also learn that if she marries before she is twenty-one all her fortune will go to her husband. Each dresses up beautifully and tries to dazzle her with his proposal. Beppo feels he has nothing to offer to an heiress sought by rich gentlemen and goes to sleep. Batista shakes him awake and declares she will marry none but him. The rascals point out that she is a minor and has to marry whomever is approved by a newly discovered uncle of hers. Her birth certificate is duly produced, proving that she was twenty-one that very day. The sweethearts marry and live happily ever after.

This flimsy two-act entertainment, in spirit more an opera bouffe than an opera, opened at the Opéra on 29 March 1844 and was found musically pleasing by the *Revue et gazette musicale*:

> In the five duets, two trios, six arias, and four or five choruses one rediscovers the distinguished and elegant hand of M. Halévy. The orchestration is subdued to agree with the non-boisterous character of the text. It is tasteful, expressive and easy to understand. The melodies stand out by their grace and naive freshness. The score leans towards the light and spontaneous. Since *L'Eclair* M. Halévy had not given us tunes so easy to grasp and retain.

Berlioz said the opposite:

> The orchestration is too grandiose, too pompous, too loud and even too slow for this kind of story. Thus in the scene where Beppo and Batista are telling each other of their fears and love, it seems to me that non-arpeggiated chords of trumpets and trombones are not suitable to express tender feelings and out of tune with the style of the scene.[7]

The Escudiers in *La France musicale* were dismissive:

> M. Halévy should not and cannot write bouffe music. This master needs strong passions, dramatic situations and violent scenes. Give him these, with plenty of time to write and re-write, and his success is assured. Opera bouffe demands from the composer a flowing melody, imagination, and continuous verve. Only four living composers have what it takes: Rossini, Auber, Donizetti and Adam.[8]

What they passed over in silence was that Halévy, yielding to instructions from above, had written the part of lethargic charming Beppo with Mme Stoltz in mind, a fiery Spanish-born mezzo soprano who was the mistress of the new Opéra Director Léon Pillet. A year earlier they briefly reported that she and M. Pillet had left for Le Havre. 'Mme Stoltz is suffering from an indisposition which would require nine months to recover from,'[9] In March 1844 they reported that she had been safely delivered of her indisposition and would be returning to the Opéra to sing in *Le Lazzarone*.

The situation behind the scenes was well known, though not openly commented upon. The reviewer of *La Revue et gazette musicale* tactfully referred to the 'dearth of tenors' afflicting the Opéra and regretted that M. Halévy had been 'forced to do without a timbre of voice so essential to an opera'. The result, he concluded, 'is a certain monotony which does no harm to the composer's name but is harmful all the same.'[10]

The part of the florist Batista was sung by Mme Dorus-Gras who had created Eudoxie in *La Juive* and Ginevra in *Guido et Ginevra*. There was no love lost between the two leading ladies. At the premiere of *Le Lazzarone* Mme Stoltz, having impeccably sung one of her arias, waited for Mme Dorus-Gras to start hers, then slowly crossed the stage eating macaroni; a riveting vulgar act performed by a large woman in man's clothes. Her rival's singing was drowned under the audience's hoots of delight and raucous laughter.

The impromptu macaroni scene was not relished by Gautier who believed that grand opera should be preserved in its pristine purity:

> Let us say at the outset that we do not approve in any way of the introduction of comic situation into opera. Opera calls for great tragic or poetic subjects, or at least for gossamer-like fantasies.[11]

The music however did not displease him:

> It is carefully thought out with the elegance and original harmony that are M. Halévy's hallmark. You will find no prettier musical babble nor a more charming instrumental prattle. Alas the singing is not so fortunate.[12]

Not one to mince his words even when writing about a singer known to be the unassailable mistress of the Opéra Director, he went on to point out the incongruity of a portly Mme Stoltz portraying a lissome youth. The following year, at thirty-two, she retired from the Opéra though not from singing. Mme Dorus-Gras lived to be ninety-two. *Le Lazzarone* quietly foundered.

14

BACK TO OPERAS COMIQUES

*A*LEXANDRE DUMAS THE ELDER (1802–1870) was one of the most prolific novelists and dramatists of his day. Of the 1,200 books he claimed to have written none were better loved than the eight volumes of *Les Trois mousquetaires* which he brought out in 1844. Inspired by a work published in Cologne in 1701–2 he initiated a mid-nineteenth-century readership into the extraordinary exploits of a seventeenth-century elite corps of musketeers who were courageous to the point of foolhardiness, loyal, chivalrous, quick to take offence, delighting in duels and derring-do adventures. Dumas was no librettist but the genre which he introduced into French literature became all the rage. Thus the opéra comique *Les Mousquetaires de la reine* penned by Saint-Georges came into being.

The story is set in the 1620's, when Louis XIII and his court temporarily moved to Poitou to await the start of the siege of La Rochelle. The Queen's musketeers have been forbidden duelling. Bored, with no duels or fighting to distract them, they drink, brag, brawl and dream of beautiful damsels.

In the royal park Athenais, a lady-in-waiting to the Queen, confides to another lady-in-waiting called Berthe that she is in love with the valiant but aloof Olivier. Her secret, though not the name of the loved one, is overheard by the musketeer Hector who, to relieve his boredom, begins to send her anonymous love letters, eventually asking for an assignation. When he turns up she rebuffs him for the impostor he is. Only then does he realise that the love-stricken musketeer he has been impersonating is none other than his best friend Olivier.

Olivier has long admired Athenais from a distance, daunted by the difference in their rank. To his delighted amazement he learns that thanks to the demise of an unknown uncle he has succeeded to the title of Duke of Monbaret. He pays his respects to Athenais who treats him frostily; she suspects that he has connived in the false love letters to make fun of her. Berthe acts as a go-between and tells Olivier that at a masked ball arranged for the evening Athenais will be expecting to hear his explanation. She will be wearing a blue domino. The arrangement misfires. When Olivier speaks to a lady in a blue domino she takes off her mask to reveal the aged face of a woman of sixty.

More subterfuges lead to more mishaps which lead to more misunderstandings. Suffice it to say that the story ends with the wedding of Athenais and Olivier celebrated in true musketeer fashion, and that Berthe the peacemaker and repentant Hector are going to be married as well.

Les Mousquetaires de la reine, an opéra comique in three acts, opened at the Opéra-Comique on 3 February 1846 to resounding success. Before expressing his warmest admiration for the score Gautier gave free rein to his wit:

> We have heard a great deal of Grey Musketeers, Black Musketeers and Infantry Musketeers. Have there ever been Queen's Musketeers? A serious question which we shall ask M. Alexandre Dumas to clarify for us as soon as we have a chance to do so. Whatever the answer, M. Saint-Georges' libretto is abundant in musical situations; hardly credible as they are, they are interesting enough to grip the attention of the audience at the expense of the music. The title has obviously brought good luck; it has inspired the librettist, found the cast in good voice, and the composer in brilliant form – a rare triple coincidence which has resulted in great success . . .

> The overture is remarkable indeed. M. Halévy has long been a past master in harmonic combinations; nobody knows better than he does how to use all the resources of the orchestra. In this work his craftmanship is happily married to an abundance of themes and inexhaustible inventiveness. The clever composer has solved the tricky problem of how to satisfy musicians as well as the general

public. The former will admire the beautiful orchestral inventiveness of the score; the latter will go home humming the tunes.[1]

Henri Blanchard of *La Revue et gazette musicale* also began his review with a reference to the source material:

> The musketeers we see have absolutely nothing to do with those of M. Alexandre Dumas, but Monsieur de Saint-Georges has done well to take the characters of his libretto from that breed of warriors, eminently brave, merry and light-hearted, who epitomise the ancient French qualities which are gradually dying out. Such characters, with their splendid costumes, chivalrous ways, gallant manners and adventurous spirit could hardly be more in tune with the genre of the opéra-comique . . .
>
> The overture, most elegant in style, is a true introduction to an opera comique, scintillating with verve and gaiety. A real overture, the like of which one no longer composes nowadays, it was excellently executed by the orchestra and spiritedly heralded the nocturnal march of the musketeers at the end of Act One.[2]

Not since *L'Eclair* had an opera comique by Halévy excited such adulation. Blanchard gave him the final accolade:

> This is the most outstanding score of our time, based on an excellent libretto which was as splendidly acted as it was sung . . . It is a clear and beautiful fusion of words, music and the rich costumes of the musketeers . . . The orchestra plays as one, because it knows how to subjugate its disparate wishes to the conductor's interpretation. Honour to Messrs Halévy and Saint-Georges who have achieved this brilliant artistic success which indisputably places the composer at the head of our French school of music.[3]

Berlioz was again silent. The enthusiastic review in *Le Journal des débats* was unsigned:

> The resounding success of this music, which the future will enhance even more, elevates M. Halévy to a summit never conquered by any of his previous operas comiques performed at the Opéra-Comique. Ought one to reproach him for the distinction and finesse of his melodies which render them less instantly popular? Ought one to reproach him for the restraint, so rare nowadays, of an orchestration which prefers impact to noise? It would be a strange criticism to make and, were I a composer, I could hardly wish for a better one.[4]

Even *La France musicale* saluted the new work, though not even now could the Escudiers refrain from reminding their readers of Halévy's past sins:

> In his new opera he gave up his cranky effects, his muddled combinations and the din of the brass for songs full of grace and vigour, for simple and beautiful harmonies, varied and intelligible . . . Honour to one of the Masters of the French school, honour to M. Halévy who this time has produced a score worthy of his talent and his name.[5]

The public loved the new work and the press commented that 'its success at the Opéra-Comique goes crescendo.'[6] The younger generation of the royal family sang its praises and on 22 February a command performance was given at the private theatre of the Tuileries palace. For Halévy, long associated with the widowed Duchess of Orleans over the education of her children, it was not his first visit to the palace nor his first audience with Louis Philippe and the Queen. For his aristocrat librettist it was. Protocol was observed. 'After the performance,' the press reported, 'M. Halévy presented M. de Saint-Georges to Their Majesties.' The Queen was most gracious. 'Her Majesty said that in spite of all the praise showered on the opera by the young princes who have seen it at the Opéra-Comique no less than three times, she still found that what she saw far exceeded their praise.'[7]

It was a whirlwind success. In July rehearsals of the opera in a German translation began for simultaneous performances in Berlin, Vienna, Strasbourg, Leipzig and Breslau. In September, when the Opéra-Comique reopened for its autumn season, the takings for the first performance of *Les Mousquetaires* amounted to 5,000 francs and three hundred people had to be turned away. In November a huge party was held to celebrate its hundredth performance, attended by anybody who had ever had anything to do with it. 'There has never been such a consistent success on any of our operatic stages,' the press enthusiastically reported. 'One hundred performances in ten months!'[8]

Not only was the composer the darling of the Opéra-Comique management but also the favourite of the Palace, virtually Master of the King's Music. When Ibrahim Pasha, the right-hand man and adopted son of Muhammed Ali ruler of Egypt visited Paris, Halévy was commissioned to compose a work in his honour. It was to mark the political finale of the long French involvement with what was known as the Eastern Question.

The Question was basically how to reconcile the demand of the rebellious Muhammed Ali to be recognised as ruler of Egypt and Syria with the adamant refusal of the crumbling Ottoman Empire to yield an inch of its territory. France, together with England, Russia, Austria and Prussia had been mediating and pulling strings. Public opinion in France was mostly for the ruler of Egypt and a French colonel drilled the Egyptian army in modern warfare. Muhammed Ali showed his political astuteness by sending the people of France a marvel of ancient Egyptian art, a 75 foot high granite obelisk which was once part of the temple of Luxor built by Rameses II. It is now one of the most familiar landmarks of Paris on Place de la Concorde.

The Eastern Question was evidently resolved through the mediation of the Five Powers. Muhammed Ali was recognised by the Ottoman Sultan as ruler of Egypt though not of Syria, and in 1846 his heir apparent Ibrahim Pasha went on tour of Western Europe. Halévy's musical offering marking the French stage of the tour was a cantata for soloists and choir, set to words by his brother Léon. *Les Plages du Nil* was performed for the visitor on 21 May 1846 at the home of the Minister of Public Education whose portfolio included the arts, and who later had the libretto translated into Turkish by a distinguished French scholar. Ibrahim Pasha died in Egypt in November 1848.

Another work of no great consequence was occasioned by the inauguration of the Opéra-National, later to be renamed the Théâtre-Lyrique, the third opera house in Paris after the Opéra and the Opéra-Comique. No fewer than two librettists and four leading composers were commissioned to contribute. The result was an operatic skit by A. Royer and G. Vaez set to music by Adam, Auber, Carafa and Halévy. One of the aims of the Opéra-National was to encourage young composers making their first steps in the operatic world, and the joint work was appropriately named *Les premiers pas*. The skit rose, or perhaps stooped, to the frivolous mood of the occasion. So did Gautier in his review following opening night on 15 November 1847:

> Four composers of established repute and proven merit joined forces to consecrate the new Temple of Music. The Masters crowned by public opinion wanted to stretch a hand to young Laureates, all

fervent disciples of unknown geniuses, so as to help them enter the Sanctuary. One scene where the aforesaid four who dominate the Opéra and Opéra-Comique are executed was surely the fulfilment of everybody's fondest dream.

We were not told which illustrious composer had written which piece, but it seems to us that the overture with its curious *vocalise* sung by the choir behind the scenes must be by Adam. The love song bears the stamp of Halévy's sober style. Quotes from Zanetta and The Duke of Olonne [both opéras comiques by Auber, 1840 and 1842 respectively] point to Auber as the author of the soprano aria, while the baritone aria is in all probability by Carafa. Among so much talent it hardly matters if we confuse one composer with another. The work is consistently good and an error in identification does nobody any harm.[9]

1847 was drawing to a close amid growing political unrest. Louis Philippe had yielded to pressure and allowed greater freedom of speech. Legitimists, radicals and republicans were arranging banquets where for the price of six francs, the equivalent of two days' wages for the average worker, people could eat, drink and make speeches against the regime. When the speeches became too provocative Louis Philippe, on the advice of his minister Guizot, prohibited them. On 24 February 1848 angry demonstrators marched through the streets of Paris demanding Guizot's dismissal. He was promptly dismissed. The masses continued to march. Louis Philippe sent out the National Guard. The National Guard joined forces with the marchers. Other troops were called out, a stray shot was fired, barricades were put up, shots were fired in anger, forty people lay dead. The maddened crowd marched on the royal palace. Louis Philippe abdicated in favour of his grandson and together with his Queen crossed the Channel under the name of Mr and Mrs Smith. The Second Republic was born.

In the course of the next few months of political rivalries and reorganisation a new name was beginning to gain popularity among the masses – Louis Napoleon Bonaparte, nephew of the Great Napoleon. During Louis Philippe's reign he had twice attempted to declare himself Emperor; after the second attempt he was condemned to life imprisonment. Six years later he took advantage of some alterations being made to the prison building, heaved a plank of wood onto his shoulder like a mason's mate and walked out. He made straight for England. On Louis Philippe's abdication he returned to Paris, had himself elected to the National Assembly and in December 1848 was elected its President by five million votes to one and a half million for the runner-up.

One of the by-products of the February Revolution was the notion that artists should be represented in the National Assembly in the same way that artisans were. Halévy was prevailed upon to stand as the musicians' candidate and one rainy April morning presented himself for nomination at an unfinished hall with a badly leaking roof. Each aspirant to the candidature professed his faith in the Republican ideals. One Abbé Duguerry graciously stood down in favour of Halévy and Halévy, in his speech of thanks, made another, unexpected, profession of faith. 'I am most touched by the sentiments expressed by Abbé Duguerry,' he said, 'particularly that although we both believe in the same God we do not follow the same faith.'[10] Catholic priest and Jewish composer embraced each other to thunderous applause.

The composer won the nomination but failed to be elected to the National Assembly – he was a good few thousand votes short. The personal benefit to him of his attempt was that he was unexpectedly revealed as a brilliant public speaker, an accomplishment which would advance his career at the Institute of France. His Republican convictions found a less ambitious outlet by his serving with Auber, Adam and Carafa on a panel of adjudicators in a competition of national songs.

While politicians and statesmen were debating reforms, the financial instability following the February Revolution had a disastrous effect on the performing arts. Musical celebrities began leaving Paris for London, among them Berlioz, Kalkbrenner, Thalberg, Hallé, Pauline Viardot and Chopin, although the latter's departure had been planned and mentioned in the press at the end of the previous year. Theatres were having a tough time, actors and singers were playing to poor houses. Halévy, buoyed up by the tremendous success of *Les Mousquetaires* a couple of years earlier, was working again with Saint-Georges on another opera comique. As Léonie was pregnant the greatest part of the score was composed in Versailles, away from home;

after the difficulties of the first two years of married life an acceptable domestic pattern prevailed, Léonie domineering, her husband acquiescing, both caring.

The plot of the new work was set in the Pyrenean semi-independent state of Andorra which since 1278 had been under the joint suzerainty of France and Spain. Traditionally it had to pay an annual due of 960 francs to France and 460 pesetas to Spain but in Saint-Georges' *Le Val d'Andorre* only the Spaniards hold on to their original due while the French demand theirs in kind; every year a French recruiting officer presses into military service fifteen young Andorrean bachelors drawn by lots.

The unlucky young bachelor who draws the Black Ticket is Stephen the hunter who is loved by three women: an attractive farm owner known as Widow Thérèse, her orphan maid Rose de Mai, and the rich heiress Georgette. Stephen, who unbeknown to her loves Rose de Mai, hides in the mountains so as not to be forced to go away. He is declared a deserter, is caught and condemned to death by firing squad. Rose de Mai learns that his pardon and discharge from military service can be bought for 1,500 francs. She 'borrows' the large sum from her mistress's money box and has Stephen released, giving out that it is rich Georgette who has contributed the money. Thérèse discovers the theft, rightly suspects her maid and brings her to justice.

The dénouement is in the best romantic tradition. As a young lass Thérèse had an illegitimate baby whom she abandoned to conceal her disgrace. An old goatheard reveals to both Thérèse and Rose de Mai that they are mother and daughter. Rose de Mai and Stephen fall into each other's arms, Thérèse embraces both with maternal love and the heiress Georgette casts her net elsewhere.

Owing to a last-minute hitch the opening night of *Le Val d'Andorre* had to be put back a few days and was held at the Opéra-Comique on 11 November 1848. It was an unprecedented success even in Halévy's latest run of successes. Many numbers were encored, the applause brought the house down, the stage was showered with bouquets, the cast were recalled time and again. Halévy, modestly enjoying the applause from behind the scenes, was grabbed by the singers and forcibly dragged onto the stage to acknowledge the unceasing acclaim. The flustered reviewer of *La Revue et gazette musicale* rushed his copy to the printer's to catch the deadline, thus scooping dailies and weeklies alike. Proudly informing his readers of his feat, he pronounced without hesitation:

> This is the most brilliant total success ever recorded at the Opéra-Comique. It is epoch-making . . . It offers that rare fusion of the frolicsome and the pathetic, with a score by a great master, written with a genius's verve and a profound knowledge of the art. It is unlike any other work of his; different aims, different effects. What we find is purity, delicacy, imagination and mastery — all of which are the elements of his musical individuality.[11]

A week later the reviewer devoted to the work a more detailed analysis:

> From the very first bars of the overture place and scene are clearly indicated. Those prolonged calls, those distant echoes, that rustic musette accompanied by slight shudderings of the strings, the mischievous frolicking of the flutes — it all lends local colour. We breathe the mountain air, we listen to the sweet simple song of the goatherd. Suddenly rhythm and character change. The allegro bubbles, bursts into a marvellous and graceful theme in a minor key which flourishes deliciously in the major key . . . The second theme of the allegro, with a drum, is one of the most felicitous numbers of the work; it heralds the refrain of the soldiers' song which frequently reappears throughout the opera.[12]

Le Ménestrel, having been scooped the week before, tackled the work from the political angle:

> Maestro Halévy, who understands the full force of a new work at these times of political anxiety, elevated himself to a higher pedestal by driving out of mind the stressful events of the present. His music will induce more confidence and calm than twenty pretty speeches by the Mirabeaux of the day . . . We foresee a long procession of Parisians and provincials gravitating towards the charming Val d'Andorre, not the one in the Pyrenees but the one in rue Favart, with the final destination being the box office.[13]

And so it was. *Le Val d'Andorre* ran for one hundred and sixty-five performances, saved the Opéra-Comique from financial ruin and restored it to solvency and profitability. The following year it was performed in a German translation in Leipzig. 'Music of a genuine dramatic character,' Moscheles noted in his diary. 'It has more flow of melody than his other operas. The subject is cleverly worked out and very impressive. It was so finely given that the entire cast was called forward.'[14] In Paris an indefatigable Halévy was already putting the finishing touches to his next work.

La Fée aux roses, publicised as 'a fairy tale opera comique in three acts,' had taxed the combined talents of Scribe and Saint-Georges. It begins in the kingdom of Kabul, in the laboratory of Atalmuc the sorcerer. He is trying for the umpteenth time to brew a love potion which would win the heart of pretty Nerilha whom he has bought in the slave market. When his latest potion fails he smashes his phials and mixing bowls and rushes out. Nerilha finds his book of magic spells and makes a broomstick and furniture hurl themselves into a boisterous dance which threatens to get our of hand. Atalmuc returns just in time to restore order – a scene which predates *L'Apprenti sorcier* by the yet unborn Paul Dukas by nearly fifty years.

Atalmuc gives Nerilha a magic metal rose in the hope of winning her love. She promptly calls up a basket of real roses which flies her to a royal garden in Kashmir where a prince rests after much travelling. The prince is dismayed to hear from his grand vizier that by the will of his late father the King he is to marry a certain princess; he yearns for a pretty slavegirl he has noticed on his travels. She is of course pretty Nerilha. Before she has a chance to reveal her presence, Atalmuc the sorcerer joins the party and puts her out of the running by transforming her into an ugly old woman.

The permutations of love and sorcery reach their zenith at a Sorcerers' Conference in Delhi. Nerilha steals Atalmuc's book of magic spells and performs a few tricks of her own. She divines that she is the intended princess who, when a baby, was snatched from her cradle and sold to slavery. Her beauty is restored to her and the fairy tale ends with two happy couples, prince and Nerilha, other princess and Vizier. Poor Atalmuc is disconsolate. Nerilha generously promises him her royal friendship.

La Fée aux roses opened on 1 October 1849 at the Opéra-Comique with its reorganised orchestra and drew some unusual adjectives from the press. *La Revue et gazette musicale* pointed out 'the savage, strange introduction which announces the world of sorcery.'[15] *Le Ménestrel* mentioned 'research into harmony, new rhythms and sounds.'[16] Berlioz, tired of other people's successes, tired of reviewing, tired of having to attend dress rehearsals to acquaint himself with unpublished scores, tired of first nights which would begin at half past eight and end at one o'clock in the morning, gave vent to his frustration in *Le Journal des débats*:

> It is not enough to listen to a three-act opera, to attend the dress rehearsal, to leave one's dinner hardly touched for fear of missing a single note of the overture on opening night . . . It is not enough to sit up half the night trying to remember the various episodes of the story, the form of the musical numbers, the names of the cast, the devil and his retinue, to dream of it if you doze off, to think of it when you are awake. Oh no, it is not enough. We critics also have to render in a more or less intelligent way what we have not had enough time to properly understand, to voice an opinion about something we shall only get to know in a month's time, explain the Whys and Hows, the Too Much and the Too Little.[17]

Having said that much he admitted that he arrived at the Opéra-Comique only towards the end of the overture and that he was 'too engrossed in the farandole of pestles, mortars and stoves' which accompanied Atalmuc's potion brewing 'to pay much attention to the music.' He paid enough attention though to praise and retract his praise in one sentence: 'M. Halévy has written a brilliant and rich score, perhaps even too rich, which would benefit from losing some numbers.'[18] The fairy tale proved to be a success as it was. After eighty-one performances in its first full year it was kept on for four more.

It was a good year for Halévy. On 26 February 1849 his second daughter Geneviève was born, and on 27 May he celebrated his fiftieth birthday. He was one of the most frequently performed opera composers of the day, a high earner, an influential public figure, a member of yet another Commission of Enquiry into the administration of the Villa Medici in Rome. The busier he was the more he took on. He wrote articles, gave lectures, attended committee meetings, and went on composing as if impelled by Atalmuc the sorcerer. By sheer coincidence a character in his next work would also be a sorcerer – Prospero in Shakespeare's *The Tempest*.

15

SEVEN WEEKS IN LONDON

*I*N THE SPRING OF 1850 HALÉVY, accompanied by wife and children, went to London to supervise the rehearsals of *La Tempesta*, his latest collaboration with Scribe. This three-act opera, based on Shakespeare's *The Tempest*, had been commissioned by Her Majesty's Theatre and was a token of the management's faith in the composer's drawing power even though his work was little known in England.

A skimpy sample of it had been offered to London audiences as early as 1835, after the recent success of *La Juive* in Paris. Alfred Bunn, the then lessee of the Drury Lane Theatre, without as much as By your leave, staged it in a two-act English adaptation called *The Jewess*. Of the vast score only two choruses were used.

During the next eleven years, while Europe was singing Halévy's praises as the leader of the French school, London turned a deaf ear. His music was given its first chance when the Brussels Opera Company included two of his operas in their season at the Drury Lane Theatre in the summer of 1846. *La Juive* was performed on 29 and 31 July, *Les Mousquetaires* on 3 and 8 August, both in French. The former, which by then had won universal acclaim, made an impact. The latter, which had opened in Paris only five months earlier and was expected to sweep the English off their feet as it had the French, produced two diametrically opposed reactions. *The Illustrated London News* wrote:

> We are still quite unable to account for the extraordinary popularity of *Les Mousquetaires* in Paris and Brussels . . . The music is heavy, and dry, although beautifully scored. The overture is much more lively than the vocal music which shows more scientific application than melodious imagery. Halévy is a musician of great talent but he is no genius; he has grace without freshness, elegance without charm.[1]

The Musical World expressed unqualified admiration, going as far as to suggest that had the season opened with this opera instead of Meyerbeer's *Les Huguenots*, the company would no have made the financial loss that it had.

> *Les Mousquetaires* is beyond comparison the happiest exhibition of all the best qualities of the composer. We have heard it twice through with pleasure, and are not therefore disposed to quarrel with the popularity it enjoys in Paris, where it has been played just short of 90 times. It is certainly one of the most perfect representations of the Brussels Opera Company and had the season commenced with it we are inclined to think matters would have gone on more prosperously.[2]

A couple of years later the manager of the Strand Theatre read with envy how *Le Val d'Andorre* had saved the Paris Opéra-Comique from financial ruin after the February Revolution. He procured an English adaptation and, hardly any more scrupulous than Mr Dunn had been with *La Juive* fourteen years earlier, presented it 'without a note of music.'[3]

In January 1850 another production of *Le Val d'Andorre* was mounted by Mr Mitchell, the lessee of the St James's Theatre, this one in French, unmutilated, unshorn of its music. *The Musical World* gave the venture moral support:

> For some unfathomable reason M. Halévy's music has never been favourably regarded by the managers of our national operas, who avoid him with studious pertinacity, although composers of less repute are essayed without hesitation. Happily Mr Mitchell has at length stepped forward as his champion.[4]

La Val d'Andorre opened on 7 January but its charms were lost on *The Musical World* reviewer who denied to Halévy what the French critics had been admiring in him most – his profound learning, originality, and gift for melody:

> Halévy often begins a melody well, but seldom finishes it effectively

. . . Yet, without genuine originality or extensive learning, without racy melody or that fluency which sometimes usurps its place, he is not a common writer. We do not yawn over Halévy as over many of the modern Germans, nor laugh at him as in Flotow, nor hold our hands on our ears as at Verdi.[5]

The society ladies and gentlemen who patronised the St James's Theatre prided themselves on their knowledge of French but many, some critics among them, were unable to follow the fast-spoken dialogue of an opera comique nor the uniquely French *esprit* which inspired it. The dramatic situations of a grand opera were easier to understand. *A Musical Times* reviewer signing himself as J. de C put the blame on the composer:

> We are inclined to the opinion that M. Halévy's powers are more in the serious than in the comic line, his instrumentation frequently overpowering the vocalist in those light passages which constitute the charm of comic opera.[6]

Le Val d'Andorre had a good run all the same and was honoured with Queen Victoria's attendance. The five soloists were hurriedly coached in the singing of the national anthem and J. de C gave two of them a pat on the back:

> Between the second and third acts *God Save the Queen* was sung by the company. Mlles Charton and Guichard acquitted themselves most creditably in the verses allotted to them and pronounced the words with remarkable distinctness and good emphasis.[7]

Halévy's real chance to prove his worth to English audiences came when Mr Lumley, lessee of Her Majesty's Theatre, asked him to write an opera based on Shakespeare's *The Tempest*. Scribe had written the libretto in French and the Italian poet P. Giannone, librettist of Halévy's *Clari* which was performed at the Paris Théâtre-Italien in 1828, translated it into Italian. The policy of Her Majesty's Theatre required operas to be performed in Italian.

While delighted with the commission, both composer and librettist were apprehensive about entrusting their work to a London theatre manager. Paris was rife with horror stories about the English way with opera. Managers were said to be only keen on publicity and 'novelty.' They had no ear for flaws, hesitations, pauses, untuned strings. Act Fast rather than Act Well was their guiding rule. If a conductor required three more days for choral rehearsals a horrified manager would tell him to cut the choruses out. If the orchestra had had no chance to go through the music of the mandatory ballet the manager would instruct the musicians to sight-read as best they could on opening night. One story, as recounted by Berlioz, was a particular favourite in Paris.

It concerned the manager of the Drury Lane Theatre who in 1848, to fill an empty house, announced a performance of Donizetti's *Linda di Chamounix*. Orchestra, soloists and choir were all at their places for the first rehearsal.

'Start,' said the manager to the conductor.

'Can't, said the conductor. 'There's no music on the music stands.'

The manager summoned the Head of the Copying Department and ordered him to distribute the music right away.

'Which music?' asked the chief copyist.

'*Linda di Chamounix* of course'

'Sorry, Sir. There isn't any. Nobody has ordered any part scores for the orchestra or vocal scores for the singers.'[8] Posters were hurriedly torn down, potential ticket buyers were turned away.

'On one side of the Channel it takes ten months to rehearse and put on a five-act opera,' Paris was saying. 'On the other side it takes ten days.'[9] Halévy and Scribe decided to go to London to oversee the rehearsals themselves. Fortunately the new conductor of Her Majesty's orchestra was their old friend the Irish composer Michael Balfe who had lived and worked in Paris, who had had an opera comique with libretto by Scribe successfully performed at the Paris Opéra-Comique, and who was known to be intolerant of shoddiness.

On 7 May 1850 Halévy, Mme Halévy, young Esther who was nearly seven, and fourteen-months old Geneviève arrived in London. 'We are here in this ancient city after an abominable crossing, a real tempest indeed.' Léonie wrote to her mother after their safe arrival. 'We were all deathly sick, my poor Esther and even the baby . . . The house we are staying in is charming, but how dull London is.'[10]

The house which had been rented for them was 16 Pall Mall. No sooner had Halévy settled his family, seen to the luggage and charmed the maids with his French courtesy than he walked unaccompanied to Her Majesty's Theatre where he sat down unobtrusively in a back seat, listening to the orchestral rehearsal. The first to notice and recognise the stranger was Balfe. Conductor and orchestra gave him a hearty welcome 'in a regular English fashion' and Halévy, touched by the warm reception, addressed the musicians in French, with Balfe interpreting:

> Gentlemen, I have just had the pleasure of hearing you play and can therefore applaud you conscientiously. You have applauded me without knowing whether I deserve it or not. I feel grateful for your courtesy but, when you have heard my music, if your feelings towards me remain the same, your applause will afford me tenfold pleasure.[11]

Before getting totally absorbed in rehearsals Halévy had to acquit himself of a mission of honour. He was to deliver a book from his friend the writer Jules Janin to Louis Philippe who after the February Revolution had been living at Claremont, near Esher, as a guest of Queen Victoria. Janin had just published his novel *La Religieuse de Toulouse* and was anxious for the exiled king to read it. Accordingly Halévy went to Esher, was received by his old friend the widowed Duchess of Orleans and heard from her that the preface to the book had appeared in a Belgian paper and that the king had had it read to him. The following day an equerry called at 16 Pall Mall to inform Monsieur Halévy that His Majesty would receive him together with his wife and daughters on Sunday 12 May.

'When I arrived the King was resting,' Halévy wrote to Janin a few days later. 'When he woke up he sent for me. He received me lying down on his bed. He seemed very tired. I was struck by the change in him . . . The King spoke at length of France, the revolution, of how he had always wished to make France happy.'

After the presentation of the book the conversation turned to *La Tempesta*. 'The king knows Shakespeare by heart,' Halévy continued and quoted what Louis Philippe had said to the Shakespearian scholar Croker who had called on him. 'Few foreigners know Shakespeare as well as I do,' the Kind had said to Mr Croker. 'Oh Ṣire,' Mr Croker answered. 'Few English people know Shakespeare as well as the King does.'[12]

The king then invited M. and Mme Halévy, together with M. and Mme Scribe who had also arrived in London, to dine with him at Claremont the following Sunday, 19 May. In fact only the

Queen dined with them; the King, seventy-seven and in poor health, had something served to him in his room and joined the guests when the meal was over. He died three months later, on 26 August.

Halévy and Scribe took their supervisory work seriously. An incredulous London press reported that they were attending rehearsals 'sedulously,' spending ten hours a day at the theatre, bestowing their attention 'on all the minor details so essential to the perfect production of a dramatic work.'[13] In his public relations Scribe was every bit as modest and gracious as Halévy was with the orchestra. A charming letter of his, in a fitting English translation, was published in the *Illustrated London News*:

> I have done the utmost to represent the inspiration of your immortal author. All the musical situations I have created are but suggestions taken from Shakespeare's ideas; and as all the honour must accrue to him, I may be allowed to state that there are but few subjects so well adapted to musical interpretation.[14]

The first night was awaited with unprecedented curiosity, as *The Musical World* explained: 'The European name of Scribe, which has been associated with so many brilliant triumphs in every branch of the dramatic art; the celebrity of Halévy, whose operas have of late years been the main support of the two great theatres in Paris; the subject, one of Shakespeare's most familiar dramas which, moreover, had already been set to music by the great English composer Purcell; these and other reasons combined in raising public expectations about *La Tempesta* to the highest pitch.[15]

The supervised rehearsals went on for a month. Opening night had to be put back by a couple of days but on 8 June – a day after Esther's seventh birthday – the curtain rose on the new opera before one of the most glittering audiences that had ever assembled in Her Majesty's Theatre. The enthusiasm knew no bounds. The soloists had to take a bow after each number; Halévy and Balfe the conductor were recalled amid 'hurricanes of applause.' Scribe and Lumley acknowledged the hurricane by gracefully bowing from their respective boxes. The cheers and applause 'rent the roof.'

The press unanimously agreed that production, scenery and performance were immaculate. No detail had been overlooked, no detail was superfluous. Never before had London seen anything like it. Halévy's and Scribe's supervision had achieved outstanding results.

The reaction to the work itself was less unanimous. *The Daily News* reviewer, like his Paris colleagues, was wary of giving a definite opinion on the strength of one hearing. He pointed out a few minor flaws, congratulated Halévy on his weaving in Arne's *Where the Bee Sucks* and ended with unstinting praise:

> Like all music of a high class it requires to be repeatedly heard before it can be fully judged. But we have no hesitation in thinking that *La Tempesta* will be regarded as the *chef d'oeuvre* of its celebrated author. It is the work of a poet as well as a musician. Like all Halévy's work it is profound in thought and masterly in construction, while it is bold, free, imaginative and dramatic, with a great deal of expressive melody, set off by the most varied and elegant instrumentation.[16]

The Times too pointed out some flaws and grandly concluded:

> Our impression of the whole work however is so favourable that were we justified in offering a decided opinion after one hearing we should feel inclined to rank *La Tempesta* higher than any previous effort of its composer. As in *La Juive*, M. Halévy has essayed to individualise each of the dramatis personae by certain peculiarities of rhythm and orchestral treatment. With Caliban, Miranda and Ariel he had been remarkably successful; less so with Prospero . . . The instrumentation of the opera throughout is a masterly example of the modern French school, of which M. Halévy is one of the most celebrated disciples; while the choral writing, in a great measure, illustrates the prevailing fault of that school – want of continuity.[17]

The Musical World was hostile. It rebuked Halévy for having failed to provide the opera with an overture though on second thoughts, it added, it was just as well since the composer was not known to have excelled in that kind of writing. The first act was good, the second less so, the third not a patch on either. The music as a whole reflected Cherubini's influence, though only those with 'an educated ear' could discern it. Balfe was praised for conducting the opera as if it were one of his own, and note was taken of the increasing attendance at every subsequent performance. 'The hit is decisive,'[18] was the reluctant conclusion.

On 19 June Queen Victoria, a day or two after 'a ruffianly assault had been committed against her,' chose to attend *La*

Tempesta in order to reassert her popularity. 'After the second act the curtain rose and the whole company came forward and sang *God Save the Queen* amid such a perfect hurricane of applause, so uproarious, continuous and interrupting, that not one word of the anthem was heard.'[19] As for the opera, 'Her Majesty appeared highly pleased.'[20] To her at least Halévy's music was not altogether new; she had heard and enjoyed *Le Val d'Andorre* at the St James's Theatre earlier that year.

The seven-week stay in London offered Halévy a taste of English social life. His letter to Janin mentioned lots of *toasts*, *clubs* and *speeches* as well as a meeting with Thackeray. In the third week of June he returned to Paris with his family and the Scribes, 'overwhelmed with words of estimation of their private worth and with public ovation'[21] and 'with the pleasant conviction that their trip to England has alike been honourable to themselves and profitable to the spirited lessee of Her Majesty's Theatre.'[22]

16

HOW LONDON SAW *LA JUIVE*

*E*IGHTEEN FIFTY WAS HALÉVY'S English year. On 7 January *Le Val d'Andorre* had opened at St James's Theatre. On 8 June *La Tempesta* opened at Her Majesty's Theatre. On 25 July *La Juive* opened at the Royal Italian Opera Covent Garden.

It was the third, and most ambitious version of *La Juive* ever presented in London. The first was put on shortly after the Paris premiere in February 1835 at the Drury Lane Theatre by its lessee Alfred Bunn who collaborated with the Frenchman M. Planche on an English translation. Between them they transformed a five-act opera into a two-act 'melodramatic spectacle'[1] from which all music but two choruses had been excised. To improve it further a happy end had been tacked on, saving Rachel from the boiling cauldron. Halévy had been powerless to do anything about it. It was only in May 1851 that Judge Lord Campbell together with eight other judges of the Courts of the Queen's Bench and Common Pleas ruled in a test case concerning Bellini's *La Somnambula* that 'pirating and using a musical composition' was an offence and that 'copyright can be enjoyed in England by foreigners and aliens.'[2]

For the presentation of his piracy Mr Bunn needed actors not singers. The part of Elazar was offered to William Macready, the star of the Drury Lane Theatre and, when he turned it down, to Mr Vanderhoff, his closest rival in the theatre's acting hierarchy.

To give the audience value for money *The Jewess* was double billed with *The Siege of La Rochelle*, a two-act opera by the young and still unknown Irish composer Michael William Balfe (1808–1870).

The double bill was a hit, the making of Balfe's name and Drury Lane's fortune. At a time when uninterrupted runs of two to three months were unheard of, it ran to seventy performances in its first thirteen weeks, from 16 November 1835 well into the new year. The weekly takings rose from £1,427 to £2,381 and Covent Garden Opera House round the corner was reported to have become a desert. Mr Vanderhoff's Elazar became a household name and a furious Macready waved his contract at Mr Bunn threatening all manner of retaliation.

The 1836 spring season started with a compromise. Instead of a double bill with no Macready a triple bill was introduced – three acts of *Richard III* which had been one of Macready's triumphs in the title role, *The Jewess* with his rival, and a curtain raiser called *Chevy Chase*. The audience had eyes and ears only for Mr Vanderhoff's Elazar. At nine o'clock in the evening of 29 April, as Mr Bunn was peacefully working in his theatre office, probably counting the day's takings, Richard III burst in shouting 'Take that' and knocked him down. *The Jewess* was eventually taken off, though not before it had scored eighty-four performances.

Two bona fide performances of *La Juive* were given by the Brussels Opera Company during the 1846 season at the Drury Lane Theatre, as part of an ambitious programme which included Meyerbeer's *Les Huguenots* and *Robert le Diable*, Adam's *Le Postillon de Lonjumeau*, Auber's *Les Diamans de la Couronne* and *Le Domino noir*, Rossini's *Guillaume Tell* and Halévy's *La Juive* and *Les Mousquetaires*. All operas were sung in French.

From the outset the four-week season of the visiting company, from mid-July to mid-August, was dogged by bad luck. *Les Huguenots*, which opened it, was unpopular and put people off seeing the company's other offerings; the two managers who had organised the tour turned out to be amateurs in the world of business, the singers were often indisposed and unable to sing, the theatre opened and closed at random and, last but not least, the summer was unaccountably hot and society deserted the stifling metropolis for fresh country air.

In spite of the difficulties *La Juive* was performed twice, on 29 and 31 July. *The Illustrated London News* singled out various numbers for special praise and gave its readers a perceptive list of situations in the final scene: 'the savage fury of the bigoted populace, the resignation of Rachel, the feverish inquietude of the Cardinal, the malignant aspect of the Jew at the gratification of his revenge, the chants of the church, the automaton attitude of the disciplined military, with the officer who gives his dreadful orders for the ceremonial as if he were only on a parade of pleasure.'[3]

That same year Covent Garden Theatre was redesigned and renovated, its auditorium given the traditional Italian horse-shoe shape. A new Royal Italian Opera was launched, to which composer and conductor Michael Costa (1808–1894) brought along some of the best players in London and his legendary baton with which he drew immaculate performances from orchestras under his tutelage. In February 1850 the Covent Garden prospectus mentioned *La Juive* as one of the forthcoming 'novelties' of the season. It was an unexpected bonus that later that year both Halévy and Scribe were working in London on *La Tempesta* and were able to meet and confer with Costa. Composer and librettist returned to Paris satisfied that *La Juive* was in safe hands.

It was intended to be, and was, 'beyond all comparison, the most gorgeous *mise-en-scène* ever known on the continent.'[4] Money was no object. The best producers, the best designers, the best costumiers, and of course the best soloists were commissioned. Pauline Viardot who had sung Rachel in French in Paris and in German in Berlin was now to sing the part in Italian to agree with the policy of the Royal Italian Opera. Italian-born Mario whose tenor voice was all the rage was to sing Elazar. The singers worked from vocal scores entitled *L'Ebrea*, published in both Italian and German by Lemoine who had bought Schlesinger's publishing rights on the latter's retirement.

As was the case in the original Paris production, the opera was found to be too long. Costa dropped the overture and with further judicious cuts reduced the running time to four hours. All boded well for the opening night on 25 July when professional jealousy nearly wrecked it.

Tenor Giovanni Mario (1810–1883) had been living with Italian soprano Giulia Grisi (1811–1869) for eleven years when the London *La Juive* was announced; they had several children and to all intents and purposes were husband and wife. Holy matrimony however was impossible because of a hasty marriage Grisi had contracted in her early youth. She and Mario sang leading parts in the same operas, travelled together on foreign assignments, and for many years had a regular season in London. When the new Royal Italian Opera was set up they both joined it, Grisi singing the title role in Rossini's *Semiramide* at the launching. It came as a shock that while Mario was given the part of Elazar in the forthcoming *La Juive*, that of Rachel was given to Pauline Viardot. It was the second time in two years that Grisi had been passed over in favour of Viardot.

The first time was when Mario was to sing at the Royal Italian Opera the part of Raoul in Meyerbeer's *Les Huguenots* to Viardot's Valentine. The performance was to take place on the first Thursday of August 1848. Grisi persuaded Mario to sham illness with a view to having the performance cancelled and Viardot denied her expected triumph. What happened that night was reported a couple of days later in *The Illustrated London News*:

> At the eleventh hour on Thursday, owing to the sudden indisposition of Signor Mario, there was the advent of Monsieur Roger in the role of Raoul. He had never played the character before but he had studied it for the French Grand Opera. He sang it in French of course as he had only three hours' notice and no rehearsal. The success was immense . . . He electrified the house in the Septuor of the duel and was rapturously encored. The duo with Viardot in the third act was wonderfully sung and was cheered from first to last . . . The beauty of the organ of the French tenor, his fine style of declamatiom and power of expression surpassed every expectation.[5]

Infuriatingly Viardot was showered with flowers and had several curtain calls. She was particularly praised for thoughtfully moving between Italian and French, thus establishing a perfect rapport with her partner. Mario was nettled. *The Illustrated London News* reported what happened during the subsequent performance:

> On Saturday night, Mario having recovered from his indisposition, he reappeared as Raoul in Meyerbeer's *Les Huguenots*. Excited probably by the great success of the French tenor M. Roger on the previous Thursday, who assumed his part at a few hours' notice, Mario exerted himself strenuously and on no previous occasion did he sing with such sweetness and power. He gave new life to the

Septuor of the duel and, for the first time, he was encored in this splendid piece, as M. Roger had been the previous Thursday.[6]

In spite of the failure of her scheming Grisi persuaded Mario to try again the same tactic in order to deprive Viardot of her expected triumph in *La Juive*. This time it was bound to succeed. On the morning of 25 July the tenor who believed himself irreplaceable at short notice sent a hurried note in French to Frederick Gye, the business manager of the Royal Italian Opera, pleading sudden indisposition.

> Mon cher M. Gye – I am in despair – it's impossible for me to sing tonight – I wanted to wait and see – it's no use – you must postpone *La Juive* to Saturday – for tonight don't even think of it – it's absolutely impossible for me to sing – it's a bad cold. Adieux.[7]

Again there was panic. again Grisi's plan was thwarted. One of the minor parts in the crowd scenes had been given to Maralti, formerly leading tenor of the Brussels Opera Company, who had sung Elazar many times in Belgium. He stepped into the breach singing in French with versatile Viardot sympathetically responding in the same language, then reverting to the mandatory Italian. He was given a tumultuous applause. As for Viardot, her fans claimed it was one of her greatest triumphs.

After the performance the press discreetly mentioned that Mario had been 'seized with hoarseness while singing on Wednesday night at Lord Landsdowne's concert.'[8] Maralti's success cured the patient of his hoarseness, though not of his vanity, the vanity of a tenor whose handsome face was part of his stock in trade. He appeared on stage with no make-up, presenting to the audience an incongruously youthful and attractive Elazar. Fifteen years earlier, when Nourrit created the part, Halévy was the first to appreciate what a sacrifice it was for a handsome tenor to appear as an old Jew bent with age:

> The tenor insists on a lover's prerogative to look attractive. When making himself up like an old man he risks losing for ever the prestige of youth, leaving the spectators – particularly those of the fair sex – with an indelible impression of an unprepossessing mask and the stamp of premature ageing ... But Nourrit was young enough and confident enough to face the risk for the sake of the common cause.[9]

TENOR MARIO

Nourrit's artistic integrity greatly impressed Delacroix, who wrote to thank him for his performance, calling him 'dear Jew, Jew from beard to toe, and with no caricature.'[10] Mario however could not bring himself to conceal his good looks for the sake of the 'common cause.' Of all contemporary tenors he was certainly the most physically attractive. His engraved picture shows him as handsome of face, slim, graceful of figure even in repose. His female admirers were legion. The English novelist Ouida had fallen for him during a performance and kept his framed picture on her desk to her dying day. He sang Elazar looking his handsome self, to the great disapproval of the critics:

> The first great mistake is in the making up of the head. The face is not furrowed as it should be by the wrinkles of age and cunning and he looks more like the brother of Rachel than her father. The form of Mario is too erect and his gait too steady for the restless, suspicious Shylock of Constance.[11]

When Elazar took no notice and continued to look young enough to be his daughter's brother, the press gave him a word of advice:

> As yet Mario's Lazaro rests mainly on his rich vocalisation. If he will make up his head differently and give his mind to the Jew's attributes, it may still be rendered his finest creation.[12]

It was no use. Mario remained a handsome young Elazar until the subscribers' season ended on 24 August. As for the opera *The Illustrated News* wrote:

> The *mise-en-scène* is the theme of universal admiration. The costumes are magnificent and are historically correct in many instances. The procession in the first act – the Emperor's cortège with civil, military and ecclesiastical authorities – is admirably managed. Grieve and Telbin have surpassed all their former scenic displays in this opera, particularly in the view of Constance and the Minster, with the ancient streets in the foreground, the gardens in which The Emperor's banquet is given – for extent of stage never approached – and the grand square filled with the vast populace, and the city in the distance, where the Jew and Jewess are led to execution. The groupings of all the scenes and the general stage business under Mr Harris's direction are worthy of every praise.[13]

Of the music the paper wrote:

> Overscored as are many of the accompaniments by the free use of the

brass and percussion instruments, the instrumentation is, on the whole, remarkable for elegance and appropriateness to the dramatic situation . . . Halévy's *Juive* is a masterpiece of its class, even if that class be not the first of lyrical compositions.[14]

The Paris press was delighted with the London success of *La Juive*. 'In the absence of the composer,' *La Revue et gazette musicale* reported after the first night, 'conductor Costa was recalled to acknowledge the applause on his behalf. This success, achieved in the face of many difficulties, proves that from now on the Italian Opera at Covent Garden can rely only on Meyerbeer and Halévy. *Le Prophète* has made its fortune; *La Juive* will double it.'[15]

There was one point which the London press made no comment on, perhaps because it was not aware of it. The final line of the final scene of the opera had been altered. In the French score, after both Rachel and Elazar perish in the boiling cauldron, the crowd sings: 'It is all over, we have taken our revenge on the Jews.' In the one-and-sixpence programme sold at Covent Garden which included the full libretto in both Italian and English the text had been moderated: 'All is over, the guilty pair are dead.'

There was no revival of that 'most gorgeous *mise-en-scène* ever known on the continent.' The entire set was destroyed in the Covent Garden fire of 1856 and not until 1871, long after Halévy's death, was a new production mounted in the rebuilt theatre. In 1900 the recently established Moody-Manners Opera Co Ltd, claiming to be the largest English Opera company in the world, put it on in an English version by Percy Pinkerton, with Madame Fanny Moody as Rachel and Mr Charles Manners as Cardinal Brogni. A programme including an explanatory introduction and a full English libretto cost twopence and patrons were 'earnestly' requested to report to the management if they were overcharged.

17

MORE OF THE SAME

*B*ACK IN PARIS AFTER HIS WORKING
visit to London, Halévy resumed his composition routine, producing three operas in as many years. The first was to a libretto by Scribe.

The London interlude introduced a social element into an association which had hitherto been primarily professional. It was after all thanks to Halévy that the Scribes were included in an invitation to a Sunday lunch with the exiled King Louis Philippe and his Queen at Claremont. Mme Scribe began to call; Scribe went as far as to suggest that the two families should spend a holiday together in Switzerland. 'Even from this distance,' he wrote jokingly, 'I can hear Mme Halévy's cry of horror.'[1] All the same he never waived the formal *vous*, as had the more approachable M. de Saint-Georges while Halévy, for his part, never omitted to weave into his letters the deferential *mon cher et illustre ami*.

Much of their correspondence after their return from London revolved round an annoying financial matter. Benjamin Lumley, the lessee of her Majesty's Theatre, had also acquired the lease of the Théâtre-Italien in Paris and proposed inaugurating his lesseeship with *La Tempesta*. Composer and librettist mentioned copyright, Lumley appeared not to hear, Halévy enlisted the help of his London agent.

The unsatisfactory negotiations went on for the best part of two years. Lumley, born Levi or Levy, formerly a solicitor specialising in company law, sent word that he would be willing to honour a demand for 6,000 francs provided he was given sole rights of *La Tempesta*. He also invoked a verbal agreement he claimed he had made with the claimants. Long before any settlement was reached he put the opera on at the Théâtre-Italien in a two-act version.

The mixture of Shakespeare, Scribe and an Italian libretto left Paris cold. The tune of *Where the Bee Sucks* which Halévy had so cleverly woven into the score to the delight of his English audiences evoked nothing. The ballet dancer who represented Ariel tripped up on the first night. Only Lablache, the most famous bass of his generation, won praise in the role of Caliban. It was one of those operas of which loyal friends later said: 'Without harming the Master's name it did nothing to enhance it.'[2] Premiered on 25 February 1851m it was taken off after eight performances. It was cold comfort to see *Le Tre Nozze* by one Alary which replaced it taken off after four. Lumley eventually gave up theatre management altogether and resumed his legal practice in London.

The work Halévy and Scribe embarked on in 1850 was an opéra comique. Some fourty years before Tchaikovsky's version, Scribe, as a basis for his libretto, used a short story by the Russian poet Alexander Pushkin, who, like Halévy, was born in 1799 but died when still in his thirties. It was *Pikovaya dama*, first published in 1834, known in France as *La Dame de pique* and in England as *The Queen of Spades*. It introduced opera audiences to the unusual set of a Russian salt mine with a lift going up and down.

The plot unfolds in 1762 during the short reign of Tsar Peter III. Neliadov, a young nobleman who is denied his rightful title because of some unproven allegation against his late father, brings a letter to the castle of Polovsk, announcing the return from Court of young Princess Polovska. A fierce snow storm makes two travellers seek hospitality in the castle. One is Prince Zizianov, the other the elderly German banker Klaremberg.

Klaremberg recalls that when he was a young man heavily in debt through gambling, old Princess Polovska, long since dead, took pity on him and discreetly indicated which three cards he should play to win. In return he had to promise never to play again, and never did.

Young Princess Polovska now turns up, lame and blatantly plain, but believed to have inherited the secret of the three winning cards. Prince Zizianov accuses Neliadov of courting her for her inheritance. Neliadov draws his sword, is overpowered and sent down to the mine prison.

Act II takes place in the mine. The young princess plans Neliadov's escape. She persuades the mine manager, an inveterate gambler, to leave the cell door unlocked, in return for which she tells him the secret of the winning cards: three, ten, Queen of Spades. Prince Zizianov overhears the secret formula. The princess persuades Klaremberg to take Neliadov up the lift disguised as his servant and allow him to escape. Prince Zizianov declares princess, banker, mine manager and Neliadov wanted criminals.

In Act III they all meet on neutral ground, at the Karlsbad casino. Zizianov and the mine manager play the secret formula and lose heavily. A mysterious vision looking like the Queen of Spades forces a confession out of Zizianov rehabilitating Neliadov and restoring him to his rightful title. The princess, having shed her assumed limp and plain looks along with her disguise as the Queen of Spades, offers him her love and her hand.

The twist of the plot is provided by the banker Klaremberg who now reveals that there has never been a secret formula. Old Princess Polovska had a standing arrangement with the Court croupier to let win any three cards she passed on to him in the name of the Tsarina. She never used the same sequence twice. Out of kindness she had given the croupier to understand that Klaremberg was her ally in the game. The revelation brings about the mandatory happy end of an opera comique. The wicked lose all, the righteous win their just reward. The mine manager, the gullible victim of the Princess's conspiracy to set Neliadov free, has his gambling debts paid off and promises to follow old Klaremberg's example and never play again.

La Dame de pique opened at the Opéra-Comique on 28 December 1850 and was an instant success. Gautier, who had been maintaining for years that Halévy should stick to grand opera and that Scribe could not write a line of decent verse, was for once content to report rather than give an opinion:

The Opéra-Comique, which has known a great many triumphs, has never had as resounding a success as that of *La Dame de pique*: book, score, performance – everything has worked out beyond anyone's wildest dreams. The evening was a non-stop ovation for composer and author. Halévy, like an Italian Maestro, was made to appear in person to receive the acclaim of the enchanted audience.[3]

Berlioz's review, apparently written without the benefit of a second hearing, was full of pinpricks:

The score of M. Halévy, like everything penned by this Master musician, is well crafted and witty. I am bound to say however that it struck me as less rich in ideas than his earlier work. It is skilful, deft, well researched as far as local colour and character are concerned. But his melodies are sometimes on the short side, lacklustre, undistinguished. The orchestration in conscientious but overloaded with percussion. A frequent use of the tambour on top of the bass drum and the kettledrum results in a crude and dry sound which totally crushes the small orchestra of the Opéra-Comique. I cannot understand such an error of judgment on the part of as eminent a composer as M. Halévy.[4]

La Revue et gazette musicale dwelled on the music of Act II which takes place in the depths of the mine:

The overture describes the subject of the opera, as does the picturesque music which introduces the second act. We hear an excellent simulation of the work down the mine, even the sound of the pickaxes. We hear a bell sounding the dominant E over a mysterious harmony in A minor, telling the miners it is time to take a break. That E sound of the bell becomes a third in the modulation of C major which now follows, tinkling on in a most original way. The clarinet and the flute sing charmingly. A crescendo in A major, with a tambour joining in, adds colour to a little symphonic drama which heralds a complicated action by variations of rhythms and the unison of clarinet and bassoon. The mysterious sound of the cellos lends a melancholy note to the brief and energetic crescendo we have already mentioned, which soars to a happy peroration.[5]

The reviewer's final judgment, two pages later, was that the opera was 'well acted, well sung, well performed and well directed.'[6] During its run there was talk of inviting Pauline Viardot to take over the lead, or engaging her to sing in a projected revival of another Halévy opera. She was too tired to accept.

George Sand approved her decision in a letter written on 16 October 1851 from her country house at Nohant:

> You are quite right to take a rest, you have been overdoing it far too long. You will be ten thousand times better off not exhausting your voice and soul singing any Halévy, the ugliest, most hook-nosed and most stupid music there ever was, so say I.[7]

It is not likely that the content of that letter was ever imparted to Halévy, or shared by his audience. During the next few seasons *La Dame de pique* had forty-seven performances. A distinguished achievement in itself, it was disappointing all the same when compared with the hundred performances of *La Fée aux roses*, nearly a hundred and thirty of *Le Val d'Andorre* and well over two hundred of *Les Mousquetaires de la reine*.

His next work was based on a text by Scribe and Saint-Georges. The two most sought-after librettists in Paris, they often relegated the completion of their work to a pool of assistants; occasionally they assisted each other, as they had in Halévy's opéra comique *La Fée aux roses*. This time they collaborated on a five-act grand opera, based on the old legend of the Wandering Jew.

The legend had been well known in one variant or another for hundreds of years. A Jewish soldier marching behind Jesus carrying his cross on the way to Golgotha prodded him from behind and said: 'Faster, why do you keep stopping?' Jesus answered: 'I walk as has been ordained and soon I shall come to rest. But you, you will keep marching until the Day of Judgment.' A learned reviewer informed his readers after the opening night of *Le Juif errant* that the first written mention of the Wandering Jew was made by the monk Matthew Paris of St Albans as early as 1228, at which time he was still nameless. He became Ahasverus in 1547. After that he was sighted in Vienna in 1599, in Lübeck in 1601, in Krakow and Moscow in 1616, in Paris in 1644 . . .

The source material used by Scribe and Saint-Georges was the novel *Le Juif errant* by Eugène Sue, published in ten volumes in 1844–45. Its popularity gave rise to a spate of plays; in 1846 the Palais-Royal put on *Le nouveau juif errant* by Varmer, and in 1849 the Ambigu put on a dramatised version of Sue's novel. It was only natural that an opera should follow.

The story concocted by Scribe and Saint-Georges is a far cry from Eugène Sue's novel though its canvas is as vast as the original. It begins in Antwerp in 1190, where a ferrywoman sings a ballad telling the story of the Wandering Jew, who can never die, who cannot stop anywhere longer than a quarter of an hour, who is always prodded on by the Avenging Angel ordering 'March, march.'

Ahasverus has long repented of his ancient callousness, he only seeks to do good and find the peace of death. On his wanderings he comes upon a band of brigands who have abducted a little girl called Irene, the lawful heiress to the Byzantine Empire. He rescues her and twelve years later he goes through an ordeal of fire to prove her claim and dethrone a usurper. The usurper treacherously asks Irene to marry him. She refuses him for Léon, a son of Ahasverus. The usurper orders his henchmen to kill his rival, but Ahasverus drives them away. The Avenging Angel takes over and is about to throw Léon from a rock into the sea. There is a heroic struggle between Angel and Ahasverus who tries to save his son's life. When he loses he dives in after him.

Léon, Irene and Ahasverus find themselves on a deserted sea shore. Ahasverus knows through some spiritual power that the usurper has died and urges Irene to go back to claim her empire. Léon and Irene refuse to leave without him. He orders them to do so, begging them to implore God to let him die. They reluctantly depart.

Left alone Ahasverus feels his strength ebbing away. He lies down on a rock awaiting sweet death. Mysterious singing is heard – the chorus of the dead, a chorus of devils, a chorus of the dammed, a chorus of the blessed. It is the Day of Judgment. The Avenging Angel appears and revives the semi-dead Ahasverus: 'March, march.' The trumpet sounds. The Wandering Jew resumes his eternal wandering.

It was a vast work and, as during his work on *La Juive* and *Charles VI*, Halévy was tense, tormented, irritated with the unpredictability of the Opéra timetable. On 10 January 1852 he wrote to Scribe:

> The Wandering Jew marches on, though slowly; all the same he is doing well. You would be very useful to us here at the Opéra; we start rehearsing in a few days' time. If there was some more activity at this

theatre, and I mean real activity, we would be making much better progress. Every instant there is some rehearsal, some scheduling requirement which involves more work. I hope it will go well, the signs bode well for it . . . Are you working a little, *mon cher et illustre?* Saint-Georges complains he has not received anything from you . . . Let me hear from you.[8]

Recovering his good spirits he ended with somewhat belated wishes for a happy new year:

Can you read my frightful scribble? Can you read that I present Mme Scribe with my affectionate respects and my cordial wishes for the New Year? What can we two wish ourselves? Thousands of years similar to the preceding ones. My warmest regards to both of you. I will now hand over to my wife to add a few words.[9]

Le Juif errant was premiered at the Opéra on 23 April 1852, after a relatively short rehearsal period of only three months. Paul Smith, the latest recruit to the editorial board of *La Revue et gazette musicale*, wrote after the first night:

For eighteen centuries the Wandering Jew had been on the move . . . He had tried them all – drama, vaudeville, epic, novel. In vain did he try to stop. Always there was this 'march, march,' chasing him away from his momentary halts, forcing him to resume his wanderings. In vain did he seek the peace of the grave. But now, arriving at the Opéra, he has found a homeland, a throne, a haven. Now he is at last persuaded by the manner of his reception that his destiny has been overcome, that his wanderings are over, that from now on it will be the crowds who would bestir themselves to come to him, to watch and listen. This is the result of a synthesis of ideas, inspirations and hard work of which only one theatre in the world has the secret, the only theatre that can put it into effect.[10]

Having singled out numerous numbers for special comment, the reviewer went on:

The music? I have told you enough, when describing each number separately, to make you sense that the score may well be a masterpiece. Perhaps it would have been enough to say that it is a work by M. Halévy. Still, I insist on saying that this distinguished composer has never been nearer this highest of all terms of art, enfolding as he does the grand within the simple, the simple within the grand. There is nothing forced, nothing tiring, nothing laboured. It is as if the music has been poured onto paper without pause or hesitation. What distinguishes this great artist is his ability to develop and go from strength to strength. God has ordered Halévy, as he has the Wandering Jew, 'March, march,' – and Halévy keeps marching.[11]

La Revue considered *Le Juif errant* so important that it devoted to it two more articles, both by the Belgian composer and musicologist Fétis, author of the encyclopedic *Biographie universelle des musiciens*. In his first article he looked askance at a curfew scene which was reminiscent of one in Meyerbeer's *Les Huguenots*. In his second article he gave a full description and analysis of each number, reserving his highest praise for the Last Judgment and the resurrection of the dead:

> The chorus singing *Qui vient donc* – Who comes to disturb the dead in their cold grave? – is one of the most beautiful numbers of the score. It is a pity that the visual impact of this scene so enthralls the viewers that it hardly allows them to absorb all the beauties of the music . . . Even when all the miracles engineered by designer and machinist have disappeared it is not all over: clouds disperse, the poor Jew is revealed crouching on the ground. He stirs, wakes up and cries to the Avenging Angel: 'Oh, my doom is not over . . . ' giving vent to his anguish in a recitative of four lines. Trumpets sound, a chorus of angels pushes him on his way with the terrible 'March, march.' He runs away, the Avenging Angel after him in hot pursuit. Thus ends this opera which in spite of the great beauties contained in *Guido et Ginevra*, *La Reine de Chypre* and *Charles VI*, is the most outstanding and complete work Halévy has written since *La Juive*.[12]

A perceptive interpretation of the work as a whole, detaching it from its literal context and elevating it to the sphere of moral philosophy, came from Gautier. '*Le Juif errant*,' he wrote, 'is a symbol of humanity marching on in search of an ideal.'[13] One of Halévy's most powerful and moving grand operas, it held the Opéra stage for two seasons and achieved forty-nine performances.

Back to opéra comique, on with Scribe and Saint-Georges. This time it was a jolly little plot, set first in British India, then in Wales. Lord Evendale, the British Commissioner stationed somewhere near Calcutta, is bored with life and fed up with his capricious wife. With what is taken for a characteristically English nonchalance he decides to commit suicide. An old friend, a doctor by profession, prescribes a one-year course of treatment away from home. The patient's last official act before leaving is to pay the return passage to Britain of a young woman called Dora, strayed in India. She is not aware that there is no official charitable fund for waifs and strays and that Lord Evendale pays out of his own pocket. The audience however understands that the Nabob is a kind man.

The scene shifts to Wales. Lord Evendale, now known as plain George Preston, is a factory hand in a tobacco plant owned by Toby. Toby thinks the world of his honest and conscientious employee and so does his niece Dora, who has made it home all the way from Calcutta. Needless to say she does not recognise the Nabob. She tells Uncle that she is in love with George and wishes to marry him; not only does he approve but he promises to promote her future husband to a managerial status. When a determined Dora informs George of his good fortune he does not know what to do.

At nearby Denbigh Manor an annual fête is held to which plebs and nobs are equally welcome. Distinguished guests from far away include Lady Evendale, her young escort Arthur and, by way of chaperoning her, the family doctor. George confronts his wife and asks for a divorce. She refuses. The doctor now confronts her, reminding her that many years ago, when she was a young woman of dubious morals and he a gullible student, they were married. Her marriage to Lord Evendale is therefore bigamous and invites prosecution. Before any more is said she disappears with young Arthur, leaving the doctor free to enjoy his single life and the one-time Nabob to contract a lawful marriage with Dora.

Le Nabab, a three-act opera comique, was premiered on 1 September 1853 and pleased G. Heguet, another newcomer to *La Revue et gazette musicale* who wrote:

> So you think a Nabob is an Indian, one of those disgustingly rich Indians who die without ever knowing how many rupees they had? Wrong. Here we have a Nabob who is really and truly English, and a high-born Englishman at that . . . The score contains items of rare merit. Of all Halévy's works *Le Nabab* is perhaps the one where this great composer has most put himself out to write melody, where he has realised his quest most felicitously, flowingly and elegantly. The music seems born more spontaneously out of the words and is

destined to enjoy instant as well as long-lasting popularity . . . It is a brilliant work and will run for a long time.[14]

Le Nabab ran for thirty-eight performances, a respectable though hardly a run-away success. It was Halévy's last collaboration with the librettist of La Juive. Scribe's last years were marred by virulent attacks on his work. 'M. Scribe, today an old man,' wrote the Escudier brothers well before Le Nabab, when the 'old man' was only fifty-five, 'has lost all the children of his spirit, all the resources of his inspiration. What he churns up now is dramatic stew . . . miserable parodies, cheap and nasty operas comiques and vaudevilles. Let him retire . . .'[15]

He died at seventy, preceding Halévy by just over a year.

18

LIFE SECRETARY

*O*N FIFTH JULY 1854 THE DEATH occurred of Raoul Rochette, Life Secretary of the Academy of Fine Arts, one of the five academies of the Institute of France. His three predecessors since the creation of the post at the beginning of the century had all been outsiders; they came from among the members of the Academy of Inscriptions and Letters. Léon, his brother's most loyal champion, felt the time was ripe to redress the balance and urged Halévy to offer his candidature for the vacancy.

Halévy was reluctant to put his name forward. Léon remembered him saying that he was unworthy of such eminence and that any one of the other candidates – there were three of them, all from other Academies – was better qualified than he. He had however two assets which they apparently lacked. Firstly he was an experienced committee man, tactful, conciliatory, genuinely interested in promoting not only music but all forms of art. Secondly, he had the gift of writing and public speaking, the very qualifications desirable in a Life Secretary who once a year had to read a paper to the open session of the Academy of Fine Arts.

That latter gift had been noticed during the lifetime of Rochette, who had twice asked him to stand in for him. On both occasions he spoke about abstruse seventeenth-century personalities, one English, one German. On both occasions he was congratulated on his writing as well as on his delivery. He had the art of the story teller, gripping attention right from the opening sentence, sometimes making his audience laugh, sometimes presenting the findings of his research as a sad winter's tale with goblins and sprites.

His first paper, read on 25 October 1852, was devoted to the life and achievement of Britton the Coalman, *Britton le Charbonnier*. A native of Northampton (1644–1714), Thomas Britton was apprenticed from the age of eight to a coal merchant in London and served his apprenticeship for seven years. On his return home at fifteen he learnt to read and write and discovered music through his church attendance. Once his apprentice's discharge money ran out he returned to London and became a plain coalman carrying a sack on his back, proclaiming his ware in the streets of Clerkenwell. In the evenings, still wearing his coalman's coarse blue jacket and carrying his empty sack, he went to various libraries in search of music scores. One free Saturday his call at Batesman's Library coincided with that of other music lovers, all from the cream of London's aristocracy. That chance encounter led to many other meetings at the Mourning Bush Tavern.

He lived in an out-of-the-way ramshackle mews where he played the viola da gamba and housed his growing collection of music books and manuscripts. His library – Halévy actually saw one of its catalogues – included such rarities as excerpts from *King Arthur* by Purcell, Matthew Lock's music for *Macbeth*, a sonata by Corelli.

His earnings were small but a commission to design and construct a portable laboratory for a neighbour of his, a French doctor turned alchemist, brought him a handsome profit as did a similar commission in Wales. He used it to convert the mews into a venue for concerts. The performers were gifted amateurs, the audience consisted of his music loving society friends who were invited to attend free of charge.

It was an unusual venue. The ground floor served as a coal store for retail trade. A ladder fixed onto an external wall led to the concert hall on the first floor, a long, narrow room with a low ceiling which was the bane of most visitors. Undeterred, fashionable ladies gathered their skirts and climbed the steep ladder, gentlemen learnt to keep their heads down until seated. Equally undeterred, Britton kept peddling coal in the streets of Clerkenwell; a portrait by Woolaston entitled The Musical Small Coalman, which Halévy may have seen at the British Museum during his stay in London, shows a distinguished-looking thin-faced behatted Britton with a lump of coal in his hand. It has since been transferred to the National Portrait Gallery.

That a street coalman entertained the cream of society in his poor home seemed odd. Rumours began to fly. The innocent recitals were alleged to be a cover for seditious activities. Britton was suspected of being a magician, an atheist, a Presbyterian, a Jesuit. He moved to safer and more comfortable premises and formed a music club, with regular meetings and a membership fee of ten shillings a year. Coffee – a new beverage at the time – was available at a penny a cup. Among his performers were the young Handel, Pepusch and many other celebrities of the day. His concerts ran from 1678 until two days before his death in 1714 and were the forerunners of the English Music Societies of the future.

The goblin of the story appeared in the shape of a ventriloquist who in the middle of a concert suddenly boomed: 'On your knees, Thomas Britton. Your hour has come. Say your prayers.' Britton had a seizure, refused to believe it was a practical joke and died two days later. He was buried in Clerkenwell, mourned by friends from all walks of life. It took three days to auction his valuable collection of books and instruments, the proceeds of which went to his widow. His grave was left anonymous, with no inscription to commemorate his life's work.

'This complex and unusual character,' Halévy said at the conclusion of his paper, 'lived at a time and in a country which made it possible for him to develop without hindrance. It seems to me that a coalman who holds concerts, gives his patronage to musicians, collects music scores and, wearing his blue working jacket, receives society ladies in a room above a coal store accessible only by ladder, could have existed nowhere else except in England.'[1]

His second paper was read on 25 October 1853 and was devoted to the German organist and composer Johann Jacob Froberger (1616–1667). Born into a family of professional musicians, he enjoyed the best musical tuition available in Stuttgart, Vienna and Rome. For many years he was the darling of the Vienna Imperial Court and was awarded the title of Emperor's Organist. His own goblin took the form of *Wanderlust*, tempting him to leave security behind and explore new pastures. In 1662 he set out for London. Before he got as far as his port of embarkation he was robbed of most of his money. During the sea voyage his ship sank. He reached English soil without a penny and begged his way to London. Wandering about he heard the sounds of an organ, followed it and found himself attending evensong at Westminster Abbey. The organist, Dr Christopher Gibbons, offered him the arduous job of an organ blower.

While the organist was satisfied with his new blower, Halévy said, the blower was far from satisfied with the master's music. He bided his time. King Charles II had just married Catherine of Portugal and was giving a series of post-nuptial celebrations in Whitehall Palace where a new organ had been installed. Dr Gibbons played away, Froberger blew hard, then stopped. The sound died away. The royal guests thought the organ was faulty, the organist knew better. He slapped his blower round the face, the blower pushed the frail old man out of the way, blew and played at the same time. His music, original Froberger music, engulfed the hall, astounded the listeners, was identified by the connoisseurs. He was brought before the King, told his story, was made to play the harpsichord, had a gold chain put round his neck. As in Vienna, he became the darling of the Court.

Here the goblin intervened again. For the second time in his life Froberger abandoned fame and security and went in search of something else. He returned to Vienna only to find himself forgotten and unwanted. He resigned his still valid title of Emperor's Organist and went into retirement, jotting down notes for an autobiography he did not really want to write, editing compositions he did not really want to see in print. They were published after his death and were highly thought of. To his dying day he missed the sound of applause, the splendour of two courts, the intoxicating tumult of success.

'Some fortunate artists,' Halévy concluded his paper, 'find the memory of past successes so sweet that they never detach themselves from it. However distant in time, they derive from it a lifelong happiness. They garland themselves with evergreen laurels, singing their own praises and getting intoxicated on the slightest handclap. The unfortunate ones however cannot think without heartache of past glories which with every passing day sink deeper into oblivion. The memory of bygone triumphs is for them so bitter and painful that it pursues them like remorse. Froberger was one of those unfortunates.'[2]

After his death Halévy's intimates said that in that final passage he was writing about himself, laying bare his own soul. In 1854 however *Froberger* was quoted, together with *Britton le Charbonnier*, as evidence of erudition, for the narrative was a framework for learned observations on comparative music patronage in seventeenth-century France, Germany and England. He was elected on 29 July, just over three weeks after his predecessor's demise.

His first public appearance in his new capacity took place on Saturday 7 October, the first Saturday in October having become the fixed day for the open session of the Academy of Fine Arts. It was a festive occasion for which Members of the Institute of France turned up in their green-embroidered black uniforms. The official uniform of the Life Secretary was more elaborate. Designed at the turn of the century, it was meant to be truly French, shedding all trace of foreign fashion. It consisted of knee breeches, a frilled shirt with ruffles, a long black coat and sword dangling down the wearer's left thigh. That was how the Life Secretary was dressed in 1819 when a young Halévy was awarded his Prix de Rome. In 1848 when Raoul Rochette, then in his ninth year of office, donned his gala dress as usual and set out for the annual session, he was booed in the streets and all but stripped of his bizarre costume which was a reminder of royalist oppression. He returned to his house, took it off and never wore it again. Four years later Halévy tacitly followed the precedent. For all his official functions as Life Secretary he wore the less conspicuous academician's suit.

The annual open session followed a pattern which had become as sacrosanct as a classic play. The prologue was spoken by the chairman. In Act One the Life Secretary would read out assessments of work despatched from the Villa Medici by laureates of all categories. In Act Two, the most exciting and eagerly awaited part of the session, he would announce the names of that year's winners of the Prix de Rome in all categories . After the excitement and the applause the audience would settle down for Act Three, the Life Secretary's learned paper. The epilogue was the performance of the cantata which had won its young composer that year's Prix de Rome for music.

Halévy's assessments of work despatched from Rome by music laureates were noted for their tactful combination of uncompromising standards and encouragement. Of a *Messe sollennelle* by Léonce Cohen, an 1852 laureate, he said: 'The style is not always as elevated as the subject demands, but he has verve and warmth. He is to be congratulated and encouraged.'[3] Of the 1851 laureate Delechelle he said: 'We invite him to show more application to his studies and not indulge a tendency for facile writing which is detrimental to his composition and nips in the bud those good qualities which we recognise in him.'[4] Of the 1850 laureate Charlet who due to a long illness could send only a fragment of a composition, he said: 'His incomplete work reveals clarity and intelligent understanding of orchestration.'[5]

The following October he continued in the same critical yet kindly vein. Of laureate Delechelle he said that 'he has profited by advice and is to be praised.'[6] From Léonce Cohen who had sent in an opera he demanded 'more individuality in his melodies.'[7] For the 1853 laureate Calibert he had a word of warning: 'Do not be facile.'[8] His judgment was later born out by his student Bizet, co-winner of the 1857 Prix de Rome, who before setting off for the Villa Medici called on earlier laureates. 'I pity those idiots,' he wrote to his mother, 'who did not realise how lucky they were to be students at the Academy in Rome. I have noticed that such idiots had not achieved a great deal. Halévy, Thomas, Gounod, Berlioz and Massé have tears in their eyes when they speak of Rome. Leforme, Galibert, L. Cohen etc say that their achievement is nil because they frittered away their time when they were at the Academy.'[9]

The new Life Secretary threw himself into his work with unwaning zeal. He pushed the publication, started and abandoned many times during the past fifty years, of the Dictionary of the Academy of Fine Arts and saw to it that the first volume was ready for distribution in 1858; it consisted of 400 pages of double columns, including more than half the entries under the letter A. He read papers at the annual open sessions of the Academy of Fine Arts, wrote learned articles for publication, chaired meetings and coped with an ever increasing volume of official correspondence.

A case which took up much of his time was that of Carpeaux,

winner of the 1854 Prix de Rome for sculpture, who failed to arrive at the Villa Medici. It appeared that he preferred to dally in Paris. When he did eventually arrive he developed such bad food poisoning that Schnetz, the director of the Villa Medici, acting on medical advice, sent him back to Paris for treatment. Once back in Paris Carpeaux stayed on but claimed his full scholarship money as if he were in Rome. There was an anxious exchange of letters between Director Schnetz and Life Secretary, Life Secretary and the Minister of Education. Meetings of the committee dealing with the case had to be called and chaired, the minutes checked and circulated. Two years later the Director of the Villa Medici informed the Life Secretary that Carpeaux was desirous of returning to Rome to resume his studies, but could not afford the fare. The Life Secretary wrote a tactful and persuasive letter to the Minister and at last, after nearly four years of official correspondence, was able to report to all concerned that the Minister had graciously agreed a travel grant of 3,000 francs.

Equally time-consuming were requests from artists who wished to be elected to the Academy of Fine Arts whenever a vacancy occurred in their special category. Delacroix, who since 1837 had failed to be elected no less then seven times, considered Halévy his best ally. 'Halévy is the only member of the Academy who has always supported me and never let me down these fifteen years,' he wrote in 1854.'[10] In 1857, with the Life Secretary staunchly backing him, he was at long last elected and donned the official dress with its 'green forest watched over by satyres.'[11] A year later when they met at the Institute of France the Life Secretary rebuked the new academician for staying away from meetings of the School of Fine Arts . . .

Another applicant for his support was Berlioz, who on his third attempt in 1854 wrote to a friend: 'I am determined to be as persistent as Eugène Delacroix . . . Halévy worked for me with one hand; what he did with the other I do not know.'[12] When yet another vacancy occurred in 1856 he tried a fourth time, again canvassing Halévy whose recent opera comique *Valentine d'Aubigny* he had damned with faint praise. Halévy graciously conceded that it was indeed a poor opera and appeared to bear no grudge. This time Berlioz was elected. A few years later they joined forced to support Liszt's application for a 'corresponding membership' of the Institute, which was not granted.

With the position of Life Secretary went a grace-and-favour apartment at the Institute of France, where a highly strung Mme Halévy gave free rein to her collector's mania and her compulsive entertaining. In 1854, the year they moved in, she had to be sent to a sanatorium for treatment. Her distraught husband consulted his brother-in-law Hippolyte Rodrigues about the advisability of bringing her back home and sending the four-year old Geneviève to stay with Rodrigues relatives. On 1 December however, when Delacroix called, he found the house 'full of company as usual,' and Mme Halévy much improved. 'They must be very pleased,'[13] he noted in his diary.

For him the Halévys were 'socialites who feel impelled to play cards every night.'[14] He knew them to be deep in debt due to domestic and social extravagance, and wondered how they could achieve a semblance of calm and contentment. All the same it was he who called their home at the Institute 'a true house of Socrates,'[15] with friends pacing up and down, discussing every topic under the sun. If, in the course of a discussion, people were at a loss for a date or a fact, Socrates would go into his study to look it up, turn his library upside down and reappear triumphant with the answer long after everybody had forgotten what the query was. Another frequent visitor remembered Halévy as a reader of dictionaries; he could not look up a word without being seduced by other words, studying them as well, ruing his insatiable inquisitiveness with disarming naivety.

The writer Léon Escudier, who commissioned Halévy to write the entry *Opera* for his Dictionary in spite of his ambivalent attitude to his operas, left a detailed description of his domestic environment at that time:

> His house was like an art gallery. The walls of his drawing room were hung with paintings by great artists as well as souvenirs from distinguished amateurs. A water colour by Princess Clothilde was propped up against a terra cotta plinth by Clodion, a seascape by Gudin was hung under a sketch by Horace Vernet. Side tables with sturdy legs and delicate nests of tables displayed antique masks, statuettes, marble busts, Florentine bronzes, bowls, jugs, ewers, gold-chased gems of every kind. Mme Halévy was the muse of this small art

gallery. From time to time her daughters would come in to brighten it up with their sweet smiles. Halévy, seated at his desk, surrounded by precious mementos, masterpieces of print and chisel, would be working on a new score, a lecture or a contribution to *La Revue*. When needing to relax he would talk to young composers anxious to hear his opinion of their first work. They never left without congratulating themselves on having had the happy idea to turn to him for advice, which was always sound and sensible.[16]

Behind this idealised façade there lurked an anxiety not unnatural in an overworked man in his mid-fifties. At a dinner party attended by a distinguished doctor the talk was of a retired wine merchant who looked seventy but was in fact only fifty-two. The notion was proposed and accepted that retirement was an ageing factor, more noticeable in workers who had been using brawn than in practitioners of intellectual occupations. At another social gathering, with another distinguished doctor present, Halévy mentioned that he had tried many times to keep a diary but every time had to give it up because of his inability to recall everyday events. From someone whose 'extraordinary retentive memory'[17] was a byword it was a staggering admission. He attributed his failing to stress and overwork, but it did not altogether escape the notice of the company that he was suppressing fear of a symptom which could well indicate the onset of early senility.

19

A TIME TO EVERY PURPOSE

*O*NE COLD FEBRUARY EVENING IN 1855, some six months after Halévy had taken up his duties as Life Secretary of the Academy of Fine Arts, Delacroix called at his sumptuous apartment at the Institute of France and left as soon as he could without seeming discourteous. To his diary he confided:

> The heating system is stifling. His poor wife clutters up the place with pots and pans and old pieces of furniture; this new craze will lead her to the poorhouse. He has changed and aged. He looks as if he has been dragged into this against his will. How can he do any serious work in the middle of all this hubbub? His new post at the Academy must take up much of his time and remove him further and further away from the serenity and tranquillity he needs for his work.[1]

Obviously Delacroix need not have worried for early the following year a new three-act opera comique called *Jaguarita* was ready to go into rehearsal. From necessity Halévy had acquired the knack of turning a deaf ear to all but the inner voice within, enabling him to work surrounded by noisy visitors just as poor frozen students were able to work in crowded cafés. 'In the midst of all that noise,' recalled one such visitor, 'he was quite imperturbable. He always kept to hand a stack of staved sheets of paper on which he rapidly broadcast notes like seeds, making them sprout into beautiful melodies.'[2]

Léon recalled occasions when his brother, working at his desk while visitors were having a lively conversation in the same room, would say to them with a disarming smile: ' "Would you mind, dear friends, leaving me on my own for a minute or two?" We knew what he meant. No sooner had we moved into another room than we heard a chord on the piano; inspiration has descended.'[3] Naturally it was not an altogether satisfactory arrangement; he worked better when he could stay at friends' houses where he found the seclusion and tranquillity he needed. Such happy escapes however became rare after he had become Life Secretary.

An interesting light on his method of composing was thrown some years ago by Karl Leich-Galland in *Observations*.[4] Many pages of Halévy's unfinished autographs, he observed, contain the vocal part or parts with the accompaniment of the instruments he considered most important for the piece, usually violins, often snatches of woodwind and brass as well. The staves for the full orchestral score were left temporarily blank. He would then go back and fill in the rest of the orchestration, the various stages of his creativity discernible through his use of different nibs and different colours of ink.

Jaguarita l'Indienne was a collaboration between Saint-Georges and Adolphe de Leuven, a prolific librettist who went on to become the director of the Opéra-Comique. The story takes place in Dutch Guyana in 1772 when Dutch troops and Red Indians were fighting each other. Jaguarita, the ferocious seductive queen of an Indian tribe, has been taken captive and plots the killing of two white officers as ordered by the Great Spirit.

Hector is a newly arrived officer who dislikes war and longs for the quiet life with his Auntie in Holland. Sent out to reconnoitre in the jungle he loses his way, stumbles on something, accidentally lets off his pistol, drops it in fright and just about manages to find his way back to base. His men give him a hero's welcome; they believe it was he who has shot dead the terrible Zam Zam, for his pistol was found next to the dead body. Hector's embarrassed denials are taken for modesty.

The Indians prepare to liberate their queen. Maurice, another Dutch officer, stands guard outside her cell and falls under her spell. She offers him drugged wine, lets in her tribesman Jumbo, and together they drag Maurice to an Indian encampment.

There they meet Hector and his men, taken prisoner during a failed expedition to the Blue Mountain. Hector cannot stop laughing; a captive Dutch doctor thinks he has gone mad; the men think that laughing in the face of death is the hallmark of courage.

Jaguarita has Maurice brought before her, tells him that she loves him, would marry him and make him King of her tribe. Jumbo wants Maurice to renounce his loyalty to the Whites. The White Man prefers death to betrayal even if the prize is the woman he loves. Jaguarita, truly in love, shows him a secret way out.

News arrives that the Dutch settlement has been taken over by the Indians. Jaguarita rushes to the danger spot, gets her Indians drunk on western 'fire water' and frees all white prisoners. Maurice embraces her tenderly; Hector goes on laughing; Jumbo vows to fight the Dutch to his last drop of blood.

Jaguarita l'Indienne was premiered on 14 May 1855 at the Théâtre-Lyrique which had been launched a few years earlier as the Opéra-National, with Halévy contributing to a skit entitled *Les premiers pas*. Its avowed aim was to put on new works which would be socially and musically more adventurous than the conventional operas comiques of the day, without encroaching on the character of grand opera. *Jaguarita* fitted the brief; it introduced the issue of colonialism and, although it bowed to convention when it made the Indian queen abandon her people and go into a white man's arms, it allowed Jumbo to develop into a true freedom fighter and Hector into a lovable coward who sees no sense in colonial antics.

As with some of Halévy's earlier successes, *Jaguarita* had a slow start. There was the usual malaise about the magnificence of the set overshadowing the originality of the music. The well-wishing reviewer of *La Revue et gazette musicale* rose to its defence. 'A pleasing text, lovely music,' he informed his readers, 'Ballets, costumes, exotic places flooded with light – something for every taste. My own preference is for the music and its interpreters. However, to satisfy the demands of the country we live in, concessions must be made to the taste of a populace who want to feast their eyes.'[5]

The Théâtre-Lyrique management felt that the opera needed a boost. Halévy, Saint-Georges and Leuven, concealing their identity under the name Alberti, provided a one-act curtain raiser called *L'Inconsolable* which on 13 June began to run jointly with *Jaguarita*. Twenty performances later it was dropped while the main work went on from strength to strength. The apparent draw was the exotic scenery but, as in the case of some earlier Halévy operas, those who came to see returned to listen. One attentive listener was Léon Kreutzer of *La Revue et gazette musicale* who wrote:

> The andante of the overture is charming; one of those sonorous edifices which M. Halévy so excels in constructing over a seemingly frail foundation. The horn sounds the dominant A, and the orchestra envelops it with all kinds of delicate lightly sketched melodies, arabesques and varied harmonies. The allegro though could be easily dropped.'

Of Hector's aria in the first act he wrote:

> Hector van Trump has only two verses to sing but they are very pretty and very jolly. His music already characterises this modest timid fellow whom the authors were pleased to make their hero.'

The young Belgian soprano Marie Cabel in the title role was a hit; even the earnest Léon Kreutzer was undecided about what he admired most – her beautiful supple voice or her stunning wardrobe:

> In the third act she wore a costume made entirely of plumage: plumes of colibri, plumes of the six-vaned Guyanese bird of paradise, plumes of other birds of paradise. The entire plumed species paid homage to the incomparable warbler, with the possible exception of ravens and geese.[6]

The one discerning voice was Berlioz's. Ignoring the satirical element of the opera he took composer and librettists to task for encouraging the cult of the 'innocent savage' and making credulous young people believe that anything savage and South American was pure and unspoilt:

> I fear that in *Jaguarita* Messrs Halévy, Saint-Georges and Leuven . . . have produced a work which is dangerous for the young men in the Boulevard de Temple [address of the Théâtre-Lyrique]. These enthusiasts rarely cross the Atlantic and have little chance to wake up to realities. Here they are, most of them, a prey to snares and delusions. Some practise archery in their garrets, other manufacture

poisoned arrows by dipping them in blue wine; some eat raw flesh, others scalp wigged heads. All would run naked in the sunshine if the sun came out; and all for the love of a Guyanese woman who has taken possession of their souls, set their hearts on fire and made their blood boil. Mme Cabel who plays this part is guilty of adding further prestige to poetical delusions by lending them the seductive power of her civilised charms.[7]

Jaguarita had eighty-four performances in its first year and many more during the next six. It was one of Halévy's greatest successes for some time and the Théâtre-Lyrique's longest run since its foundation. Reports of its continuing popularity inspired an English adaptation by A.G. Harris and T.J. Williams who transformed the Red Indian Jaguarita into the Red Indian Pocahontas and the Dutch officers into American settlers. Shorn of the satirical element which was part of its charm, the libretto was set to music by the Irish composer Wallace and premiered at London's Covent Garden in October 1863 under the title *The Desert Flower*. It made little impact.

Writing was another aspect of Halévy's many-faceted personality. His early essays were mostly about Cherubini, but his insatiable quest for knowledge widened his scope to include early music, history of the French opera, painting, architecture. 'He was one of the small number of artists who had the gift of writing,' recalled his archaeologist friend Vinet. 'For most artists writing entails inextricable difficulties and unsuspected pitfalls. For Halévy it was just another talent in which he excelled, beautifully complementing his musical achievement. To those who congratulated him on an accomplishment which could well be the envy of the most skilful of professional writers he would say with a smile that he owed it to necessity which forced musicians to wield a pen more often than sculptors or painters.'[8] In twenty-seven years his published output did not fall far short of half a million words.

His writing did not have Wagner's heavy intellectualism, Berlioz's entertaining wickedness or Marmontel's honeyed turn of phrase; it did have the lucidity of a good brain and the art of the pedagogue who knew how to impart his erudition in a beguiling form. In 1857 he published his *Leçons de lecture musicale*, a textbook commissioned by the Ministry of Education for the teaching of singing in the municipal schools of Paris. His mixture of clarity and imaginative explanations – the first musicians known to mankind were the birds, the octave was created by God, an orchestra is a family whose members are not always in accord – was new and refreshing. Three years later the book was enlarged and reprinted. 'To this day it is one of the most outstanding and useful works in the music teaching profession,'[9] wrote Léon Escudier, the younger of the Escudier brothers who compiled and published a distinguished musical dictionary.

In *Lettres sur la musique* Halévy proposed the musical re-organisation of the universe according to the gospel of Gervasius, a learned German composer invented for the purpose. It was sheer fantasy into which he wove his views on the place of music in a modern society, the instruments of the orchestra, the range of the human voice. In Gervasius's brave new world, at the Hour of Music, everything would come to a standstill – work, intrigues, passions. The artisan would drop his hammer, the legislator would step down from his dais, the writer would put aside his pen, the soldier his sword. Everybody would join in the singing. There would be no rank, discrimination, or political parties. The singers would be known by the range: soprano, mezzo-soprano, alto, tenor, baritone, bass. At the signal all voices of the choir would soar up to heaven.

A serious piece of writing which affected western music all over the world was his excellent report entitled *Le Diapason normal*. In July 1858 the Ministry of Education appointed a twelve-member commission 'to explore the means of establishing in France a uniform standard pitch, determine an unchangeable measure of sound which would serve as a norm, and suggest ways and means to ensure its adoption and observance.' What prompted the Ministry to take action was the growing tendency to raise the pitch which 'presents difficulties to music, composers, singers and manufacturers of music instruments,' and the realisation 'that the difference which exists in the pitch used by various countries, musical institutions and factories is a constant source of discord for ensembles and commercial contracts.'[10]

The Commission included Auber, Berlioz, Meyerbeer, Rossini and Thomas, two physicists, a general in charge of military music, and two theatre advisers. Its titular President was a Ministerial Counsellor but its virtual head was Halévy who made the project known to music institutions in Germany, England, Belgium, Holland, Italy, Russia and America and obtained their co-operation. His report, presented to the Ministry within six months, traced the history of the rising pitch from 1699 to 1856 and gave tables illustrating the comparative differences noted in various institutions and countries. France used a wide range of pitches; London used three, with Covent Garden's too high for some visiting French singers; Berlin and St. Petersburg used the highest, Karlsruhe the lowest.

The conclusion was that it was desirable to lower the pitch and have the lowered pitch generally adopted as an unchangeable norm. As worded by Halévy, 'The Commission recommends the establishment of a uniform pitch for all music institutions in France and having it fixed at 870 vibrations per second [equivalent to 435Hz] for the sound of *la* [A] at a temperature of 15 centigrades.'[11]

On 16 February 1859 the recommendations became law and an Imperial decree proclaimed its enforcement as from 1 July 1860 in Paris and 1 December 1860 in the provinces. The French decree encouraged international recognition of the need for universal standard pitch. It has since been revised and fixed differently, the accepted frequency now being 440 Hz for the sound of A directly above middle C. Of all Halévy's contributions to the advancement of music his work on the *Diapason normal* is perhaps the least known and the most universally beneficial.

In between composing, writing, teaching and attending to the never-ending concerns of a Life Secretary, he found time to contribute to the developing liturgical music of the Paris Jewish consistory.

He had drifted away from religious observance in his early twenties, but like many of his emancipated coreligionists he retained an inalienable loyalty to his faith and heritage. *La Juive* engulfed him more than any other work of his ever did. Helpful as he was to those who sought his advice he was perhaps even more so if they were Jewish. When the young brothers Offenbach made their first steps in Paris he went as far as to write to their father Isaac Offenbach, a cantor in a Cologne synagogue, that he would gladly do what he could for them, particularly for Jacques for whom he foresaw a great future.

His marriage to Léonie in 1842, celebrated in a synagogue, marked the beginning of his involvement with Jewish cultural life. Soon he was asked by the Jewish consistory of Paris, as was the Jewish pianist composer Alkan (1813–1888), to audition the young cantor Samuel Naumbourg, recently arrived from Germany, for the post of director of music at the synagogue in rue Notre-Dame-de-Nazareth. Alkan's report has not been found but Halévy's, dated 19 June 1845, was most favourable:

> I was able for form an opinion of his musical studies, and read his compositions. I am of the opinion that he is most suitable to be called to the important position now vacant and that he is capable of elevating it to the height of its true aim. He is keen, motivated by a desire to do well, and should give the organisation good musical service, talent and commitment.[12]

On his appointment Naumbourg began compiling an anthology of traditional liturgical songs. His great innovation was to include, for the first time in the history of Jewish liturgy in France, songs for soloists and choir commissioned from professional composers. Among the hundreds of traditional ones published in the first two volumes of his *Zemirot Yisrael* (Chants of Israel) in 1847 and the third volume published in 1865 under the sub-title *Shirey Kodesh* (Sacred Songs) there were two or three by Alkan, one by Meyerbeer, and seven by Halévy. His 1874 anthology *Aggudat Shirim* (A Posy of Songs) posthumously included three more Halévy settings.

For Halévy it was a return to the book of Psalms which had inspired his youthful De Profundis, and a fresh look at the Pentateuch and the prayer book. Now as then he used the original Hebrew text. His published settings were:

Psalm 100, 1–4	:	*Hariu la'adonay*
Psalm 115, 12–17	:	*Adonay zecharanu* in A flat
Psalm 115, 12–17	:	*Adonay zecharanu* in G
Psalm 118, 1–4	:	*Hodu la'adonay ki tov*
Psalm 118, 5–24	:	*Min hametsar*
Psalm 118, 25	:	*Ana adonay*
Psalm 122, 2–4	:	*Samahti be'omrim li*
Numbers 10, 35	:	*Vayehi binso'a ha'aron*
Deuteronomy 6, 4	:	*Shema Israel*
Prayer	:	*Yigdal*

The setting of *Adonay zecharanu* in A flat, calling for soloists, choir and an orchestra, was composed for the grand wedding ceremony on 2 May 1858 of Edgard Rodrigues, a nephew of Léonie's. The other nine settings, less ambitiously scored, were written for either tenor, bass, treble, soprano solos, or a combination of them, with or without organ, sometimes with harp, mostly with a choir. The three settings of Psalm 118 and the *Shema Israel* arranged for cantor and treble were reprinted in 1879 in a Book of Songs produced by the synagogue in rue de la Victoire and remained in use for many years.

Involvement with synagogue music led to further demands on his time. He assisted and sometimes chaired committees which selected songs for inclusion in the traditional service, participated in discussions about the rights and wrongs of introducing an organ into synagogue. When the issue was favourably resolved Alkan was offered the position of organist, which he promptly accepted and just as promptly gave up. It was Halévy's duty to invite him to his house to elicit the reason for his resignation.

In due course an anthology was published of Sephardi (oriental) liturgical melodies, as distinct from the mostly Ashkenazi (western) ones in Naumbourg's collection. The anthologist Emile Jonas, a Conservatoire graduate, sent Halévy a pre-publication copy for his opinion. On 7 August 1854, only a week after his election, the Life Secretary of the French Academy of Fine Arts graciously wrote to his coreligionist:

> The songs you have composed are simple, expressive and easy to perform, which adds to their merit . . . Do continue to devote your studies and young talent to the service of the faith to which we both belong.[13]

Driving himself as hard as he did, an occasional holiday was essential. For some years past the Halévys, like all good Parisians, made a habit of spending at least part of the summer away from the metropolis. Once of twice they stayed at Bougival or Auteuil, but their favourite retreat was Fromont, a vacant château with vast grounds sloping down to the Seine near Corbeil, within easy reach of Paris. In 1853, after several successful holidays with wife and daughters, Halévy acquired it jointly with his wealthy stockbroker brother-in-law Hippolyte Rodrigues. A landscape gar-

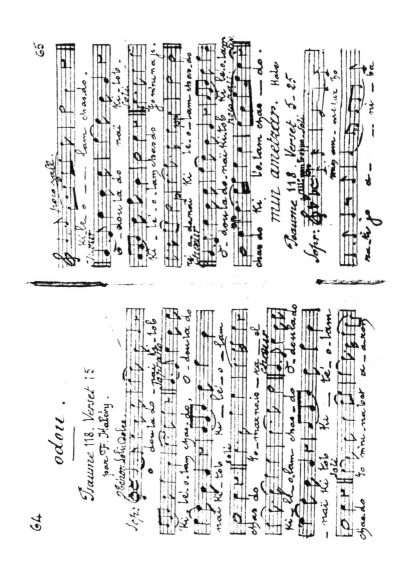

dener gradually turned the grounds into a horticulturist's paradise. On the other bank of the river was Champrosay, Delacroix's country retreat, where he worked and grew vegetables. It was a goodly walk from one residence to the other, but neighbourly visits were paid and returned, sometimes by arrangement, sometimes on the spur of the moment.

Delacroix's diary mentions many such visits. In October 1853, as he was working in his studio, in burst Mme Halévy, her two daughters and a Mme Villet with a brother and a large umbrella. At first he was annoyed, then rather pleased. On the 11th of that month he dined at Fromont and wondered, not for the first time either, how the Halévys could keep 'such a magnificent establishment.'[14] Another dinner guest, a general, loudly informed his hosts that the house was falling apart and needed a thorough overhaul. Some sixty or seventy years later it was demolished by developers to make way for a housing estate.

After the opening of *Jaguarita* Halévy's stays at Fromont were short and unpredictable. On 3 June 1855 Delacroix met Rodrigues and his son riding in the woods and was told that Halévy was in residence. By 14 June both he and his brother-in-law had already returned to Paris; Delacroix dined with Mme Rodrigues and her artist son and noticed that the grounds included 'some of the most beautiful trees in the world' and that 'the view of the Seine from the terrace is lovely, even grand.'[15] On the 17th Halévy was back at Fromont but unusually taciturn; the fate of *Jaguarita* hung in the balance, depending on *L'Inconsolable* which had opened a few days earlier. By 1 July the news from Paris was heartening and friends were entertained in the shade of the trees away from the heat of the sun.

In September the family returned to Paris. Halévy was back in harness, attending to his voluminous official correspondence, putting the final touches to a paper on the French composer of English descent Georges Onslow (1784–1853) he was due to read at the forthcoming open session of the Academy of Fine Arts and, above all, immersing himself in a new opéra comique.

20

LAST WORKS

*J*ULES BARBIER AND MICHEL CARRE were two young librettists who turned out insubstantial plots which often proved successful pegs for charming music. In the late 1850's and early 60's they would graduate to dramatic work for Gounod and Bizet; for Halévy they wrote *Valentine d'Aubigny*, a three-act opera comique set at the beginning of the eighteenth century.

Valentine is an orphan country girl of aristocratic stock who is going to Paris to find her childhood sweetheart Gilbert de Mauleon. Gilbert sets out to the country with the same object in mind. They put up at the same halfway inn but, as they have not met since childhood, they fail to recognise each other.

Other guests at the inn are the Chevalier de Boisrobert and his mistress Sylvia the actress whom he has rashly promised to marry. He points out that young Gilbert would be a better catch and persuades her to impersonate the unknown Valentine. Valentine discovers the deception and under a false name becomes Sylvia's companion. The four return to Paris.

In Paris Valentine, concealed from view, sings an old folk song which Gilbert remembers from his childhood visits. He believes Sylvia is the singer and asks her to marry him, but both she and the Chevalier have second thoughts. After a great many complications, including forged letters, two identical bouquets of flowers and a harmless duel, the truth comes out. Gilbert and the real Valentine are blissfully in love, the repentant actress and her Chevalier bow out.

Opening night on 26 April 1856 at the Opéra-Comique was a glittering occasion. The Emperor Louis Napoleon honoured it with his presence and 'was not one of the last to applaud.'[1] Claque and high society went on clapping, composer and singers took many curtain calls. The music was praised by Saint-Yves of *La Revue et gazette musicale*:

> The score M. Halévy wrote for this romantic subject is worthy of its predecessors, *L'Eclair*, *Les Mousquetaires* and *Le Val d'Andorre*. Again we hear his inspired melodies, lyrical, elegant, perfectly crafted . . . Nobody will be surprised to learn that M. Halévy has treated with a masterly touch all the dramatic situations which need energy and breadth; nobody will be surprised when we add that his more impressive numbers are those which are naive, lively and light.[2]

Berlioz began with double-edged praise and ended with his usual peroration:

> The score is one of M. Halévy's best, written with remarkable care and delicacy . . . nothing banal, petty, Parisian. It is the music of a Master whom we can hardly rebuke except for the fierceness of the accompaniment in certain scenes, particularly in the third act.[3]

After twenty-three performances the opera was taken off. Paris audiences, brought up on the French tradition which set store by a good libretto, were getting intolerant of operas comiques with little substance. In January they had welcomed Adam's *Falstaff*, in February Auber's *Manon Lescaut*. The so-called poem of *Valentine d'Aubigny* could not bear comparison. The same Saint-Yves who had praised the music described the libretto as futile, false, improbable, a comic work masquerading as drama. Léon Halévy explained what had prompted his brother to accept it:

> It was another of those errors of judgment about a libretto which, oddly enough, he made with his eyes wide open and which he would long regret; it turned people away from his most beautiful music. When working on a conventional opera comique whose nature is somewhat akin to vaudeville he favoured the Spanish-inspired comedy of intrigue which calls for the development of character. If the plot did not lend itself to the expression of passion he would not content himself with depicting just the grotesque and the ridiculous; he wanted to express some aspects of the heart and soul, with a touch

of original buffoonery . . . He put his theory to the test by accepting *Valentine*.[4]

Halévy was despondent; he had taken a calculated risk and lost. The public who for twenty years had adored his operas comiques from *L'Eclair* to *Jaguarita* kept away from his latest. He had to prove himself all over again. Little did he suspect that *Valentine d'Aubigny* would unleash unremitting revulsion and hostility.

Spurred on as he had been all his life by failure as much as by success he immediately embarked on a new work. In fact he embarked on two new works, both provisionally accepted by the Opéra. The first was *Vanina d'Ornano* with libretto by his brother Léon; the second was *La Magicienne* with libretto by Saint-Georges.

Vanina d'Ornano was set in Corsica and told the story of one of the island's many attempts to overthrow the rule of Genoa. The brothers Halévy worked hard and soon had two acts ready. Just then the Opéra management changed its plans and indicated preference for the other. The two acts were jettisoned, sharing the fate of *Erostrate*, the brothers' youthful collaboration of 1825.

La Magicienne was based on the legend of Melusine Countess of Lusignan who had sold her soul to the devil; beautiful by day, she turned into a repellent sorceress by night. It was a popular legend which Mendelssohn had used some twenty-five years earlier in his overturn *Die schöne Melusine*.

In Saint-Georges' version a crusader called René is on his way home from Palestine to marry his fiancée Blanche de Poitou. On her nightly prowl Melusine notices him asleep in a forest and falls in love with him. Her Master, Stello the necromancer, fears he may lose his hold over her.

René arrives safely at Château Poitou and renews his vows to Blanche. A disguised and veiled Melusine whispers in his ear: 'Your fiancée has been deceiving you. Meet me at midnight in the château garden.' When he does she conjures up an image of Blanche throwing a bunch of flowers to her page. The following morning René accuses the real Blanche of infidelity and she seeks refuge in a convent. Before Melusine has a chance to enjoy her triumph Stello the necromancer exposes her to René for what she is. The horrifying transformation of a beautiful woman into a repellent sorceress was a triumph of stagecraft, achieved by an ingenious use of green lights and dark shadows.

The final scene takes place outside a deserted castle near the convent where Blanche has been hiding. Melusine, touched by grace, affirms her belief in God. Stello and his devils try to wrench her back; Blanche, René and the nuns pray for her soul. In a foretaste of *Götterdämmerung* the castle comes crumbling down, the powers of evil are engulfed in flames. Fire and brimstone dissolve into three beautiful processions: village girls with the bride, her father the Count with his knights, the Abbess with her nuns. Melusine dies forgiven by God and man.

The five-act *La Magicienne* was premiered at the Opera on 17 March 1858. Berlioz gave his readers an entertaining account of High Society's way with five-act operas whoever the composer:

> People complain of the immense length of a five-act opera. What they actually see is a three-and-a-half act opera, because High Society strolls in only in the middle of Act II, or even later. Whatever time it starts, be it seven, half past seven or eight, they take up their seats only at nine o'clock . . . What matters is to be seen on Opening Night and being able to say *I was there* . . . A composer who has written an admirable first act is sure to see it performed to a hall three-quarters empty and receive nothing better than the approbation of the claque . . . Nowadays we are given a new opera only once in two years. The public should abandon its habits and hear a first performance of a new work in its entirety. Naturally this is too much to ask. Even the most marvellous inspiration of a great composer will not induce gentlemen and ladies to put forward by as little as a quarter of an hour the dinner time of their horses.[5]

Berlioz, who was known to miss the occasional overture because of his own lingering over dinner, was put out when he realised that Halévy had not written one for *La Magicienne*. 'I think he is right to dispense with an overture,' he decided on second thoughts. 'Works of such magnitude, which offer a composer so many opportunities to be prodigal with his gifts, can do without such an introduction. In any case Mendelssohn has already written an overture for Melusine.'[6] As usual he disliked the orchestration and complained that Halévy, not content with his habitual complement of loud instruments, added an oriental tom-tom as well.

Saint-Yves thought that the libretto was 'not exactly a master-piece of invention,' while the music was disappointing:

> *La Magicienne* has not fulfilled its expectations. This is not a judge-ment, just a statement. It is impossible to base an irrevocable opinion on the strength of a single hearing. However, when an opera conceals somewhere in its depths beauties of the first order, it is rare for at least some of them not to surface right away. We kept looking for them but could not find any.[7]

The most damning judgment was pronounced by a former student of Halévy's in a letter to another — the forty-year old Gounod in Paris to the twenty-year old Prix de Rome laureate Bizet at the Villa Medici:

> I have heard it twice, the third and fourth acts three times. It seems to me that this work which at times still bears witness to the high intelligence of its author shows a regrettable drying up of the source of inspiration; the melody is starved of life, top-heavy and leaning on the claque.[8]

Happily for Halévy, and not for the first time either, the public trusted a word of mouth recommendation more than a pro-fessional assessment. When Berlioz attended the second night he noticed that most of the boxes were occupied well before the start of Act II, which was 'an indication of remarkable success.'[9] Parisians liked both legend and music so well that *La Magicienne* had forty-five performances. The regulations of the Opéra stipu-lated that any work which exceeded a run of forty was considered a financial success and awarded its composer points on his pension fund. Of Halévy's ten, from the ballet opera *Manon Lescaut* in 1830 to *La Magicienne* in 1858, eight had qualified for the award.

His next choice of subject was unusual for him — the Old Testament story of the flood as dramatised and embellished by Saint-Georges. The Opéra management originally scheduled it as the 'novelty' of the 1860 season but after four acts had been completed decided to postpone it for a year or two. Halévy offered it to the Théâtre-Lyrique and while negotiations were in progress began looking for a new subject. The score of *Noé* was put away in cardboard boxes.

Knowing of his quest, the writer and music critic Blaze de Bury sent him a copy of his book *Le Koenigsmark* offering to turn it into a libretto. It was the latest romanticised version of a scandal which had been intriguing the courts of Europe for more than a hundred-and-fifty years. In 1682 sixteen-year old Princess Sophie Dorothea of Celle was married to Prince George Louis of Hanover for dynastic reasons and bore him a son and a daughter. The palace protocol was stultifying, the mother-in-law Electress Sophia was hostile, George Louis kept mistresses. After nine years of unhappy married life Sophie Dorothea fell in love with the dashing Swedish Count Koenigsmark and planned to elope with him. On the night of the elopement he failed to turn up, murdered on the orders of his one-time mistress Countess Platen, or so myth would have it. The errant husband punished his unfaithful wife by putting her under house arrest for the rest of her life. De Bury made no mention of the historical fact that in due course George Louis Elector of Hanover became King George I of England.

The plot had all the ingredients of a successful grand opera – an innocent young bride, scornful mistress, scheming courtiers, love's awakening, jealousy, murder and revenge. Halévy was enthralled. 'I read it, I believe in it, I see it,' he wrote to Blaze de Bury on 5 May 1860. 'When shall we talk?'[10] The talk led to a working plan which three months later yielded the libretto for the first two acts of a five-act opera called *Koenigsmark*.

That summer the Halévys spent their holiday at Le Tréport, an up-and-coming seaside resort near Dieppe. Halévy took de Bury's first two acts with him and on 22 August 1860 he wrote:

> A thousand thanks for the material you sent and the charming writing of these two acts. Countess Platen's aria is excellent and I composed the music while reading the words. Please do not stop and send more nourishment to one who has a voracious appetite.[11]

De Bury sent off arias, trios, quartets and a finale. Halévy was enthusiastic:

> Bravo! And thanks again. It is a splendid scenario and I keep turning it round in my mind. I should be pleased if I could enter into the spirit of it as successfully as you did. Everything has turned out well with your part of the work; you are condemning me to compose a masterpiece.[12]

His euphoric mood soon evaporated. He was beset by doubts. On his return from his summer holiday he wrote to de Bury:

> Opera fans fancy themselves as persons of great erudition, so we must not show them up. We must offer them stories of well-known heroes. Give them a Medici in Florence, an Este in Ferrara, a Visconti in Milan and they will be able to follow and understand without difficulty. But these fiendish German and Swedish words! How does one pronounce them in music? And who cares about a Hanoverian court anyhow? What rank is an Elector in operatic hierarchy? Hardly higher than your ordinary Parisian from any of the twenty Paris arrondissements. An Electress is hardly more noteworthy than any lady from the Faubourg St. Germain.[13]

He felt it would be wiser to transfer the background to Renaissance Italy and set it on the banks of the Po or the Arno. While in this mood he tried to rekindle interest in *Noé* and approached the Minister of Fine Arts who was a friend and an admirer. The Opéra Director was nudged into acquiescence and scheduled it for the 1862 season. *Koenigsmark* was dropped, cardboard boxes were retrieved. He worked feverishly on the fifth act, the dramatic climax of the flood, steeling himself to six months of rehearsals, staging problems, arguments with singers demanding more arias or longer arias than he felt their parts warranted. He did not live to see the work through. Some ten years later it was completed by Bizet as a three-act opera called *Le Déluge*. Paris was not interested. It was not until 1885, when Halévy and Bizet had both been long dead, that it had its first performance, in Karlsruhe.

Halévy's contemporaries often accused him of being a butterfly, never settling for long on any one subject. He was said to be inclined to follow the whim of the moment, drop one project for another, abandon something halfway through, start on a new idea, drive himself ruthlessly for a while only to drop whatever he had started in order to resume a work earlier abandoned. Whether it was a fault which affected the quality of his compositions or, on the contrary, an instinct which allowed his subconscious a period of gestation while he was engaged on something totally different, is a moot point. Some said it was sheer indolence. At the height of his glory, when he put off correcting Wagner's proofs of a piano reduction of *La Reine de Chypre* in order to do something more creative, his publisher Schlesinger accused him of incorrigible laziness. By contrast, friends who survived him said that it was overwork that hastened his death. Whichever way one looked at it, his output was not that of a truant; his thirty-odd performed operas were interspersed with as many small vocal pieces, cantatas, piano and instrumental works.

Among his last was a cantata set to words by his librettists of the day Jules Barbier and Michel Carré, composed while *Valentine d'Aubigny* was in rehearsal. It was performed at the Opéra-Comique on Monday 17 March 1856, the day on which Paris theatres opened their doors to the public free of charge. Halévy's cantata was the fourth item on a long programme and the only one noticed by the press: 'Its impact was such that it had to be encored.'[14]

Three other works were inspired by France's foreign policy of the time. Louis Napoleon had come to a secret understanding, which did not stay secret for long, with Cavour, Minister to Victor Emmanuel King of Sardinia, to liberate Italy from the yoke of the Austrians and help it to achieve unification. When the Italian War broke out in April 1859 French troops played an active part. Two months later a joint victory was won. On Sunday, Monday and Tuesday, 5, 6 and 7 June, Paris theatres were brightly illuminated and celebratory works were performed. Halévy's cantata *Italie*, to words by Saint-Georges, was performed at the Opéra-Comique on the Tuesday by four of its leading soloists and choir.

The following year, when Nice and Savoy were returned to French rule in consideration of Louis Napoleon's help, there were further celebrations. Immersed as he then was in *Koenigsmark*, he marked the occasion with two works for four voices, *La Nouvelle alliance* and *France et Italie*. Both were composed for the Orphéon, France's great choral society which had branches all over the country.

In the fantasy world described in *Lettres sur la musique*, Halévy had erected a Temple to Music. That was the temple where he worshipped; composition was an act of faith, something to cling to in good times and in bad, in youth and in old age. He had his composer's blocks, he allowed himself to be lured hither and thither, but he never strayed from the path of artistic integrity.

Talent was a privilege bestowed by providence, not to be trivialised or misused. 'Whether composing something grand or small,' Léon wrote, 'he worked scrupulously and conscientiously. He served his art with respect, faith and fervour.'[15]

21

AND TIME TO DIE

AFTER AN ABSENCE OF EIGHTEEN
years Wagner returned to Paris where in late January and early
February 1860 the Théâtre-Italien gave three concerts of his
music. The press was scathing but Halévy, Wagner heard, had
expressed approval. He called on him at his residence at the
Institute Palace and later wrote:

> He seemed particularly eager to learn from my own lips what my new
> theory about music really was, of which he had heard such wild
> rumours. For his own part, he said, he had never found anything in
> my music but music, with this difference that mine had generally
> seemed very good. This gave rise to a lively discussion on my part, to
> which he good-humouredly agreed.[1]

It was their first meeting since the early 1840's, when a young
Wagner was making ends meet by working on a piano reduction
of *La Reine de Chypre* and a successful Halévy was a fêted composer. Wagner was appalled to see how much he had aged, how
life's experience had sapped his resilience. 'From this final visit,'
he recalled, 'I carried away a depressing sense of enervation, both
moral and aesthetic, which had overcome one of the last great
French composers.'[2]

By that time he had published in Germany the first edition of
his essay *Das Judenthum in der Musik*, of which Halévy would have
been aware even though it contained no covert personal insinua-

tions against him. That he received Wagner graciously would have been in character; that he was interested in his music was only natural. In the spring of 1861 the Opéra gave three performances of *Tanhäuser* for which Wagner had composed a new Bacchanale and Venusberg scene. The first, on 13 March, was an Imperial Command performance and the distribution of tickets was mainly, though not solely, in the hands of court officials. Halévy wrote to the Opéra for tickets for the first night and also managed to obtain a dress circle box for the dress rehearsal for Léonie's relative the Jewish philanthropist Edouard Rodrigues. Wagner was reported highly gratified.

They had both been long dead when their names were jointly invoked. In 1933, in a Paris where German Jews were already seeking refuge from Nazism, the Opéra revived *La Juive* after more than forty years. It had mixed reviews. The music critic of *Le Temps* did not mince his words: 'Let's open our eyes and, except for the second act and part of the third, let's shut our ears.' However, conscientious reviewer that he was, he took notice of what Wagner had written some ninety years earlier and quoted his judgment to justify some favourable comment of his own about other sections of the work. 'Paradoxically,' writes musicologist D. Van Moere, 'it is perhaps Wagner who has saved Halévy from oblivion.'[3]

1861 was drawing to a close. Halévy's health was giving cause for concern. His energy was failing, the spark had gone. At the Musicians Monday Dinners the once witty conversationalist would sit listless, barely addressing a word to his fellow diners on the right or left. Medical opinion was that he had been driving himself too hard too long and that a rest would help him recover. The few weeks at Le Tréport the previous summer had been so beneficial that he thought of applying for leave of absence from his duties as Life Secretary of the Academy of Fine Arts and professor at the Conservatoire, and return to the seaside, not to idle, but to complete *Noé* without pressure. 'I'm better,' he told friends, 'I'm happy. I must take a good long holiday of two or three months. I'll go back to this little village, I'll take along an opera and finish it. I must do it before I die.'

'You mustn't say things like that,' exclaimed one of his daughters.

'Would you rather have me say I will finish it after I die?' he quipped.[4]

It was decided that a few months' rest-cure in the warm winter sunshine of the South of France would be more beneficial than the unreliable climate of a resort on the Channel coast. A large villa surrounded by trees and flower beds was rented in Nice from a Polish lady who kept part of it for herself and her children. On 23 December 1861 patient, wife, daughters and some indispensable household staff set out for Nice, stopping at Toulon and continuing the rest of the journey by easy stages.

Before his departure Halévy wrote to his old friend the writer and music critic Fiorentino, alluding to the hostility of the press towards him since *Valentine d'Aubigny*. Not only had there been vicious attacks on his work in general but also barbed comments on his persona. Fiorentino recalled:

> He was calm, resigned, somewhat sad. Recently he had been a butt of attacks which he neither provoked nor deserved. He was no more spared than the late Scribe had been. It was not a question of legitimate criticism. I am referring to gratuitous, personal and insulting attacks, meant to draw blood. There was no justification for such violent polemics or heated altercations. I know one should treat such excesses with the contempt they deserve, but there comes a point in life when one is more vulnerable than one cares to admit, when injustice is rendered even more bitter because it is mixed with ingratitude. After years of hard work and success, having earned an indisputable right to contemporary esteem and gratitude, even a steeled soul when feeling forgotten and ignored by a new generation, cannot but succumb to sadness.[5]

Sadness and resignation were not in character. Time and again Halévy had shaken off the pain and bitterness of relative failure, rising up like the just man in Proverbs. Once in Nice, with a better perspective of what was going on in a younger Paris, he regained hope and was looking forward to a speedy return to his busy creative life. His mind was primarily on *Noé*. On 6 January, having heard from his librettist Saint-Georges that the Opéra production team had made some cuts in text and score, he wrote practically, using the informal *tu*:

> I suggest that you begin simply and grandly with Noah's prayer. I am sorry about the cuts because I've given Japheth some lovely little

$\underline{2}$

AUTOGRAPH LETTER OF HALEVY

numbers to sing. Obviously we have to be brief in order to survive. I
hope we will be beautiful. All my love, your old friend F. Halévy.[6]

Life at the Villa Mascet in rue de France soon fell into a pattern. A
local doctor instructed by an eminent Paris physician was in
attendance, the complement of household staff was supple-
mented by a maid whose duty was to help look after the patient.
He took walks, followed a diet, grimaced at his medicines. Esther
gave lessons to her younger sister Geneviève, Léonie issued the
order of the day. Everybody was busily writing letters to friends
and relatives. On fine days a family outing to the local beauty
spots would be arranged. On Sundays they would listen to the
municipal military band playing bits of Halévy, Bellini, Donizetti,
walk up and down the Promenade, exchange greetings with
other promenaders. At four o'clock, the hour of sunset, the
promenaders would hurry away, at five minutes past four everybody would be indoors. In the evening distinguished Niçois
burghers would call to pay their respects, passing Paris singers
would stop by. The great baritone Tamburini who had retired to
Nice entertained the family with his well-preserved voice, the
Master accompanying him at the piano.

He missed the turbulence of Paris life. 'What is new in that
abyss?' he wrote to his close friend Monnais on 4 January, barely
two weeks after his departure. 'How does this huge workshop
behave itself? Do the opera houses sing properly? Has a new star
risen? Do satisfy my curiosity even if you have to embroider a
bit.'[7]

What he was particularly anxious to hear was the latest gossip
about himself, he had to know whether this or that critic was still
pursuing his private vendetta against him. The odd numbers of
Le Constitutionnel which had been sent to him from Paris did not
satisfy his curiosity any more than Monnais did. On 31 January
he circumspectly repeated his request:

> You are bound to know a lot of stories, gossip, anecdotes . . . Surely
> there is a lot of grumbling going on, storms brewing up. Do send me
> some, they won't disturb the serenity of our clear blue sky . . . My
> affectionate regards to you, my dear Monnais, and my respects to
> Mme Monnais. Remember me to those who think of me; no need to
> bother about the others.[8]

At first there seemed to be an improvement in his condition. In

February, when he received from Léon a summary of a tiresome letter from one Ferdinando Morini concerning a monument in Florence to Cherubini, in which he was repeatedly referred to as 'His Most Illustrious Life Secretary' and 'His Most Illustrious Lordship,' he answered in kind:

> My dear brother, this is what I should like you to do. Kindly write to the Lord Morini. Tell him that My Most Illustrious Lordship is in Nice for recuperation and that he should approach the Most Illustrious M. Auber, Director of the Conservatoire; also that the Most Illustrious Prince Poniatowski is only vice-chairman, an honour which I share with him, however undeservedly . . . Also tell him that as soon as my health improves I should be delighted to write a piece for a fund-raising concert in Florence . . .[9]

It was only a remission. The weather was inclement, the coldest spring in years, the Niçois said. There was talk of returning him to Paris. He spent his days on a divan, dependent on others for the slightest service. Communication was difficult. When he once wanted to recline back on the cushions he tried to indicate that he should be lowered gradually: 'like a scale – C, D, E, F. No, you don't understand. It's so simple, like a scale: C, D, E, F.'[10]

Léonie was unable to cope. They had hardly been at the villa three full weeks when she wrote to her brother Hippolyte in Paris:

> Fromental is still weak, does not like his prescribed walks, his prescribed food, his prescribed medicines; he is irritable . . . From time to time two or three people drop in for a game of whist, but we do not wish to see anybody else. We want to rest so that as soon as he feels better he can go back to working on his opera . . .[11]

She was not used to being a *garde-malade*; it was she who had always been taken care of, waited upon hand and foot, sent to various sanatoriums for treatment whenever her precarious mental balance was upset. In spite of Esther and the maid carrying the brunt of the burden she complained:

> You see, my dear Hippo, how busy I am with my Fromental, with his health, with what he thinks, with what he eats, with what might entertain him. I no longer have any other thought in my head . . .[12]

Hippolyte had a word with Léon and a few weeks later reinforcement arrived from Paris in the form of Léon's son Ludovic who was Esther's fiancé, and a Rodrigues relative called Henri Vieyra. Shortly after their arrival Halévy had two attacks of convulsions, the second one fatal. His last hours were described by Ludovic in a letter written to his mother immediately after the demise:

> Last night's attack gave way to a considerable diminution of pain. This morning, from seven to nine, he was better than he was yesterday. He spoke a little, thanked us for looking after him, was very loving to Léonie. Nothing gave us any reason to think that he was aware of his condition. Léonie was beginning to hope again, but the rest of us realised only too well that the peace and calm were the sign of the end.[13]

Léonie retired to take a rest after the exertions of the night's vigil and Esther went to look after her, tiptoeing into her father's room just once. He appeared to understand what was said to him but was no longer able to respond. At about 10 a.m. he indicated that he wished to be got out of bed. He was put on a couch by the window. It was a beautiful spring morning. The children of the Polish lady were playing in the garden, their happy laughter mingling with the chirping of the birds. The lemon trees were in full bloom, their scent rising to the window through which Halévy was taking his last look at the world. Ludovic kept watch.

> There he lay from ten in the morning to three in the afternoon, his life ebbing away . . . You cannot imagine a death more gentle, calm, free of pain . . . He was so quiet at his last moments that the doctor who was with us had to tell us it was all over.[14]

He died in the afternoon of Monday 17 March. Telegrams were sent to relatives who notified the press, arrangements were made to transfer the body to Paris. Three days later coffin and mourners were back at the grand apartment at the Institute Palace from where the funeral would start. An elegant black-edged invitation was sent to a vast number of friends and colleagues:

> You are invited to attend the funeral procession and burial ceremony of Monsieur Jacques-Elie-Fromental Halévy, member of the Institute, Life Secretary of the Academy of Fine Arts, professor at the Imperial Conservatoire of Music, Commander of the Imperial Order of the *Légion d'honneur*, deceased 17 March 1862 in Nice, Maritime Alps, in the sixty-third year of his life, which will be held on Monday,

the 24th instant, at 12 a.m. precisely. Point of assembly – the Institute Palace, 25 quai Conti.[15]

The invitation was sent out on behalf of the family. First on the long list were the chief mourners, the Halévys: Mme Léonie Halévy; Mlles Esther and Geneviève Halévy; M. and Mme Léon Halévy; Mlles Flore and Melanie Halévy [the unmarried sisters]; M. Ludovic Halévy, Mlle Valentine Halévy [Léon's son and daughter]. Then came the Rodrigues clan: M. Hippolyte Rodrigues Henriques [Léonie's brother]; M. and Mme Edgard Rodrigues Henriques; M. Fernand Rodrigues Henriques; M. Adolphe Vieyra Molina; M. and Mme Henri Vieyra [the relative who had come down to Nice for the final stages of Halévy's illness]; M. Alfred Vieyra Molina; M. William Busnach; M. Edouard Rodriques Henriques and Mme Henri Rodrigues Henriques, their respective daughters, brother, sisters, sisters-in-law, nephews, nieces, brother-in-law, cousin, a female cousin – the list offered an interesting insight into the ramifications of Léonie's family. The main text was inserted in the press with a tactful addition: 'The family begs M. Halévy's numerous friends who have not received a letter to regard this announcement as an invitation.'[16]

It was like a state funeral. Contemporary reports estimated that fifteen thousand people attended it; the coffin had already reached the Place de la Concorde when the end of the procession was still stationery at the Institute Palace. At the Jewish section of the cemetery of Montmartre three orchestras and choirs were deployed. A *De Profundis* was sung, composed by Halévy's former students, Jewish and Christian: Gounod, Victor Massé, Bizet, François Bazin, Jules Cohen, Jonas. Rabbis and Jewish choristers performed the burial rites. When the coffin was lowered into the grave the massed orchestras played the *Marche funèbre* from Act V of *La Juive*. No less than eight funeral orations were spoken: by Couder, President of the Academy of Fine Arts; colonel Cerfberr, President of the Central Jewish Consistory; Edouard Monnais, representing the Conservatoire; Ambroise Thomas, representing the Committee of Authors and Dramatic Composers; Baron Taylor, representing the Society of Dramatic Artists; Perrin, Director of the Opéra-Comique; Saint-Georges the librettist; and, for the final word of farewell, Rabbi Ulmann, Chief Rabbi of France.

Even before the funeral Paris started recounting stories about Halévy's premonitions of death, his fortitude, his gift of repartee. To the young Belgian composer Gevaert who was highly thought of in Paris he reportedly said just before his departure for Nice: 'My dear Gevaert, I rather think you will have to do for me what I have done for the dying Hérold. I completed his Ludovic, you will complete my *Noé*'[17] To Jouvin of *Le Figaro* who had been one of his harshest critics he said 'with his gentle and rather sad smile: I do not appear on your calendar of saints but you have early placed me among your martyrs.'[18] To a long-winded chairman who introduced him before a lecture and later said to him: 'What a beautiful piece you have played to us,' he said without batting an eyelid: 'Yes, but what an overture.'[19] He bore no grudge. Whenever confronted by yet another virulent criticism he would ask: 'Is that journalist fellow an honest man?' When assured that he was, Halévy would shrug his shoulders and say: 'Well, if that's what he really thinks, too bad.'[20]

The obituaries were kind in the way that obituaries are: 'Never was a great artist more sincerely and unaffectedly modest. He was a man of high intelligence, erudite, witty, with simple affable manners.'[21] The literary critic Sainte-Beuve, hinting at the frustrations and professional attacks which had embittered Halévy's last years, left an interesting assessment of his character:

> Meeting him as I did only in society, I thought he was the happiest of artists, wholly fulfilled. Now I know that he was not. I can now understand why that face of his, as photographed in repose, is grave, sad, heavily lined. I only saw his social side, articulate, animated, charming . . . This agreeable person, inquisitive, accessible, totally committed to his art, harboured an inner hurt, a hidden wound.[22]

Another interesting assessment was made by the archaeologist Vinet who was closely associated with Halévy when he was Life Secretary. Unlike Sainte-Beuve who sensed a hurt and a wound caused by circumstances, he saw perseverance and inborn zeal, which he ascribed to Halévy's Jewishness:

> One often mentions nowadays the influence of race. Some admit it, some deny it . . . Four great composers have enriched our French opera as well as the operas of other European countries. One was Italian, another was Paris-born. The other two were hard-working individuals from first to last. Everything spurred them on, success as

well as criticism. If they stopped it was only to wipe the sweat of their brow, after which they resumed their work with unabated ardour. Both were fired with an obstinate conviction and a deep faith which are the distinct traits of strongly-moulded characters. Both were Jews.[23]

The Jewish organ *Archives Israëlites* saw a side of Halévy that no Sainte-Beuve or Vinet could either comment on or fully appreciate. In its assessment of the deceased it quoted Colonel Cerfberr who, like Halévy during his lifetime, achieved a distinguished career in a gentile world. In his funeral oration the Jewish colonel had put it in a nutshell:

> We are happy to count him as one of us, not only because he brought honour to France, but because he held high the flag of his religion. In these sad times of religious indifference he had the good sense not to deny the faith of his fathers.[24]

It was as if the spirit of old Elie Halévy had inspired those words echoing the slogan of the Jewish Enlightenment in which he so fervently believed: *Tiens au pays et conserve ta foi* – be loyal to your country and true to the faith of your fathers. Without being a practising Jew, Fromental Halévy, bearer of a name recalling the music-makers of the ancient Temple of Jerusalem, fulfilled that precept. He was a credit to France and a credit to his race.

22

A DESCENDANT OF B — A — C — H

*T*HE FICTITIOUS 19TH-CENTURY German composer whom Halévy invented in his *Lettres sur la musique* was a foundling. A staved note tucked into his swaddling clothes read: 'My name is Gervasius. I am a descendant of *si bémol, la, ut, si naturel.*' [B flat, A, C, B natural]. Neither his adoptive father nor any of his colleagues, all players in the Vienna theatre orchestra, could make any sense out of it. Only years later did it occur to a music-loving doctor that since in German notation the four notes were rendered as B, A, C, H, the message meant that the foundling was a descendant of Bach.

This fairly tale introduction to a learned essay was Halévy's way of claiming that he himself was a spiritual descendant of Bach – for Gervasius was his alter ego – and that his music had been formed and inspired by Bach's heritage. It was a claim not many of his contemporaries could have made at the beginning of the 19th century, when Bach was not as universally known as he would be a few decades later. Not many would have understood his allusion to the fugue which Bach had improvised on the letters of his surname, as commanded by Frederick the Great during a court recital.

Right from his student days in the late 1810's Halévy studied Bach's music in depth as well as the works of 'all the other Bachs.' 'My aim,' he wrote, 'was to study all the secrets of the masters and then, away from the tumult of the world, devote myself to new and persistent study of music itself; not the mechanics of music, but its very essence, its nature, its resources, its haven inside the human heart, its place in the vast framework of human intelligence.'[1]

The body of his work testifies to the success of his aims. He was a master craftsman who had penetrated the deepest secrets of his craft; he was a sensitive artist who sought to express in music the emotions, conflicts and drama which poets expressed in words. He translated human experience into opera.

His music was considered 'innovative', which meant that he had the courage to try out new ideas, and 'complex', which meant that he often questioned, and sometimes departed from received doctrines. Time and again reviewers stressed that it could not be easily understood. 'One needs to have acquired an intelligent experience and a trained ear to be able to grasp all the ingenuity, wealth and distinction of his musical thinking.'[2], wrote *La Revue et gazette musicale* after *La Reine de Chypre*. 'Let us say right away,' wrote *Le Ménestrel* after *Le Guitarrero*, 'that it needs to be heard many times to be properly appreciated. This goes for everything he has written, including *La Juive*.'[3]

The two criteria by which a composer was judged were harmony and melody. The reaction to his search for new harmonic permutations fluctuated between admiration and total disapproval. While *L'Eclair* was hailed as a masterpiece well ahead of its time, *La Fée aux roses* made some of his critics gasp with horror at his unorthodox harmony and utter ambivalent praise for his 'savage' rhythms. After *Les Mousquetaires de la reine* he was rebuked for using a major key and a minor key in the same piece. After *Le Val d'Andorre* he was taken to task for starting the overture in C minor and ending it in D. The most disapproving of all was the music critic of the London Times, who, after the premiere of *La Tempesta*, complained of 'a habit in which M. Halévy indulges of beginning a piece in one key and ending it in another.' He pointed faults and reminded the errant composer of textbook rules:

> The trio of Miranda, Prospero and Caliban, which begins in G minor ends in B flat, though praised for its dramatic effectiveness, is commented upon for an indifference to the rules of 'tonality', unprecedented in the work of the great masters . . . No piece of music can

with propriety begin in a minor key and end in the relative key, or vice versa. If in the course of the composition a movement, or a phrase in the relative, succeeds the delivery of the principal theme in the tonic, another movement or a return to the first phrase in the tonic must follow, or the composition remains unfinished. This is the principle of the symphonic form, the only true one in music . . . Thus Miranda's first *cavatina*, which open in D and finished in A — is a plain violation of a law that should be absolute and irrefragable.[4]

Halévy however was no rigid theoretician as some of his reviewers appeared to be, but an erudite composer blessed with imagination and an inquiring mind. A Bach scholar, professor of fugue and counterpoint since 1833 and of composition since 1840, he may have been inspired by a duet written by the Master in canon at the fifth, which 'gave the impression of two separate keys succeeding one another, then becoming superimposed and contrasted, while the harmonic texture remained tonal.'[5] Having studied 'all the secrets of the masters,' he may have been similarly inspired by the second movement of Haydn's Symphony No 103 in E flat (Drum roll) in which C major alternates with C minor. In *Prométhée enchainé*, a cantata written in 1849 to his brother's translation of Aeschylus, he went as far as to use quarter tones. The martinets of the profession accused him of muddled combinations and cranky effects; the open-minded listened again and welcomed his originality.

His gift for melody, the second criterion by which a composer was assessed, never led him astray into sentimentality or trendiness. That was something he owed to Cherubini's influence. Whether writing for a tormented father or a woman in love, a simple shepherd or a Red Indian temptress, he found the right note, the right key, the right mode. From Méhul and Catel, his first teachers at the Conservatoire, he learnt the use of a recurrent melodic theme, a device which only long after his death was named *Leitmotif*.

His melodies, like his orchestration, had their admirers and their detractors. Some critics found them lyrical and moving, other dismissed them as bland. The public liked them. Not only were they played by music lovers in every home which had a piano, but also by grinders of street organs in every corner of Paris. There came a time when music publishers, fearful for the sales of sheet music, sought an injunction restraining street organists from playing melodies by composers on their lists. Writing to Counsel for the Defence Adolphe Crémieux, a fellow Jew, a personal friend and a future Minister of Justice, Halévy sided with the organ grinders.

> Tunes thus transmitted to the public, far from injuring composers' reputation actually add to their popularity . . . Let composers compose, publishers publish and street organs grind for the delectation of the less discriminate. The art of music will be none the worse for it, publishers' sales will not fall because of it, and composers will lose nothing by having their work widely performed, however uncouth the execution may be.[6]

Local colour was another of his strong points. As early as 1828, when *Clari* was staged at the Théâtre-Italien, his ability to evoke in music the character and ambience of a distant country was noticed and admired. Often it was expressed in a skilful handling of folk music, as in *Le Guitarrero*, or in the *Le Val d'Andorre*. It was used to great effect in *La Reine de Chypre*, where the two locations of the story were characterised by two distinct kinds of music, one evoking Venice, the other Cyprus. It was less obvious in *La Juive*, to this day probably the only opera in which the *Seder*, the Passover ritual meal, is celebrated. Although written in the responsorial style of the psalmody, it was the text rather than the music which evoked a Jewish ambience. In view of his background and familiarity with both Ashkenazi (western) and Sephardi (oriental) liturgical music, it would appear that the absence of a recognisable Jewish element in the *Seder* scene was due to a conscious decision.

Always striving to enrich the texture of his orchestration, he was quick to make use of the wider range offered by technically improved instruments. He was among the first in France to use the valve trumpet, and the first to use the valve horn. His scores favoured strong wind and brass sections, and a variety of percussion instruments. Berlioz repeatedly criticised what he considered the overpowering sound of the brass, scoffed at his introduction of an organ into his orchestration of *La Juive* and a tom-tom into that of *Jaguarita*. Never one to pander to popular taste, Halévy made no concessions to the pundits either. He knew his resources – the instruments of the orchestra and the human voice.

In his *Musiciens du passé* Blaze de Bury suggested that good musical ideas were never wasted; if they failed in one work the composer would use them in another. 'A work of music is like a ship sailing the seas.' he wrote. 'When there is a shipwreck one salvages what one can and gives it new life somewhere else. Thus Rossini salvaged bits from *Il Viaggio a Reims* and put them into *Le Comte Ory*; Boieldieu salvaged a tune from a piece of incidental music and used it for the tenor's opening aria in *La Dame blanche*; and Auber enriched *Les Chaperons blancs* with what he had salvaged from *Fra Diavolo*.'[7] A legitimate and acceptable ploy, it was not one which Halévy was said to use even though he had quite a few shipwrecks during his career. The bubbling source of his inspiration never dried up.

Many composers who were well known in their day have since been forgotten either because taste has changed or because their style and idiom quickly dated. In theory music like Halévy's, often judged 'modern' by his contemporaries, should have appealed to later generations whose ears would no longer be offended by his 'kinky' or 'savage' sounds. That his operas gradually disappeared all the same was perhaps due to an entirely different factor − the prohibitive cost of their production.

Of his thirty-two operas and opéras comiques, most were meant to be a feast to eye and ear, the magnificence of the sets complementing the effects of the music. Even in his lifetime evil tongues whispered that of all contemporary composers he alone knew how to cajole and press theatre managers into unprecedented lavishness. That lavishness was counter-productive; the more sumptuous the production the less likely it was to be staged. While praising the music of *La Magicienne*, a realistic critic correctly predicted that the prohibitive cost involved would ban it from all provincial opera houses. In due course even the Paris Opéra had to make cuts. *Noé* was shelved before it was completed because the management would not envisage a set requiring a flood, an ark and all manner of beast and fowl making a brief appearance on stage. The live horses in *La Juive*, the ship sailing into the harbour of Nicosia in *La Reine de Chypre*, the fire and brimstone in *La Magicienne*, were becoming a thing of the past. A policy of retrenchment was adopted in foreign opera houses as well.

What was true then is even truer now; not long ago a projected

London revival of *La Juive* had to be shelved for the same reason. Only the opera comique *L'Eclair*, which requires four singers, no choir, one main set, and a small orchestra, was performed and recorded in our own generation, its freshness and instrumentation making it easy to understand why in 1836 it was considered ahead of its time. For some of Halévy's grand operas the solution is perhaps a semi-staged concert performance, a practice which in London has proved itself this decade with Saint-Saëns's *Samson et Dalila*, Richard Strauss's *Electra* and in December 1993 with Berlioz's *Les Troyens*.

Among Halévy's papers an incomplete article on music was found, commissioned by the editors of a new encyclopedia. It called attention to the fact that music appreciation was no longer the prerogative of the few. 'Nowadays the future of music is no longer in doubt,' he confidently predicted. 'Musical education has made great progress in all countries and all walks of life . . . Harmony is no longer a mysterious science reserved for the clever; it reveals itself to everybody. Music will soon be what it should be – poetry which is universally understood.'[8]

That was written in 1861. Nearly a century and a half later, when opera has evolved from an elitist form of art into popular entertainment, occasionally even mass entertainment, the time has come to acquaint new audiences with unjustly neglected classics. Among Halévy's grand operas there are some which can still hold their own against works by Bellini, Bizet, Gounod and Saint-Saëns, as they did until the turn of the century. Based on conflict, whether moral, religious or national, they are timeless because of their imaginative fusion of subject and music. They live up to their creator's aims: beautifully crafted, they spring from the heart and fall into the framework of human intelligence. They depict in music the dramas of life.

23

EPILOGUE

*I*N ACCORDANCE WITH CUSTOM the Academy of Fine Arts elected a new Life Secretary within three or four weeks of the last incumbent's demise. Léonie ceded the sumptuous residence at the Institute Palace to the new incumbent F. Beulé, moving out with her antique furniture, pictures, sculptures, masks and knick-knacks. Loss and stress aggravated her extravagance. A Nice newspaper mentioned that her 'coreligionists' settled her outstanding debts, presumably those left unpaid to the landlady of the villa and the local tradesmen. A concerned Paris journalist wrote that Halévy who had given his all to music and made the fortune of the Opéra, the Opéra-Comique and the Théâtre-Lyrique had left his widow nothing but his name. The unprecedented idea of a State pension for a composer's widow began to be mooted. Influential friends pulled strings, the Academy of Fine Arts lobbied the Minister of State Count Walewski, Louis Napoleon was advised to refer the matter to the State Council. On 11 June, less than three months after Halévy's death, a bill was published:

Article 1: Granting, by way of a national award, to Madame Rodrigues-Henriques, (Hannah-Léonie), widow of M. Jacques-Elie-Fromental Halévy, a pension of five thousand francs.

Article 2: This pension shall be entered in the Pension Books of the

Public Treasury with effect as from 17 March 1862, date of M. Halévy's demise.[1]

To become statutory the bill had to be ratified by the state legislative body and the Senate. The Emperor issued the necessary decree:

> Napoleon, by the grace of God and the will of the people Emperor of the French —
> To all those present and those due to arrive — greetings. We have decreed and are decreeing as follows:
>
> Article 1: Shall be sent to the Legislative Body by our Minister of State the Bill discussed at the State Council proposing to grant Mme Rodrigues-Henriques, widow of M. F. Halévy, a pension of 5,000 francs as a National Award.
>
> Article 2: Counsellors of State Viscount de Rouge, M. de Lavenay and M. Eugène Marchand are charged with supporting this Bill during the debate at the Legislative Body and Senate.
>
> Article 3: Our Minister of State is charged with the execution of this decree.
>
> Given at the Palace of Fontainebleau on 14 June 1862.[2]

While waiting for the ratification of the pension Léonie applied herself to sculpting a posthumous bust of Halévy, earmarked for the Opéra performance of *La Juive* on 28 May, commemorating the anniversary of his birth on the 27th. The management was trying to atone for a faux pas which had shocked both friends and foes: on the day of the funeral, while the Opéra-Comique and the Théâtre-Lyrique closed as a mark of respect for the deceased, the Opéra, putting business before sentiment, was open as usual.

The cult of the dead continued. On the first Saturday of October 1862, at the annual open session of the Academy of Fine Arts, the new Life Secretary F. Beulé chose Halévy as the subject of his paper. A nation-wide subscription was organised for a memorial fund. The elderly architect Le Bas, distinguished Member of the Institute of France and Léon Halévy's father-in-law, designed a grand monument which was to serve also as a family grave. The sculptor Duret, also a member of the Institute, sculpted a statue to be placed on top of it.

The unveiling ceremony took place on 17 March 1864, on the second anniversary of Halévy's death. A dense crowd assembled in the Jewish section of the cemetery of Montmartre – musicians, singers, actors, writers, artists, members of the Institute, students and teachers of the Conservatoire, members of the Jewish community. At three o'clock precisely the Conservatoire students orchestra and choir struck up *Les Choeurs des tombeaux* from *Guido et Genevra* which was followed by a Jewish choir singing a French translation of the Hebrew prayer for the dead. With the last reverberation of the final word the shroud was flung back to reveal the memorial.

It was a tall structure of Jura granite, with a bronze door into which three star-shaped windows had been cut. Over a flat roof engraved with the name Fromental Halévy three white marble tiers rose. The lower two displayed thirty-two garlands in bas-relief, each bearing a title from his thirty-two performed operas. The top tier served as a pedestal for the statue, also in white marble, depicting Halévy in the uniform of a member of the Institute of France, his hands crossed, the left holding a half-unrolled sheet of music, the right clasping a pen. Against his feet rested a lyre and a mask.

Le Figaro complimented Le Bas on his design and Duret on the statue. The *Archives Israëlites* however, recalling God's injunction to the Children of Israel *Thou shalt not make unto thee any graven image*, expressed disapproval:

> We said it when the idea of a statue was first mooted, and we repeat it now that it has been erected. The principle of commemoration was good; the way it was executed is questionable. We concede that in 1864 the features of a Jewish man of genius may be reproduced in any form or material, but we definitely do not accept that the place for such an image is a Jewish cemetery . . . Had the statue been positioned at the Opéra foyer like Rossini's statue, or at the Conservatoire, where the defunct has taught so brilliantly, or anywhere else, it would have given us cause for rejoicing. But there, where it is now, it contradicts the very spirit of Judaism. We are not referring to bigoted, out-of-date orthodoxy but to a reasoned faith which strives to conserve its original purity and the integrity of its fundamental doctrines.[3]

Apparently the editor of the *Archives Israëlites* was not aware that the Opéra, the Conservatoire and the Institute of France already

HALEVY'S MONUMENT AS IT WAS IN 1864

had busts of Halévy in their respective foyers; nor could he have foreseen that a time would come when Duret's sculpture which so offended him would inexplicably disappear. In 1922 the monument suffered extensive damage which made it necessary to remove the three tiers with the thirty-two bas-relief garlands, and reduce the statue to a bust. It was duly positioned on top of the monument, with the administrative identification *Sépulture Halévy* replacing name and surname. Some fifty years later the bust was removed together with the base carrying the two-word inscription, and today only the single word Halévy remains, engraved on the top left hand side of the granite monument.

The unveiling ceremony at the cemetery of Montmartre was attended by Esther and Geneviève without their mother. Léonie, who for two years had taken an active part in the fund raising, design and execution of the monument, ended by having a nervous breakdown and was being cared for at a sanatorium. A month later, on 19 April, twenty-year old Esther died in a nursing home of an unspecified illness. Her funeral, at the Jewish section of the Montmartre cemetery, drew a large Jewish crowd of mourners in spite of the fact that it coincided with the first day of Passover. Rabbi Isidor, the Chief Rabbi of Paris, made a moving speech. She was buried in the family vault beneath the memorial, next to her father.

Geneviève, aged fifteen, grew up under the domination of an unstable, self-centred mother. When Bizet and she fell in love and wanted to get married a united Halévy-Rodrigues clan objected to a gentile husband. The only tolerant voice was that of Hippolyte Rodriques, Léonie's brother, author of a learned work entitled *The Three Daughters of the Bible − Judaism, Islam and Catholicism*. It was he who eventually persuaded the family to withdraw their objection. When a well-meaning acquaintance suggested to the twenty-year old bride that she should convert to Catholicism she reportedly retorted: 'I have too little religion of my own to convert it into anything.' They were married in the summer of 1869 at the registry of the 9th arrondissement. Léonie did not attend; she was at a nursing home. She died in 1884 and was buried in the family vault next to her husband and her eldest daughter.

Geneviève had been married only six years when Bizet died. After eleven years of widowhood she married the wealthy Jewish lawyer Emile Straus. The wedding, held on 7 October 1886 at the synagogue of rue de la Victoire, was a grand affair. As Léonie had died two years earlier the bride's side of the family was represented by Hippolyte Rodrigues, her uncle on her mother's side, and her cousin Ludovic Halévy. The bridegroom's best man was his relative Baron Edmond de Rothschild. The religious ceremony was conducted by Rabbi Zadoc Kahn, the current Chief Rabbi of Paris.

As Mme Straus, Geneviève became one of the leading hostesses of Parisian society, attracting to her salon many of the great cultural figures of the day. Marcel Proust used her as a model for the Duchess of Guermantes in the third part of his *A la recherche du temps perdu*. Jacques Bizet, the only issue of her first marriage, committed suicide in 1922, pre-deceasing her by four years. She died in 1926 at the age of seventy-seven.

SOURCES

UNPUBLISHED LETTERS BY HALÉVY

Bibliothèque Nationale, Paris: NAF 14345–14355, NAF 14383–14386, NAF 15799, NAF 22547, NAF 24641, NAF 16274, NAF 10177, NAF 1304, Hahnemann–Harndorf, Lettres autographes vol 50
The Jewish National and University Library, Jerusalem: Halévy, The Lobbenberg Autograph Collection
The British Library, London: Add 29804, Add 33965

OTHER UNPUBLISHED DOCUMENTS

Archives de L'Opéra de Paris: Les Cancans de l'Opéra, Diary of M. Gentil
Covent Garden Opera House Archives: letter from Mario

PUBLISHED WORKS
All works published in Paris unless otherwise stated

Barzun, J M: Pleasures of Music, New York 1952
Berlioz, H: Les Musiciens et la musique, 1903
— Au Milieu du chemin, 1930
— Les Grotesques de la musique, 1859
— Les Soirées de l'orchestre, 1852
— A travers chants, 1862

— Memoirs, tr. & annotated David Cairns, London 1969
— New Letters of Berlioz, J M Barzun, New York 1954
Beulé, C E: Notice sur la vie et les oeuvres de M F Halévy, 1862
Blaze de Bury: Les Koenigsmark, 1855
— Meyerbeer, 1865
— Les Musiciens du passé, 1880
Boigne, P C B: Petits mémoires de l'Opéra, 1857
Bunn, A: The Stage, London 1840
Carmouche, P F & De Courcy: Les Souvenirs de Lafleur, 1833
Carré, M & Barbier, P J: Valentine d'Aubigny, 1856
Catelin, A: Le Dilettante d'Avignon, 1863
Chants en Usage au temple Israëlite de la rue de la Victoire, 1874
Chants en Usage dans les temples consistoriaux Israëlites de Paris, 1879
Chopin, F: Correspondance, ed. Sydow B E 1953 etc
Chorley, H F:Autobiography, London 1873
— Thirty Years of Musical Recollections, London 1862
Coleridge, A D: Life of Moscheles, London 1873
Coralli, J & Cave, E L R: La Tentation, 1832
Curtiss, M: The World of Bizet, London 1959
— Fromental Halévy, The Musical Quarterly, New York April 1953
— Unpublished letters by Bizet, ibid, July 1950
Davison J W: Music During the Victorian Era, London 1912
Delaborde H: L'Académie des Beaux-Arts depuis la fondation de l'Institut de France, 1891
Delacroix E: Journal, 1932
— Lettres Intimes, 1954
— Correspondance Générale, 1936–8
Delavigne C & G: Charles VI, 1854
Ebers J: Seven Years of the King's Theatre, London 1828
Escudier L: Mes Souvenirs, 1863–68
Escudier M & L: Vie et Aventures de Cantatrices, 1856
— Dictionnaire de Musique, 1854
Fiorentino P A: in F. Halévy, Derniers Souvenirs, 1863
Fulgence H & Ruolz H: Attendre et courir, 1830
Ganvert G: La Musique synagogale à Paris (1822–1872). thèse de doctorat, IV-Sorbonne, 1984
Gautier T: Histoire de l'art dramatique en France, 1858–9
— Les Beautés de l'Opéra, 1845

Halévy E: Limudey Dat U-mussar, Instructions religieuses et morales à l'usage de la jeunesse Israëlite, in Hebrew and French, 1820

Juxtaposed translations from Hebrew into French of:
— Prière au temple de la rue de Ste-Avoie, 1808
— Discours prononcé le 13 May 1809 par R. Cologne,
— Prière de Mordoché Roque-Martin, 1813

Halévy F: Opéra, in Dictionnaire de la musique, Escudier M & L, 1854
— Leçons de lecture musicale, 1859
— Souvenirs et Portraits, 1861
— Derniers Souvenirs, 1863
— Académie des Beaux-Arts, Séances publiques 1853–1859

Halévy L: Le Dilettante d'Avignon, after F B Hoffman 1829
— F. Halévy: Sa vie et ses oeuvres, 1863

Halphen A E: Recueil des lois concernant les Israëlites depuis la revolution de 1789, 1851

Hertzberg A: The French Enlightenment and the Jews, New York & London 1968

Jordan R: Sophie Dorothea, London 1970

Klein J W: Jacques Fromental Halévy, MR XXII 1962 (13)

Lapauze H: Histoire de l'Académie de France à Rome, 1924

Legouvé Ernest: Soixante ans de souvenirs, 1886–7

Leich-Galland K: Quelques observations sur les autographes des grands opéras de Fromental Halévy, Les Sources en musicologies, 1891
— Fromental Halévy – La Juive, Dossier de presse Parisienne (1835), Saarbrucken 1987

Levy P: Les Noms des Israëlites en France, 1960

Monnais G Ed: Souvenirs d'un ami, 1863

Morgan, Lady: Italy, London 1821
— France, London 1830
— Memoirs, London 1862

Naumbourg S: Zemiroth Yisrael, Chants religieux, 1847
— Shirey Kodesh, Nouveau recueil, 1865
— Aggudat Shirim, Recueil religieux, 1874

Periodicals, English: The Illustrated London News 1846, 1850
— The Musical Quarterly, 1950, 1953
— The Musical Times, 1846, 1848–1851, 1895
— The Musical World, 1846, 1849–1850

Periodicals, French: Archives Israëlites, 1862, 1864, 1884–6
— L'Artiste, 1855
— L'Avant-Scène, Opéra vol 100–103, 1987
— Le Constitutionnel, 1828–1858
— Le Figaro, 1862, 1864
— La France musicale, 1843–1851
— L'Illustration, Journal Universel, 1864
— Le Journal des débats, 1829–1858
— Le Ménestrel, 1835–1849
— Le Renovateur, 1835
— La Revue et gazette musicale, 1835–1858
— La Revue de Paris, 1899
Pinkerton P: The Jewess, London 1900
Planard F A E & Saint-Georges: L'Eclair, 1841
Pougin A: Halévy Ecrivain, 1865
Quicherat L: Adolphe Nourrit, 1863
Sainte-Beuve C A: Nouveaux Lundis, 1869–78
Saint-Georges Vernoy de: L'Artisan, 1827
— Le Roi et le batelier, 1827
— Ludovic, 1833
— L'Eclair, with Planard, 1836
— La Reine de Chypre, 1842
— Le Lazzarone, 1844
— Les Mousquetaires de la Reine, 1846
— Le Val d'Andorre, 1849
— La Fée aux roses, with Scribe, 1849
— Le Juif errant, with Scribe, 1852
— Le Nabab, with Scribe, 1853
— Jaguarita, with Leuven, 1855
— La Magicienne, 1858
Saint-Saëns C: Ecole buissonière: notes et souvenirs, 1913
Saint-Yves: La Langue musicale, 1831
Sand George: Correspondance, ed. Lubin G, 1964 etc
Scribe, E A: Magasin théâtral, 1834 etc
— Oeuvres complètes, 1840–47
— Oeuvres illustres, 1854–55
— Manon Lescaut, 1830
— La Juive, 1844
— Le Guitarrero, 1843
— Le Nabab, with Saint-Georges, 1853

— Le Shérif, 1841
— Le Juif errant, with Saint-Georges, 1852
Soubies A: Soizante-sept ans de l'Opéra, 1893
— Soixante-neuf ans de l'Opéra-Comique, 1894
— Histoire du Théâtre-Lyrique, 1899
— Le Théâtre-Italien, 1913
— Les Membres de L'Académie des Beaux-Arts, 1904/7
Tiersot J: Lettres de musiciens écrites en français du XV–XX siècle, 1924, 1936
Veron L: Mémoires d'un bourgeois de Paris, vol III, 1853–55
Vinet E: L'Art et l'archéologie, 1874
Wagner, Cosima: Diaries 1869–77, ed & annotated M Gregor-Dellin & D Mack, tr. G Skelton, London 1978
— Diaries 1878–83, ibid, London 1980
Wagner R: La Revue et gazette musicale, 1842
— Prose Works vols 7–8, tr. W A Ellis, London 1892
— My Life, Authorised Translation, London 1911
Wolff H C: Halévy als Kunst und Musikschriftsteller, Musicae scientiae collectanea, Cologne 1973 (697)

REFERENCES

CHAPTER 1:

1 Halphen: *Recueil des lois concernant les Israëlites,* 7
2 Ibid.

CHAPTER 2:

1 Halévy L: *F Halévy sa vie et ses oeuvres,* 13 ff
2 Lapauze: *Histoire de l'académie de France,* II, 147
3 Ibid.
4 Hahnemann-Harndorf: *Lettres autographes,* No. 50, 53

CHAPTER 4:

1 NAF 14347
2 Lady Morgan: *Italy,* II, 235
3 Ibid, 236
4 Ibid, 237–8
5 NAF 14347
6 Ibid.
7 Ibid.
8 Tiersot: *Lettres de musiciens,* II, 70–1

CHAPTER 5:

1 Lapauze: *Histoire de l'académie de France,* II, 148
2 Ibid.
3 Escudier L: *Mes souvenirs,* I, 306
4 Catelin: *Le Dilettante d'Avignon,* 6

5   Escudier M & L: *Vie et aventures des cantatrices*, 17
6   Hoffman & Halévy L: *Le Dilettante d'Avignon*
7   *Journal des débats*, 8 November 1829
8   Ibid.
9   Catelin: op. cit., 4
10   Tiersot: *Lettres de musiciens*, II, 92
11   Ibid.
12   Ibid.

CHAPTER 6:

1   Tiersot: *Lettres de musiciens*, II 97–8
2   Chopin: *Correspondance*, II, 72
3   Halévy L: *F Halévy sa vie et ses oeuvres*, 21

CHAPTER 7:

1   Halévy F: *Derniers souvenirs*, xi
2   Ibid, 166
3   Scribe: *La Juive*
4   Halévy F: op. cit., 166
5   Monnais: *Souvenirs d'un ami*, 16

CHAPTER 8:

1   *La Quotidienne*, February 1835
2   Quicherat: *Adolphe Nourrit*, III, 174
3   *Le Courrier français*, February 1835
4   *Revue des Deux Mondes*, February 1835
5   Ibid.
6   *Le Constitutionnel*, February 1835
7   *Le Renovateur*, March 1835
8   Ibid.
9   *Revue et gazette musicale*, March 1835
10   Quicherat: op. cit., 174–5
11   *Revue et gazette musicale*, March 1835
12   *Le Ménestrel*, March 1835
13   *Le Courrier français*, March 1855
14   Quicherat: op. cit., 173
15   *L'Artiste*, March 1835
16   Gautier: *Histoire de l'art dramatique*, I, 21
17   *Revue et gazette musicale*, August 1837
18   Ibid, June 1840
19   Ibid.
20   *Revue et gazette musicale,* March/April 1842
21   Ibid, March 1855

CHAPTER 9:

1   *Revue et gazette musicale*, 1840, 122–3
2   Ibid, December 1835
3   Ibid, August 1842
4   Ibid, May 1838
5   Tiersot: *Lettres de musiciens*, II, 95–6
6   Ibid, 95
7   Ibid, 261
8   Quicherat: *Adolphe Nourrit*, III, 365
9   Tiersot: op. cit., II, 129
10 Quicherat: op. cit., III, 365
11 Ibid, 366
12 *Les Cancans de l'Opéra*, II, 338–9
13 Chopin: *Correspondance*, II, 229
14 Hahnemann-Harndorf: *Lettres autographes*, No. 50, 38
15 *Revue et gazette musicale*, March 1857

CHAPTER 10:

1   Boigne: *Petits mémoires de l'Opéra*, 128
2   Tiersot: *Lettres de musiciens*, II, 96
3   *Revue et gazette musicale*, March 1838
4   Ibid.
5   Ibid, April 1838
6   Gautier: *Histoire de l'art dramatique*, I, 114
7   Ibid.
8   Boigne: op. cit., 165–6
9   Gautier: op. cit., II, 13
10 *Revue et gazette musical*, January 1840
11 Ibid.
12 George Sand: *Correspondance*, V, 529–30
13 *Journal des débats*, December 1841
14 Gautier: op. cit., 199
15 *Revue et gazette musicale*, December 1841
16 Wagner R: *My Life*, 252
17 *Revue et gazette musicale*, April/May 1842
18 Wagner R: op. cit., 254
19 Ibid.
20 Wagner R; *Prose Works*, VIII, 172

CHAPTER 11:

1   Gautier: *Histoire de l'art dramatique*, II, 185
2   *Journal des débats*, April 1839
3   Gautier: op. cit., I, 256
4   *Journal des débats*, September 1839
5   Ibid.

6   Gautier: op. cit., 300
7   *Revue et gazette musicale*, May 1840
8   Monnais: *Souvenirs d'un ami*, 25
9   Saint-Saëns: *Ecole Buissonière*, 12–13
10 *Le Ménestrel*, January 1841
11 *Revue et gazette musicale*, January 1841
12 *Journal des débats*, January 1841
13 Wagner R: *Prose Works*, VII, 114–15
14 Wagner R: op. cit., 124
15 Ibid, 172
16 *Journal des débats*, December 1841
17 George Sand: *Correspondance*, V, 231

CHAPTER 12:

1   Halévy L: *F Halévy sa vie et ses oeuvres*, 41
2   Ibid, 36
3   Coleridge: *Life of Moscheles*, II, 55
4   Halévy L: op. cit., 42–3
5   Wagner R: *My Life*, 255
6   Coleridge: op. cit., 113

CHAPTER 13:

1   Tiersot: *Lettres de musiciens*, II, 97
2   *Revue et gazette musicale*, March 1843
3   Gautier: *Histoire de l'art dramatique*, III, 24
4   *La France musicale*, March 1843
5   Ibid.
6   *Revue et gazette musicale*, March 1844
7   *Journal des débats*, April 1844
8   *La France musicale*, March 1844
9   Ibid, April 1843
10 *Revue et gazette musicale*, March 1844
11 Gautier: op. cit., III, 171
12 Ibid, 172

CHAPTER 14:

1   Gautier: *Histoire de l'art dramatique*, V, 207–8
2   *Revue et gazette musicale*, February 1846
3   Ibid.
4   *Journal des débats*, February 1846
5   *La France musicale*, February 1846
6   *Revue et gazette musicale*, February 1846
7   Ibid, March 1846
8   Ibid, November 1846
9   Gautier: op. cit., V, 178

10 Monnais: *Souvenirs d'un ami*, 29
11 *Revue et gazette musicale*, November 1848
12 Ibid.
13 *Le Ménestrel*, March 1848
14 Coleridge: Life of Moscheles, II, 203
15 *Revue et gazette musical*, October 1849
16 *Le Ménestrel*, October 1849
17 *Journal des débats*, October 1849
18 Ibid.

CHAPTER 15:

1   *Illustrated London News*, August 1846
2   *Musical World*, August 1846
3   Ibid, January 1850
4   Ibid.
5   Ibid.
6   *Musical Times*, January 1850
7   Ibid.
8   Berlioz: *Les Soirées de l'Orchestre*, 123
9   Ibid, 121
10 NAF 14383
11 *Musical World*, May 1850
12 Hahnemann-Harndorf, *Lettres autographes*, No. 50, 213
13 *Illustrated London News*, June 1850
14 Ibid.
15 *Musical World*, June 1850
16 *The Daily News* in the *Musical World*, June 1850
17 *The Times* in the *Musical World*, June 1850
18 *Musical World*, June 1850
19 Ibid.
20 Ibid.
21 *Illustrated London News*, June 1850
22 *Musical World*, June 1850

CHAPTER 16:

1   *Illustrated London News*, August 1845
2   *Musical Times*, June 1851
3   *Illustrated London News*, August 1846
4   Ibid, July 1850
5   Ibid, August 1848
6   Ibid, August 1846
7   Autograph letter, Covent Garden Archives
8   *Illustrated London News*, July 1850
9   Halévy F: *Derniers souvenirs*, 167
10 Quicherat: *Adolphe Nourrit*, III, 364
11 *Illustrated London News*, August 1850

12 Ibid.
13 Ibid.
14 Ibid.
15 *Revue et gazette musicale*, July 1850

CHAPTER 17:

1   *Musical Quarterly*, July 1850
2   Halévy L: *F Halévy sa vie et ses oeuvres*, 48
3   Gautier: *Histoire de l'art dramatique*, VI, 209–10
4   *Journal des débats*, January 1850
5   *Revue et gazette musicale*, January 1850
6   Ibid.
7   George Sand: *Correspondance*, X, 496
8   NAF 22547
9   Ibid.
10 *Revue et gazette musicale*, April 1852
11 Ibid.
12 Ibid, May 1852
13 *L'Avant-Scène, Opéra*, No. 100, 10
14 *Revue et gazette musicale*, September 1853
15 *La France musicale*, February 1846

CHAPTER 18:

1   Halévy F: *Souvenirs et portraits*, "Britton le Charbonnier", 43
2   Ibid, "Froberger", 84
3   *Académie des Beaux-Arts, Séances publiques*, 7 October 1854
4   Ibid.
5   Ibid.
6   Ibid, 6 October 1855
7   Ibid.
8   Ibid.
9   Lapauze: *Histoire de l'Académie de France*, II, 345
10 Delacroix: *Correspondance générale*, III, 216
11 Delacroix: *Lettres intimes*, 177
12 Berlioz: *Au milieu du chemin*, 231–2
13 Delacroix: *Journal*, II, 305
14 Delacroix: *Correspondance générale*, III, 19
15 Delacroix: *Journal*, II, 422
16 Escudier L: *Mes souvenirs*, 186–7
17 Vinet: *L'Art et l'archéologie*, 490

CHAPTER 19:

1   Delacroix: *Journal*, II, 313
2   Vinet: *L'Art et L'archéologie*, 490
3   Halévy L: *F Halévy sa vie et ses oeuvres*, 42

4   Leich-Galland: *Observations*, 161
5   *Revue et gazette musicale*, May 1855
6   Ibid.
7   Berlioz: *Les Grotesques de la musique*, 70
8   Vinet: *L'Art et l'archéologie*, 487
9   Escudier L: *Mes souvenirs*, 187
10   Halévy F: *Souvenirs et portraits*, 339–40
11   Ibid, 361
12   Ganvert: *La Musique synagogale à Paris*, 325
13   Ibid, 231
14   Delacroix: *Journal*, II, 84
15   Ibid, 336

CHAPTER 20:

1   *Revue et gazette musicale*, May 1856
2   Ibid.
3   *Journal des débats*, May 1856
4   Halévy L: *F Halévy sa vie et ses oeuvres*, 53
5   *Journal des débats*, March 1858
6   Ibid.
7   *Revue et gazette musicale*, March 1858
8   *Revue de Paris*, December 1899, in the *Musical Quarterly*, April 1953
9   *Journal des débats*, March 1858
10   Blaze de Bury: *Les Musiciens du passé*, 224
11   Ibid, 225
12   Ibid.
13   Ibid.
14   *Revue et gazette musicale*, March 1856
15   Halévy L: op. cit., 38

CHAPTER 21:

1   Wagner R: *My Life*, 255
2   Ibid, 256
3   *L'Avant-Scène, Opéra*, No. 100, D van Moere, *"La Juive au feu de la presse"*
4   Sainte-Beuve: *Nouveaux Lundis*, II, 243
5   Fiorentino: in Halévy F, *Derniers souvenirs*, xiv
6   *Le Figaro*, 23 March 1862
7   Monnais: *Souvenirs d'un ami*, 34
8   Ibid, 35
9   Halévy L: *F Halévy sa vie et ses oeuvres*, 70
10   *Le Figaro*, 27 March 1862
11   NAF 14384
12   Ibid.
13   Halévy L: op. cit., 72
14   Ibid.

15   Hahnemann-Harndorf, *Lettres autographes*, No. 50, *Faire-part*
16   *Le Figaro*, 23 March 1862
17   Ibid, 20 March
18   Ibid, 27 March
19   Sainte-Beuve: op. cit., 243
20   *Le Figaro*, 27 March 1862
21   Ibid.
22   Sainte-Beuve: op. cit., 241
23   Vinet: *L'Art et l'archéologie, 494–5*
24   *Archives Israëlites*, 1 April 1862, 190

CHAPTER 22:

1   Halévy F: *Souvenirs et portraits, "Lettres sur la musique"*, 226
2   *Revue et gazette musicale*, January 1841
3   *Le Ménestrel*, January 1841
4   *Musical World*, June 1850
5   Milhaud D: *Notes sans musique*, 78
6   *Archives Israëlites*, 20 August 1886
7   Blaze de Bury: *Les Musiciens du passé*, 55
8   Halévy L: *F Halévy sa vie et ses oeuvres*, 68

CHAPTER 23:

1   Halévy F: *Derniers souvenirs*, 414
2   Ibid, 407–8
3   *Archives Israëlites*, April 1864, 274

INDEX